Nagios Core Administration Cookbook

Develop an integrated monitoring solution for virtually any kind of network

Tom Ryder

BIRMINGHAM - MUMBAI

Nagios Core Administration Cookbook

First published: January 2013

Production Reference: 1180113

Published by Packt Publishing Ltd.
Livery Place
35 Livery Street
Birmingham B3 2PB, UK.

ISBN 978-1-84951-556-6

www.packtpub.com

Cover Image by Gavin Doremus (gdoremus24@gmail.com)

Credits

Author

Tom Ryder

Reviewers

Emmanuel Dyan

John C. Kennedy

Pierguido Lambri

Acquisition Editor

Jonathan Titmus

Commissioning Editor

Shreerang Deshpande

Lead Technical Editor

Kedar Bhat

Technical Editor

Lubna Shaikh

Project Coordinator

Abhishek Kori

Proofreaders

Bernadette Watkins

Maria Gould

Indexer

Monica Ajmera

Graphics

Aditi Gajjar

Production Coordinator

Manu Joseph

Cover Work

Manu Joseph

About the Author

Tom Ryder is a systems administrator and former web developer from New Zealand. He uses Nagios Core as part of his "day job" as a systems administrator, monitoring the network for a regional Internet Service Provider. Tom works a great deal with UNIX-like systems, being a particular fan of GNU/Linux, and writes about usage of open source command line development tools on his blog **Arabesque**: http://www.blog.sanctum.geek.nz.

Thanks are of course due to Ethan Galstad and the Nagios Core development team for writing and maintaining Nagios Core, along with the reference manual against which the book's material was checked.

Thanks are also due to my loving partner Chantelle Potroz for her patience and support as this book was being written, and to my employer James Watts of Inspire Net Limited for permission to write it.

Thanks also to Shreerang Deshpande and Kedar Bhat from Packt for their patience and technical guidance during the book's development.

The map of Australia used for the background to the network map in *Chapter 8, Managing Network Layout*, is sampled from the public domain images available on the superb Natural Earth website, viewable at http://www.naturalearthdata.com/.

About the Reviewers

Emmanuel Dyan is an expert in web development and in all the technologies gravitating around the Web: servers, network infrastructures, languages, and software.

He has been managing his own company, iNet Process, since 2004. He opened a branch in India in 2006 for its development needs, and recruited the staff. He then had to define the working procedures as well as the tools and set up the work environment. iNet Process implements and hosts CRM solutions based on SugarCRM. Its clients are mainly from France and are big, medium, as well as small companies.

Emmanuel teaches development languages, IT strategies, and CMS (Drupal) in a French University (Paris-Est Marne-la-Vallée) for students preparing for a Master's degree.

John C. Kennedy has been administering UNIX and Linux servers and workstations since 1997. He has experience with Red Hat, SUSE, Ubuntu, Debian, Solaris, and HP-UX. John is also experienced in BASH shell scripting and is currently teaching himself Python and Ruby. John has also been a technical editor for various publishers for over 10 years specializing in open source related books.

When John is not geeking out in front of either a home or work computer, he helps out with a German Shepherd rescue centre in Virginia by fostering some great dogs or helping the centre with their IT needs.

I would like to thank my family (my wonderful wife, Michele, my intelligent and caring daughter Denise, and my terrific and smart son, Kieran) for supporting the (sometimes) silly things and not so silly things I do. I'd also like to thank my current foster dogs for their occasional need to keep their legs crossed a little longer while I test things out from the book and forget they are there.

Pierguido Lambri has more than 10 years of experience with GNU/Linux and with the system administration side. He has worked with many operating systems (proprietary and open source), but he's a fan of the open source movement. Interested in everything that has to do with IT, he always likes to learn about new technologies.

Thanks to Abhishek Kori and Kedar Bhat for the opportunity of the book review.

www.PacktPub.com

Support files, eBooks, discount offers and more

You might want to visit www.PacktPub.com for support files and downloads related to your book.

Did you know that Packt offers eBook versions of every book published, with PDF and ePub files available? You can upgrade to the eBook version at www.PacktPub.com and as a print book customer, you are entitled to a discount on the eBook copy. Get in touch with us at service@packtpub.com for more details.

At www.PacktPub.com, you can also read a collection of free technical articles, sign up for a range of free newsletters and receive exclusive discounts and offers on Packt books and eBooks.

http://PacktLib.PacktPub.com

Do you need instant solutions to your IT questions? PacktLib is Packt's online digital book library. Here, you can access, read and search across Packt's entire library of books.

Why Subscribe?

- ▶ Fully searchable across every book published by Packt
- ▶ Copy and paste, print and bookmark content
- ▶ On demand and accessible via web browser

Free Access for Packt account holders

If you have an account with Packt at www.PacktPub.com, you can use this to access PacktLib today and view nine entirely free books. Simply use your login credentials for immediate access.

Table of Contents

Preface

Nagios Core, the open source version of the Nagios monitoring framework, is an industry standard for network monitoring hosted on Unix-like systems, such as GNU/Linux or BSD. It is very often used by network and system administrators for checking connectivity between hosts and ensuring that network services are running as expected.

Where home-grown scripts performing network checks can rapidly become unmaintainable and difficult for newer administrators to customize safely, Nagios Core provides a rigorous and configurable monitoring framework to make checks in a consistent manner and to alert appropriate people and systems of any problem it detects.

This makes Nagios Core a very general monitoring framework rather than an out-of-the-box monitoring solution, which is known to make it a little unfriendly to beginners and something of a "black box", even to otherwise experienced administrators. Busy administrators charged with setting up a Nagios Core system will often set it up to send PING requests to a set of hosts every few minutes and send them an e-mail about any problem, and otherwise never touch it. More adventurous administrators new to the system might instate a few HTTP checks to make sure that company websites respond.

Nagios Core is capable of a great deal more than that, and this book's recipes are intended to highlight all of the different means of refining and controlling checks, notifications, and reporting for Nagios Core, rather than being a list of instructions for using specific plugins, of which there are many hundreds available online at the Nagios Exchange at `http://exchange.nagios.org/`. The book's fundamental aim is to get administrators excited about the possibilities of Nagios Core beyond elementary default checking behavior, so that they can use much more of the framework's power, and make it into the centerpiece of their network monitoring.

This also includes installing and even writing custom plugins beyond the standard Nagios Plugins set, writing and refining one's own checks, working with the very powerful **Simple Network Management Protocol** (**SNMP**), recording and reporting of performance data, refining notification behavior to only send appropriate notifications at appropriate times to appropriate people or systems, basic visualization options, identifying breakages in network paths, clever uses of the default web interface, and even extending Nagios Core with other open source programs, all in order to check virtually any kind of host property or network service on any network.

Where possible, this book focuses on add-ons written by the Nagios team themselves, particularly NRPE and NSCA. It omits discussion of the popular NRPE replacement check_mk, and of popular forks of Nagios Core such as Icinga. In the interest of conferring an in-depth understanding of advanced Nagios Core configuration, it also does not discuss any configuration frontends or wizards such as NConf. Finally, as a Packt open source series book focusing on the use of the freely available Nagios Core, it also does not directly discuss the use of Nagios XI, the commercial version of the software supported by the Nagios team. This is done to instill a thorough understanding of Nagios Core itself, rather than to reflect personal opinions of the author; curious administrators should definitely investigate all of these projects (particularly check_mk).

What this book covers

Chapter 1, Understanding Hosts, Services, and Contacts, explains the basic building blocks of Nagios Core configurations and how they interrelate, and discusses using groups with each one.

Chapter 2, Working with Commands and Plugins, explains the architecture of plugins and commands, including installing new plugins, defining custom uses of existing ones, and walks us through for writing a new plugin with Perl.

Chapter 3, Working with Checks and States, explains how Nagios Core performs its checks and how to customize that behavior, including scheduling downtime for hosts and services, and managing "flapping" for hosts or services that keep going up and down.

Chapter 4, Configuring Notifications, explains the logic of how Nagios Core decides on what basis to notify, and when and to whom, including examples of implementing a custom notification method, escalating notifications that aren't fixed after a certain period of time, and scheduling contact rotation.

Chapter 5, Monitoring Methods, gives examples of usage of some of the standard Nagios Plugins set, moving from basic network connectivity checks with PING and HTTP to more complex and powerful checks involving SNMP usage.

Chapter 6, Enabling Remote Execution, shows how to use NRPE as a means of working around the problem of not being able to check system properties directly over the network, including a demonstration of the more advanced method of check_by_ssh.

Chapter 7, Using the Web Interface, shows some less-used features of the web interface to actually control how Nagios Core is behaving and to see advanced reports, rather than simply viewing current state information. Use of the network map is not discussed here but in the next chapter.

Chapter 8, Managing Network Layout, explains how to make Nagios Core aware of the structure and function of your network, with a focus on hosts and services depending on one another to function correctly, including monitoring clusters, and using that layout information to build a network status map, optionally with icons and a background.

Chapter 9, Managing Configuration, shows how to streamline, refine, and control Nagios Core configuration at a low level without the use of frontends. It focusses on the clever use of groups, templates, and macros, and gives an example of generating configuration programmatically with the templating language m4.

Chapter 10, Security and Performance, shows how to manage simple access control, debugging runtime problems, and keeping tabs on how Nagios Core is performing, as well as a demonstration of basic monitoring redundancy.

Chapter 11, Automating and Extending Nagios Core, explains how to submit check results from other programs (including NSCA) to provide information about external processes via the commands file, and an introduction to a few popular add-ons (**NDOUtils**, **NagVis**, and **Nagiosgrapher**).

What you need for this book

In an attempt to work with a "standard" installation of Nagios Core, this book's recipes assume that Nagios Core 3.0 or later and the Nagios plugins set have been installed in /usr/local/nagios, by following the Nagios Quickstart Guides available at http://nagios.sourceforge.net/docs/3_0/quickstart.html.

If your system's package repositories include a package for Nagios Core 3.0 or later that you would prefer to use, this should still be possible, but the paths of all the files are likely to be very different. This is known to be a particular issue with the nagios3 package on Debian or Ubuntu systems. If you are familiar with the differences in the installation layout that your packaging system imposes, then you should still be able to follow the recipes with only some path changes.

For the screenshots of the web interface, the familiar Nagios Classic UI is used (with white-on-black menu), which was the default from Version 3.0 for several years before the newer "Exfoliation" style (with black-on-white menu) became the default more recently. Some of the graphical elements and styles are different, but everything has the same text and is in the same place, so it's not necessary to install the Classic UI to follow along with the recipes if you already have the Exfoliation style installed.

If you really want the Classic UI so that what you're seeing matches the screenshots exactly, you can install it by adding this as the final step of your installation process:

```
# make install-classicui
```

This book was written while the alpha of Nagios Core 4.0 was being tested. I have reviewed the change logs of the alpha release so far, and am reasonably confident that all of the recipes should work in this newer version's final release. If after Nagios Core 4.0 is released you do find some issues with using some of the recipes for it, please see the "Errata" section to let the publisher and author know.

Who this book is for

This book is aimed at system and network administrators comfortable with basic Unix-like system administration via the command line. It is best suited for GNU/Linux administrators, but should work fine for BSD administrators too. It has particular focus on the kind of administrator identified in the preface: one who is comfortable working with their Unix-like system, may well have a basic Nagios Core installation ready with some PING checks, and now wants to learn how to use much more of the framework's power and understand its configuration in more depth.

Administrators should be comfortable with installing library dependencies for the extensions, plugins, and add-ons discussed in the book. An effort is made to mention any dependencies; however, how these are best installed will depend on the system and its package repository. In almost all cases this should amount to installing some common libraries and their headers from a packaging system. Debian and Ubuntu package names are given for some more complex cases.

The easier recipes in the first five chapters involve some recap of the basics of configuring Nagios Core objects. Users completely new to Nagios Core who have just installed it will almost certainly want to start with *Chapter 1, Understanding Hosts, Services, and Contacts*, after completing the Nagios Quickstart Guide, as latter chapters assume a fair amount of knowledge.

Conventions

In this book, you will find a number of styles of text that distinguish between different kinds of information. Here are some examples of these styles, and an explanation of their meaning.

Code words in text are shown as follows: "Nagios Core will only need whatever information the PING tool would need for its own `check_ping` command".

A block of code is set as follows:

```
define service {
    use                    generic-service
    host_name              sparta.naginet
    service_description    HTTP
    check_command          check_http
}
```

When we wish to draw your attention to a particular part of a code block, the relevant lines or items are set in bold:

```
define host {
    host_name              sparta.naginet
    alias                  sparta
    address                10.128.0.21
    max_check_attempts     3
    check_period           24x7
    check_command          check-host-alive
    contacts               nagiosadmin
    notification_interval  60
    notification_period    24x7
}
```

Any command-line input or output is written as follows:

```
# cd /usr/local/nagios/etc/objects
# vi sparta.naginet.cfg
```

New terms and **important words** are shown in bold. Words that you see on the screen, in menus or dialog boxes for example, appear in the text like this: "If the server restarted successfully, the web interface should show a brand new host in the **Hosts** list, in **PENDING** state as it waits to run a check that the host is alive".

Reader feedback

Feedback from our readers is always welcome. Let us know what you think about this book—what you liked or may have disliked. Reader feedback is important for us to develop titles that you really get the most out of.

To send us general feedback, simply send an e-mail to feedback@packtpub.com, and mention the book title through the subject of your message.

If there is a topic that you have expertise in and you are interested in either writing or contributing to a book, see our author guide on www.packtpub.com/authors.

Customer support

Now that you are the proud owner of a Packt book, we have a number of things to help you to get the most from your purchase.

Downloading the example code

You can download the example code files for all Packt books you have purchased from your account at http://www.packtpub.com. If you purchased this book elsewhere, you can visit http://www.packtpub.com/support and register to have the files e-mailed directly to you.

Errata

Although we have taken every care to ensure the accuracy of our content, mistakes do happen. If you find a mistake in one of our books—maybe a mistake in the text or the code—we would be grateful if you would report this to us. By doing so, you can save other readers from frustration and help us improve subsequent versions of this book. If you find any errata, please report them by visiting http://www.packtpub.com/support, selecting your book, clicking on the **errata submission form** link, and entering the details of your errata. Once your errata are verified, your submission will be accepted and the errata will be uploaded to our website, or added to any list of existing errata, under the Errata section of that title.

Piracy

Piracy of copyright material on the Internet is an ongoing problem across all media. At Packt, we take the protection of our copyright and licenses very seriously. If you come across any illegal copies of our works, in any form, on the Internet, please provide us with the location address or website name immediately so that we can pursue a remedy.

Please contact us at copyright@packtpub.com with a link to the suspected pirated material.

We appreciate your help in protecting our authors, and our ability to bring you valuable content.

Questions

You can contact us at questions@packtpub.com if you are having a problem with any aspect of the book, and we will do our best to address it.

1
Understanding Hosts, Services, and Contacts

In this chapter we will cover the following recipes:

- ▶ Creating a new network host
- ▶ Creating a new HTTP service
- ▶ Creating a new e-mail contact
- ▶ Verifying configuration
- ▶ Creating a new hostgroup
- ▶ Creating a new servicegroup
- ▶ Creating a new contactgroup
- ▶ Creating a new time period
- ▶ Running a service on all hosts in a group

Introduction

Nagios Core is appropriate for monitoring services and states on all sorts of hosts, and one of its primary advantages is that the configuration can be as simple or as complex as required. Many Nagios Core users will only ever use the software as a way to send PING requests to a few hosts on their local network or possibly the Internet, and to send e-mail or pager messages to the administrator if they don't get any replies. Nagios Core is capable of monitoring vastly more complex systems than this, scaling from simple LAN configurations to being the cornerstone for monitoring an entire network.

However, for both simple and complex configurations of Nagios Core, the most basic building blocks of configuration are **hosts**, **services**, and **contacts**. These are the three things that administrators of even very simple networking setups will end up editing and probably creating. If you're a beginner to Nagios Core, then you might have changed a hostname here and there or copied a stanza in a configuration to get it to do what you want. In this chapter, we're going to look at what these configurations do in a bit more depth than that.

In a Nagios Core configuration:

- ▸ Hosts usually correspond to some sort of computer. This could be a physical or virtual machine accessible over the network, or the monitoring server itself. Conceptually, however, a host can monitor any kind of network entity, such as the endpoint of a VPN.

- ▸ Services usually correspond to an arrangement for Nagios Core to check something about a host, whether that's something as simple as getting PING replies from it, or something more complicated such as checking that the value of an SNMP OID is within acceptable bounds.

- ▸ Contacts define a means to notify someone when events happen to our services on our hosts, such as not being able to get a PING response, or being unable to send a test e-mail message.

In this chapter, we'll add all three of these, and we'll learn how to group their definitions together to make the configuration more readable, and to work with hosts in groups rather than having to edit each one individually. We'll also set up a custom time period for notifications, so that hardworking system administrators like us don't end up getting paged at midnight unnecessarily!

Creating a new network host

In this recipe, we'll start with the default Nagios Core configuration, and set up a host definition for a server that responds to PING on our local network. The end result will be that Nagios Core will add our new host to its internal tables when it starts up, and will automatically check it (probably using PING) on a regular basis. In this example, I'll use my Nagios Core monitoring server with a **Domain Name System** (**DNS**) name of `olympus.naginet`, and add a host definition for a webserver with a DNS name of `sparta.naginet`. This is all on my local network – `10.128.0.0/24`.

Getting ready

You'll need a working Nagios Core 3.0 or greater installation with a web interface, with all the Nagios Core Plugins installed. If you have not yet installed Nagios Core, then you should start with the QuickStart guide: `http://nagios.sourceforge.net/docs/ 3_0/quickstart.html`.

We'll assume that the configuration file that Nagios Core reads on startup is located at `/usr/local/nagios/etc/nagios.cfg`, as is the case with the default install. It shouldn't matter where you include this new host definition in the configuration, as long as Nagios Core is going to read the file at some point, but it might be a good idea to give each host its own file in a separate objects directory, which we'll do here. You should have access to a shell on the server, and be able to write text files using an editor of your choice; I'll use `vi`. You will need root privileges on the server via `su` or `sudo`.

You should know how to restart Nagios Core on the server, so that the configuration you're going to add gets applied. It shouldn't be necessary to restart the whole server to do this! A common location for the startup/shutdown script on Unix-like hosts is `/etc/init.d/nagios`, which I'll use here.

You should also get the hostname or IP address of the server you'd like to monitor ready. It's good practice to use the IP address if you can, which will mean your checks keep working even if DNS is unavailable. You shouldn't need the subnet mask or anything like that; Nagios Core will only need whatever information the PING tool would need for its own `check_ping` command.

Finally, you should test things first; confirm that you're able to reach the host from the Nagios Core server via PING by checking directly from the shell, to make sure your network stack, routes, firewalls, and netmasks are all correct:

```
tom@olympus:~$ ping 10.128.0.21
PING sparta.naginet (10.128.0.21) 56(84) bytes of data.
64 bytes from sparta.naginet (10.128.0.21): icmp_req=1 ttl=64 time=0.149 ms
```

How to do it...

We can create the new host definition for `sparta.naginet` as follows:

1. Change directory to `/usr/local/nagios/etc/objects`, and create a new file called `sparta.naginet.cfg`:

   ```
   # cd /usr/local/nagios/etc/objects
   # vi sparta.naginet.cfg
   ```

2. Write the following into the file, changing the values in bold as appropriate for your own setup:

   ```
   define host {
           host_name               sparta.naginet
           alias                   sparta
           address                 10.128.0.21
           max_check_attempts      3
   ```

```
check_period          24x7
check_command         check-host-alive
contacts              nagiosadmin
notification_interval 60
notification_period   24x7
}
```

3. Change directory to `/usr/local/nagios/etc`, and edit the `nagios.cfg` file:

   ```
   # cd ..
   # vi nagios.cfg
   ```

4. At the end of the file add the following line:

   ```
   cfg_file=/usr/local/nagios/etc/objects/sparta.naginet.cfg
   ```

5. Restart the Nagios Core server:

   ```
   # /etc/init.d/nagios restart
   ```

If the server restarted successfully, the web interface should show a brand new host in the **Hosts** list, in **PENDING** state as it waits to run a check that the host is alive:

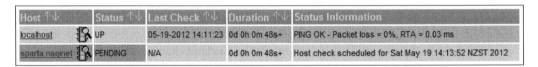

In the next few minutes, it should change to green to show that the check passed and the host is **UP**, assuming that the check succeeded:

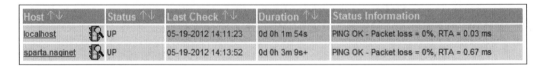

If the test failed and Nagios Core was not able to get a PING response from the target machine after three tries, for whatever reason, then it would probably look similar to the following screenshot:

Host	Status	Last Check	Duration	Status Information
localhost	UP	05-19-2012 14:26:52	0d 0h 18m 18s	PING OK - Packet loss = 0%, RTA = 0.04 ms
sparta.naginet	DOWN	05-19-2012 14:30:27	0d 0h 0m 18s	CRITICAL - Host Unreachable (10.128.0.21)

How it works...

The configuration we included in this section adds a host to Nagios Core's list of hosts. It will periodically check the host by sending a PING request, checking to see if it receives a reply, and updating the host's status as shown in the Nagios Core web interface accordingly. We haven't defined any other services to check for this host yet, nor have we specified what action it should take if the host is down. However, the host itself will be automatically checked at regular intervals by Nagios Core, and we can view its state in the web interface at any time.

The directives we defined in the preceding configuration are explained as follows:

- ▶ `host_name`: This defines the hostname of the machine, used internally by Nagios Core to refer to its host. It will end up being used in other parts of the configuration.

- ▶ `alias`: This defines a more recognizable human-readable name for the host; it appears in the web interface. It could also be used for a full-text description of the host.

- ▶ `address`: This defines the IP address of the machine. This is the actual value that Nagios Core will use for contacting the server; using an IP address rather than a DNS name is generally best practice, so that the checks continue to work even if DNS is not functioning.

- ▶ `max_check_attempts`: This defines the number of times Nagios Core should try to repeat the check if checks fail. Here, we've defined a value of 3, meaning that Nagios Core will try two more times to PING the target host after first finding it down.

- ▶ `check_period`: This references the time period that the host should be checked. 24x7 is a time period defined in the default configuration for Nagios Core. This is a sensible value for hosts, as it means the host will always be checked. This defines how often Nagios Core will check the host, and not how often it will notify anyone.

- ▶ `check_command`: This references the command that will be used to check whether the host is UP, DOWN, or UNREACHABLE. In this case, a QuickStart Nagios Core configuration defines `check-host-alive` as a PING check, which is a good test of basic network connectivity, and a sensible default for most hosts. This directive is actually not required to make a valid host, but you will want to include it under most circumstances; without it, no checks will be run.

- ▶ `contacts`: This references the contact or contacts that will be notified about state changes in the host. In this instance, we've used `nagiosadmin`, which is defined in the QuickStart Nagios Core configuration.

- ▶ `notification_interval`: This defines how regularly the host should repeat its notifications if it is having problems. Here, we've used a value of 60, which corresponds to 60 minutes or one hour.

> ▶ notification_period: This references the time period during which Nagios Core should send out notifications, if there are problems. Here, we're again using the 24x7 time period; for other hosts, another time period such as workhours might be more appropriate.

Note that we added the definition in its own file called sparta.naginet.cfg, and then referred to it in the main nagios.cfg configuration file. This is simply a conventional way of laying out hosts, and it happens to be quite a tidy way to manage things to keep definitions in their own files.

There's more...

There are a lot of other useful parameters for hosts, but the ones we've used include everything that's required.

While this is a perfectly valid way of specifying a host, it's more typical to define a host based on some template, with definitions of how often the host should be checked, who should be contacted when its state changes and on what basis, and similar properties. Nagios Core's QuickStart sample configuration defines a simple template host called generic-host, which could be used by extending the host definition with the use directive:

```
define host {
    use                 generic-host
    name                sparta
    host_name           sparta.naginet
    address             10.128.0.21
    max_check_attempts  3
    contacts            nagiosadmin
}
```

This uses all the parameters defined for generic-host, and then adds on the details of the specific host that needs to be checked. Note that if you use generic-host, then you will need to define check_command in your host definition. If you're curious to see what's defined in generic-host, then you can find its definition in /usr/local/nagios/etc/objects/templates.cfg.

See also

- ▶ The *Using an alternative check command for hosts* recipe in *Chapter 2, Working with Commands and Plugins*
- ▶ The *Specifying how frequently to check a host* recipe in *Chapter 3, Working with Checks and States*
- ▶ The *Grouping configuration files in directories* and *Using inheritance to simplify configuration* recipes in *Chapter 9, Managing Configuration*

Creating a new HTTP service

In this recipe, we'll create a new service to check on an existing host. Specifically, we'll check our sparta.naginet server to see if it's responding to HTTP requests on the usual HTTP TCP port 80. To do this, we'll be using a predefined command called check_http, which in turn uses one of the standard set of Nagios Core plugins, also called check_http. If you don't yet have a web server defined as a host in Nagios Core, then you may like to try the *Creating a new network host* recipe in this chapter.

After we've done this, not only will our host be checked for a PING response by check_ command, but Nagios Core will also run a periodic check to ensure that an HTTP service on that machine is responding to requests on the same host.

Getting ready

You'll need a working Nagios Core 3.0 or greater installation with a web interface, all the Nagios Plugins installed, and at least one host defined. If you need to set up a host definition for your web server first, then you might like to read the *Creating a new network host* recipe in this chapter, for which the requirements are the same.

It would be a good idea to test that the Nagios Core server is actually able to contact the web server first, to ensure that the check we're about to set up should succeed. The standard **telnet** tool is a fine way to test that a response comes back from TCP port 80 as we would expect from a web server:

```
tom@olympus:~$ telnet sparta.naginet 80
Trying 10.128.0.21...
Connected to sparta.naginet.
Escape character is '^]'.
```

How to do it...

We can create the service definition for sparta.naginet as follows:

1. Change to the directory containing the file in which the sparta.naginet host is defined, and edit it as follows:

   ```
   # cd /usr/local/nagios/etc/objects
   # vi sparta.naginet.cfg
   ```

2. Add the following code snippet to the end of the file, substituting in the value of the host's host_name directive:

   ```
   define service {
        host_name              sparta.naginet
   ```

```
        service_description       HTTP
        check_command             check_http
        max_check_attempts        3
        check_interval            5
        retry_interval            1
        check_period              24x7
        notification_interval     60
        notification_period       24x7
        contacts                  nagiosadmin
}
```

3. Restart the Nagios Core server:

    ```
    # /etc/init.d/nagios restart
    ```

If the server restarted successfully, the web interface should show a new service under the **Services** section, in **PENDING** state as the service awaits its first check:

sparta.naginet HTTP	PENDING	N/A	0d 0h 0m 4s+	1/3	Service check scheduled for Sat May 19 14:48:25 NZST 2012

Within a few minutes, the service's state should change to **OK** once the check has run and succeeded with an **HTTP/1.1 200 OK** response, or similar:

sparta.naginet HTTP	OK	05-19-2012 14:48:25	0d 0h 0m 16s	1/3	HTTP OK: HTTP/1.1 200 OK - 453 bytes in 0.008 second response time

If the check had problems, perhaps because the HTTP daemon isn't running on the target server, then the check may show **CRITICAL** instead. This probably doesn't mean the configuration is broken; it more likely means the network or web server isn't working:

sparta.naginet HTTP	CRITICAL	05-19-2012 14:54:25	0d 0h 1m 16s	2/3	Connection refused

How it works...

The configuration we've added adds a simple service check definition for an existing host, to check up to three times whether the HTTP daemon on that host is responding to a simple **HTTP/1.1** request. If Nagios Core can't get a response to its check, then it will flag the state of the service as **CRITICAL**, and will try again up to two more times before sending a notification. The service will be visible in the Nagios Core web interface and we can check its state at any time. Nagios Core will continue testing the server on a regular basis and flagging whether the checks were successful or not.

It's important to note that the service is like a property of a particular host; we define a service to check for a specific host, in this case, the `sparta.naginet` web server. That's why it's important to get the definition for `host_name` right.

The directives we defined in the preceding configuration are as follows:

- `host_name`: This references the host definition for which this service should apply. This will be the same as the `host_name` directive for the appropriate host.

- `service_description`: This is a name for the service itself, something human-recognizable that will appear in alerts and in the web interface for the service. In this case, we've used `HTTP`.

- `check_command`: This references the command that should be used to check the service's state. Here, we're referring to a command defined in Nagios Core's default configuration called `check_http`, which refers to a plugin of the same name in the Nagios Core Plugins set.

- `max_check_attempts`: This defines the number of times Nagios Core should attempt to re-check the service after finding it in a state other than `OK`.

- `check_interval`: This defines how long Nagios Core should wait between checks when the service is `OK`, or after the number of checks given in `max_check_attempts` has been exceeded.

- `retry_interval`: This defines how long Nagios Core should wait between retrying checks after first finding them in a state other than `OK`.

- `check_period`: This references the time period during which Nagios Core should run checks of the service. Here we've used the sensible `24x7` time period, as defined in Nagios Core's default configuration. Note that this can be different from `notification_period`; we can check the service's status without necessarily notifying a contact.

- `notification_interval`: This defines how long Nagios Core should wait between re-sending notifications when a service is in a state other than `OK`.

- `notification_period`: This references the time period during which Nagios Core should send notifications if it finds a host in a problem state. Here we've again used `24x7`, but for some less critical services it might be appropriate to use a time period such as `workhours`.

Note that we added the service definition in the same file as defining the host, and directly after it. We can actually place the definition anywhere we like, but this happens to be a good way of keeping things organized.

There's more...

The service we've set up to monitor on `sparta.naginet` is an HTTP service, but that's just one of many possible services we could monitor on our network. Nagios Core defines many different commands for its core plugin set, such as `check_smtp`, `check_dns`, and so on. These commands, in turn, all point to programs that actually perform a check and return the results to the Nagios Core server to be dealt with. The important thing to take away from this is that a service can monitor pretty much anything, and there are hundreds of plugins available for common network monitoring checks available on the Nagios Exchange website: `http://exchange.nagios.org/`.

There are a great deal more possible directives for services, and in practice it's more likely for even simple setups that we'll want to extend a service template for our service. This allows us to define values that we might want for a number of services, such as how long they should be in a `CRITICAL` state before a notification event takes place and someone gets contacted to deal with the problem.

One such template that Nagios Core's default configuration defines is called `generic-service`, and we can use it as a basis for our new service by referring to it with the `use` keyword:

```
define service {
    use                    generic-service
    host_name              sparta.naginet
    service_description    HTTP
    check_command          check_http
}
```

This may work well for you, as there are a lot of very sensible default values set by the `generic-service` template, which makes things a lot easier. We can inspect these values by looking at the template's definition in `/usr/local/nagios/etc/objects/templates.cfg`. This is the same file that includes the `generic-host` definition that we may have used earlier.

See also

- ▶ The *Creating a new servicegroup* recipe in this chapter
- ▶ The *Specifying how frequently to check a service* and *Scheduling downtime for a host or service* recipes in *Chapter 3, Working with Checks and States*
- ▶ The *Monitoring web services* recipe in *Chapter 5, Monitoring Methods*

Creating a new e-mail contact

In this recipe, we'll create a new contact with which hosts and services can interact, chiefly to inform them of hosts or services changing states. We'll use the simplest example of setting up an e-mail contact, and configuring an existing host so that this person receives an e-mail message when Nagios Core's host checks fail and the host is apparently unreachable. In this instance, I'll make it e-mail me at `nagios@sanctum.geek.nz` whenever my host, `sparta.naginet`, goes from DOWN to UP state, or vice-versa.

Getting ready

You should have a working Nagios Core 3.0 or greater server running, with a web interface and at least one host to check. If you need to do this first, see the *Creating a new network host* recipe in this chapter.

For this particular kind of contact, you'll also need to have a working SMTP daemon running on the monitoring server, such as **Exim** or **Postfix**. You should verify that you're able to send messages to the target address, and that they're successfully delivered to the mailserver you expect.

How to do it...

We can add a simple new contact to the Nagios Core configuration as follows:

1. Change to Nagios Core's object configuration directory; ideally it should contain a file that's devoted to contacts, such as `contacts.cfg` here, and edit that file:

   ```
   # cd /usr/local/nagios/etc/objects
   # vi contacts.cfg
   ```

2. Add the following contact definition to the end of the file, substituting your own values for the properties in bold as you need them:

   ```
   define contact {
        contact_name                  spartaadmin
        alias                         Administrator of sparta.naginet
        email                         nagios@sanctum.geek.nz
        host_notification_commands    notify-host-by-email
        host_notification_options     d,u,r
        host_notification_period      24x7
        service_notification_commands notify-service-by-email
        service_notification_options  w,u,c,r
        service_notification_period   24x7
   }
   ```

3. Edit the definition for the `sparta.naginet` host, and add or replace the definition for `contacts` for the appropriate host to our new `spartaadmin` contact:

```
define host {
        host_name               sparta.naginet
        alias                   sparta
        address                 10.128.0.21
        max_check_attempts      3
        check_period            24x7
        check_command           check-host-alive
        contacts                spartaadmin
        notification_interval   60
        notification_period     24x7
}
```

4. Restart the Nagios Core server:

```
# /etc/init.d/nagios restart
```

With this done, the next time our host changes its state, we should receive messages similar to the following:

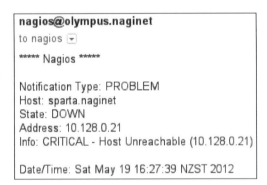

When the host becomes available again, we should receive a recovery message similar to the following:

If possible, it's worth testing this setup with a test host that we can safely bring down and then up again, to check that we receive the appropriate notifications.

How it works...

This configuration adds a new contact to the Nagios Core configuration, and references it in one of the hosts as the appropriate contact to use when the host has problems.

We've defined the required directives for the contact, and a couple of others as follows:

- ▶ `contact_name`: This defines a unique name for the contact, so that we can refer to it in host and service definitions, or anywhere else in the Nagios Core configuration.

- ▶ `alias`: This defines a human-friendly name for the contact, perhaps a brief explanation of who the person or group is and/or for what they're responsible.

- ▶ `email`: This defines the e-mail address of the contact, since we're going to be sending messages by e-mail.

- ▶ `host_notification_commands`: This defines the command or commands to be run when a state change on a host prompts a notification for the contact. In this case, we're going to e-mail the contact the results with a predefined command called `notify-host-by-email`.

- ▶ `host_notification_options`: This specifies the different kinds of host events for which this contact should be notified. Here, we're using `d,u,r`, which means that this contact will receive notifications for a host going DOWN, becoming UNREACHABLE, or coming back UP.

- ▶ `host_notification_period`: This defines the time period during which this contact can be notified of any host events. If a host notification is generated and defined to be sent to this contact, but it falls outside this time period, then the notification will not be sent.

- ▶ `service_notification_commands`: This defines the command or commands to be run when a state change on a service prompts a notification for this contact. In this case, we're going to e-mail the contact the results with a predefined command called `notify-service-by-email`.

- ▶ `service_notification_options`: This specifies the different kinds of service events for which this contact should be notified. Here, we're using `w,u,c,r`, which means we want to receive notifications about the services entering the WARNING, UNKNOWN, or CRITICAL states, and also when they recover and go back to being in the OK state.

- ▶ `service_notification_period`: This is the same as `host_notification_period`, except that this directive refers to notifications about services, and not hosts.

Note that we placed the definition for the contact in `contacts.cfg`, which is a reasonably sensible place. However, we can place the contact definition in any file that Nagios Core will read as part of its configuration; we can organize our hosts, services, and contacts any way we like. It helps to choose some sort of system, so we can easily identify where definitions are likely to be when we need to add, change, or remove them.

There's more...

If we define a lot of contacts with similar options, it may be appropriate to have individual contacts extend contact templates, so that they can inherit those common settings. The QuickStart Nagios Core configuration includes such a template, called `generic-contact`. We can define our new contact as an extension of this template, as follows:

```
define contact {
    use     generic-contact
    alias   Administrator of sparta.naginet
    email   nagios@sanctum.geek.nz
}
```

To see the directives defined for `generic-contact`, you can inspect its definition in the `/usr/local/nagios/etc/objects/templates.cfg` file.

See also

▸ The *Creating a new contact group* recipe in this chapter

▸ The *Automating contact rotation* and *Defining an escalation for repeated notifications* recipes in *Chapter 5, Monitoring Methods*

Verifying configuration

In this recipe, we'll learn about the most basic step in debugging a Nagios Core configuration, which is to verify it. This is a very useful step to take before restarting the Nagios Core server to load an altered configuration, because it will warn us about possible problems. This is a good recipe to follow if you're not able to start the Nagios Core server at any point because of configuration problems, and instead get output similar to the following:

```
# /etc/init.d/nagios restart

Running configuration check... CONFIG ERROR!  Restart aborted.  Check
your Nagios configuration.
```

Getting ready

You should have a working Nagios Core 3.0 or better server running.

How to do it...

We can verify the Nagios Core configuration as follows:

1. Run the following command, substituting the path to the Nagios binary file and our primary `nagios.cfg` configuration file, if necessary:

    ```
    # /usr/local/nagios/bin/nagios -v /usr/local/nagios/etc/nagios.cfg
    ```

2. If the output is very long, then it might be a good idea to pipe it through a pager program, such as `less`:

    ```
    # /usr/local/nagios/bin/nagios -v /usr/local/nagios/etc/nagios.cfg
    | less
    ```

3. Inspect the output and look for warnings and problems. Here's an example of part of the output we can expect, if our configuration is correct:

    ```
    Checking for circular paths between hosts...
    Checking for circular host and service dependencies...
    Checking global event handlers...
    Checking obsessive compulsive processor commands...
    Checking misc settings...

    Total Warnings: 0
    Total Errors:   0

    Things look okay - No serious problems were detected during the pre-flight check
    root@olympus:/usr/local/nagios# 
    ```

    If there's a problem of some sort, then we might see an output similar to the following, which is just an example of a possible error; my configuration is wrong because I tried to add a service for a host called `athens.naginet`, when I hadn't actually configured that host yet. So Nagios Core is quite right to yell at me:

    ```
    Error: Could not find any host matching 'athens.naginet' (config file '/usr/local
    /nagios/etc/objects/athens.naginet.cfg', starting on line 9)
    Error: Could not expand hostgroups and/or hosts specified in service (config file
     '/usr/local/nagios/etc/objects/athens.naginet.cfg', starting on line 9)
        Error processing object config files!

    ***> One or more problems was encountered while processing the config files...

        Check your configuration file(s) to ensure that they contain valid
        directives and data defintions.  If you are upgrading from a previous
        version of Nagios, you should be aware that some variables/definitions
        may have been removed or modified in this version.  Make sure to read
        the HTML documentation regarding the config files, as well as the
        'Whats New' section to find out what has changed.

    root@olympus:/usr/local/nagios# 
    ```

How it works...

The configuration is parsed as though Nagios Core were about to start up, to check that the configuration all makes sense. It will run basic checks such as looking for syntax errors, and will also check things like having at least one host and service to monitor. Some of the things it reports are warnings, meaning that they're not necessarily problems; examples include hosts not having any services monitored, or not having any contacts defined.

This is the quickest way to get an idea of whether the Nagios Core configuration is sane and will work correctly. Whenever there's trouble restarting the Nagios Core server, it's a good idea to check the output of this command first. In fact, it's a good habit to check the configuration before restarting, particularly if we're unsure about the configuration changes, or if the monitoring server is checking something very important! This means if it turns out that our configuration is broken, then the Nagios Core daemon will keep running with the configuration from the point before we changed it, and we can fix things before we restart.

There's more...

The program at `/usr/local/nagios/bin/nagios` is actually the same program that runs the Nagios Core server, but the `-v` part of the command is a switch for the program that verifies the configuration instead, and shows any problems with it. The second path is to the configuration file with which Nagios Core starts, which in turn imports the configuration files for objects, such as contact, host, and service definitions.

See also

> ▸ The *Writing debugging information to Nagios Core log file* recipe in *Chapter 10, Security and Performance*

Creating a new hostgroup

In this recipe, we'll learn how to create a new hostgroup; in this case, we'll do this to group together two webservers. This is useful for having distinct groups of hosts that might have different properties, such as being monitored by different teams, or running different types of monitored services. It also allows us to view a group breakdown in the Nagios Core web interface, and to apply a single service to a whole group of hosts, rather than doing so individually. This means we can set up services for a new host simply by adding it to a group, rather than having to specify the configuration manually.

Getting ready

You should have a working Nagios Core 3.0 or better server running, with a web interface.

You should also have at least two hosts that form a meaningful group; perhaps they're similar kinds of servers, such as webservers, or are monitored by the same team, or all at a physical location.

In this example, we have two webservers, `sparta.naginet` and `athens.naginet`, and we're going to add them to a group called `webservers`.

How to do it...

We can add our new hostgroup `webservers` to the Nagios Core configuration as follows:

1. Create a new file called `/usr/local/nagios/etc/objects/hostgroups.cfg`, if it doesn't already exist:

   ```
   # cd /usr/local/nagios/etc/objects
   # vi hostgroups.cfg
   ```

2. Add the following code into the new file, substituting the names in bold to suit your own layout:

   ```
   define hostgroup {
         hostgroup_name    webservers
         alias             Webservers with Greek names
   }
   ```

3. Move a directory up, and then edit the `nagios.cfg` file:

   ```
   # cd ..
   # vi nagios.cfg
   ```

4. Add the following line to the end of the file:

   ```
   cfg_file=/usr/local/nagios/etc/objects/hostgroups.cfg
   ```

5. For each of the hosts we want to add to the group, find their definitions, and add a `hostgroups` directive to put them into the new hostgroup. In this case, our definitions for `sparta.naginet` and `athens.naginet` end up looking as follows:

   ```
   define host {
         use           linux-server
         host_name     sparta.naginet
         alias         sparta
         address       10.128.0.21
         hostgroups    webservers
   }
   ```

```
define host {
        use             linux-server
        host_name       athens.naginet
        alias           athens
        address         10.128.0.22
        hostgroups      webservers
}
```

6. Restart Nagios:

    ```
    # /etc/init.d/nagios restart
    ```

We should now be able to visit the **Host Groups** section of the web interface, and see a new hostgroup with two members:

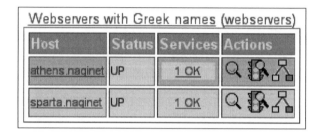

How it works...

The configuration we added includes a new file with a new hostgroup into the Nagios Core configuration, and inserts the appropriate hosts into the group. At the moment, all this is doing is creating a separate section in the web interface for us to get a quick overview of only the hosts in that particular group.

There's more...

The way we've added hosts to groups is actually not the only way to do it. If we prefer, we can name the hosts for the group inside the group definition, using the `members` directive, so that we could have a code snippet similar to the following:

```
define hostgroup {
        hostgroup_name  webservers
        alias           Webservers with Greek names
        members         athens.naginet,sparta.naginet
}
```

This extends to allowing us to make a hostgroup that always includes every single host, if we find that useful:

```
define hostgroup {
    hostgroup_name   all
    alias            All hosts
    members          *
}
```

If we're going to use hostgroups extensively in our Nagios Core configuration, then we should use whichever method is going to be easiest for our configuration. We can use both, if necessary.

It's worth noting that a host can be in more than one group, and there is no limit on the number of groups we can declare, so we can afford to be quite liberal with how we group our hosts into useful categories. Examples could be organizing servers by function, manufacturer, or colocation customer, or routers by BGP or OSPF usage; it all depends on what kind of network we're monitoring.

See also

▶ The *Creating a new host* and *Running a service on all hosts in a group* recipes in this chapter

▶ The *Using inheritance to simplify configuration* recipe in *Chapter 9, Managing Configuration*

Creating a new servicegroup

In this recipe, we'll create a new servicegroup. This allows us to make meaningful groups out of a set of arbitrary services, so that we can view the status of all those services in a separate part of the web administration area.

Getting ready

You should have a working Nagios Core 3.0 or better server running, with web interface.

You should also have at least two services defined that form a meaningful group; perhaps they're similar kinds of services, such as mail services, or are monitored by the same team, or all on the same set of servers at a physical location.

In this example, we have three servers performing mail functions: `smtp.naginet`, `pop3.naginet`, and `imap.naginet`, running an SMTP, POP3, and IMAP daemon, respectively. All three of the hosts are set up in Nagios Core, and so are their services. We're going to add them into a new servicegroup called `mailservices`.

Here are the definitions of the hosts and services used in this example, so you can see how everything fits together:

```
define host {
     use                    linux-server
     host_name              smtp.naginet
     alias                  smtp
     address                10.128.0.31
     hostgroups             webservers
}
     define service {
          use                    generic-service
          host_name              smtp.naginet
          service_description    SMTP
          check_command          check_smtp
     }
define host {
     use                    linux-server
     host_name              pop3.naginet
     alias                  pop3
     address                10.128.0.32
     hostgroups             webservers
}
     define service {
          use                    generic-service
          host_name              pop3.naginet
          service_description    POP3
          check_command          check_pop
     }
define host {
     use                    linux-server
     host_name              imap.naginet
     alias                  imap
     address                10.128.0.33
     hostgroups             webservers
}
     define service {
          use                    generic-service
          host_name              imap.naginet
          service_description    IMAP
          check_command          check_imap
     }
```

How to do it...

We can add our new servicegroup with the following steps:

1. Change to our Nagios Core configuration objects directory, and edit a new file called `servicegroups.cfg`:

   ```
   # cd /usr/local/nagios/etc/objects
   # vi servicegroups.cfg
   ```

2. Add the following definition to the new file, substituting the values in bold with your own values:

   ```
   define servicegroup {
       servicegroup_name   mailservices
       alias               Mail services
   }
   ```

3. Move a directory up, and then edit the `nagios.cfg` file:

   ```
   # cd ..
   # vi nagios.cfg
   ```

4. Add the following line to the end of the file:

   ```
   cfg_file=/usr/local/nagios/etc/objects/servicegroups.cfg
   ```

5. For each of the services we want to add to the group, find their definitions and add a `servicegroups` directive to put them into the new servicegroup. The definitions may end up looking similar to the following code snippet:

   ```
   define service {
       use                   generic-service
       host_name             smtp.naginet
       service_description   SMTP
       check_command         check_smtp
       servicegroups         mailservices
   }
   define service {
       use                   generic-service
       host_name             pop3.naginet
       service_description   POP3
       check_command         check_pop
       servicegroups         mailservices
   }
   ```

```
define service {
    use                  generic-service
    host_name            imap.naginet
    service_description  IMAP
    check_command        check_imap
    servicegroups        mailservices
}
```

6. Restart Nagios with the following command:

```
# /etc/init.d/nagios restart
```

We should now be able to visit the **Service Groups** section of the web interface, and see a new servicegroup with three members:

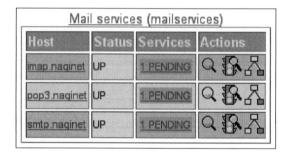

How it works...

The configuration we added includes a new file with a new servicegroup into the Nagios Core configuration, and inserts the appropriate services into the group. This creates a separate section in the web interface for us to get a quick overview of only the services in that particular group.

There's more...

The way we've added services to the groups is actually not the only way to do it. If we prefer, we can name the services (and their applicable hosts) for the group inside the group definition, using the members directive, so that we could have a code snippet similar to the following:

```
define servicegroup {
    servicegroup_name   mailservices
    alias               Mail services
    members             smtp.naginet,SMTP,pop3.naginet,POP3
}
```

Note that we need to specify both the host that the service is on, and then the services to monitor on it, comma-separated. The hostname comes first, and then the service.

This extends to allowing us to make a servicegroup that always includes every single service, if we find that useful:

```
define servicegroup {
    servicegroup_name  all
    alias              All services
    members            *
}
```

If we're going to be using servicegroup definitions extensively in our Nagios Core configuration, we should use whichever of the two methods to add services to groups that we think is going to be easiest for us to maintain.

It's worth noting that a service can be in more than one group, and there is no limit on the number of groups we can declare, so we can afford to be quite liberal with how we group our services into categories. Examples could be organising services by the appropriate contact for their notifications, for internal functions, or customer facing functions.

See also

▶ The *Creating a new service* and *Running a service on all hosts in a group* recipes in this chapter

▶ The *Using inheritance to simplify configuration* recipe in *Chapter 9, Managing Configuration*

Creating a new contactgroup

In this recipe, we'll create a new contactgroup into which we can add our contacts. Like hostgroups and servicegroups, contactgroups mostly amount to convenient shortcuts. In this case, it allows us to define a contactgroup as the recipient of notifications for a host or service definition. This means that we could define a group `ops`, for example, and then even if people joined or left the group, we wouldn't need to change any definitions for the hosts or services.

Getting ready

You should have a working Nagios Core 3.0 or better server running.

You should also have at least two contacts that form a meaningful group. In this case, we have two staff members, John Smith and Jane Doe, who are both a part of our network operations team. We want both of them to be notified for all the appropriate hosts and services, so we'll add them to a group called `ops`. Here are the definitions with which we're working:

```
define contact {
      use            generic-contact
      contact_name   john
      alias          John Smith
      email          john@naginet
}
define contact {
      use            generic-contact
      contact_name   jane
      alias          Jane Doe
      email          jane@naginet
}
```

How to do it...

We can create our new `ops` contactgroup as follows:

1. Change to our Nagios Core object configuration directory, and edit the `contacts.cfg` file:

    ```
    # cd /usr/local/nagios/etc
    # vi contacts.cfg
    ```

2. Add the following definition to the file, substituting your own values in bold as appropriate:

    ```
    define contactgroup {
          contactgroup_name   ops
          alias               Network operators
    }
    ```

3. For each of the contacts that we want to add to the group, find their definitions and add the `contactgroups` directive to them. The definitions will end up looking similar to the following code snippet:

    ```
    define contact {
          use            generic-contact
          contact_name   john
          alias          John Smith
          email          john@naginet
          contactgroups  ops
    }
    ```

```
define contact {
    use             generic-contact
    contact_name    jane
    alias           Jane Doe
    email           jane@naginet
    contactgroups   ops
}
```

4. Restart the Nagios Core server:

    ```
    # /etc/init.d/nagios restart
    ```

How it works...

With this group set up, we are now able to use it in the `contactgroups` directive for hosts and services, to define the contacts to which notifications should be sent. Notifications are sent to all the addresses in the group. This can replace the `contacts` directive where we individually name the contacts.

There's more...

This means, for example, that instead of having a service definition similar to the following:

```
define service {
    use                   generic-service
    host_name             sparta.naginet
    service_description   HTTP
    check_command         check_http
    contacts              john,jane
}
```

We could use the following code snippet:

```
define service {
    use                   generic-service
    host_name             sparta.naginet
    service_description   HTTP
    check_command         check_http
    contact_groups        ops
}
```

If John Smith were to leave the operations team, then we could simply remove his contact definition, and nothing else would require changing; from then on, only Jane Doe would receive the service notifications. This method provides a layer of abstraction between contacts and the hosts and services for which they receive notifications.

See also

- ▸ The *Creating a new contact* recipe in this chapter
- ▸ The *Automating contact rotation* recipe in *Chapter 4, Configuring Notifications*
- ▸ The *Using inheritance to simplify configuration* recipe in Chapter 9, *Managing Configuration*

Creating a new time period

In this recipe, we'll add a new time period definition to the Nagios Core configuration to allow us to set up monitoring for hosts and services only during weekdays. There's a default configuration defined as workhours that would almost suit us, except that it doesn't include the evenings. We'll make a new one from scratch, and we'll make another one to cover the weekends too.

Getting ready

You should have a working Nagios Core 3.0 or better server running.

How to do it...

We can set up our new time period, which we'll call weekdays, as follows:

1. Change to our Nagios Core configuration objects directory, and edit the file called timeperiods.cfg:

```
# cd /usr/local/nagios/etc/objects
# vi timeperiods.cfg
```

2. Add the following definitions to the end of the file:

```
define timeperiod {
    timeperiod_name   weekdays
    alias             Weekdays
    monday            00:00-24:00
    tuesday           00:00-24:00
    wednesday         00:00-24:00
    thursday          00:00-24:00
    friday            00:00-24:00
}
```

```
define timeperiod {
    timeperiod_name    weekends
    alias              Weekends
    saturday           00:00-24:00
    sunday             00:00-24:00
}
```

3. Restart the Nagios Core server:

   # /etc/init.d/nagios restart

How it works...

In our host and service definitions, there are two directives, `check_period` and `notification_period`. These directives are used to define the times during which a host or service should be checked, and the times when notifications about them should be sent. The `24x7` and `workhours` periods are defined in the `timeperiods.cfg` file that we just edited, and are used in several of the examples and templates.

We've just added two more of these time periods, which we can now use in our definitions for hosts and services. The first is called `weekdays`, and corresponds to any time during a weekday; the second is called `weekends`, and corresponds to any time that's not a weekday. Note that in both cases, we specified the dates and times by naming each individual day, and the times to which they corresponded.

There's more...

The definitions for dates are quite clever, and can be defined in a variety of ways. The following are all valid definitions for days and time periods:

- `june 1 - july 15 00:00-24:00`: Any time from June 1st to July 15th, inclusive
- `thursday -1 00:00-24:00`: Any time on the last Thursday of every month
- `day 1 - 10 13:00-21:00`: From 1 PM to 9 PM on any day from the 1st of any month to the 10th of any month, inclusive

It's likely that the standard `24x7` and `workhours` definitions will be fine for day-to-day monitoring, maybe with a `weekdays` and `weekends` definition added. However, there may well come a time when we need a specific host or service monitored on an unusual schedule, particularly if we're debugging a specific problem that only manifests around a certain time, or have a lot of contacts to manage, or a complex on-call roster.

Note that Nagios Core can behave in unusual ways, particularly with uptime reporting, if the time periods for our monitoring of hosts and services don't add up to 24 hours. Ideally, we should check and notify all our hosts and services in at least some way around the clock, but dealing with the notifications in different ways depending on schedule; for example, we could page the systems administrators about a non-critical system during work hours, but just e-mail them when they're asleep!

See also

> ▸ The *Automating contact rotation*, *Configuring notification periods*, and *Configuring notification groups* recipes in *Chapter 4, Configuring Notifications*

Running a service on all hosts in a group

In this recipe, we'll create a new service, but instead of applying it to an existing host, we'll apply it to an existing hostgroup. In this case, we'll create a group called `webservers`. The steps for this are very similar to adding a service for just one host; only one directive is different.

Getting ready

You should have a working Nagios Core 3.0 or better server running, with a web interface. You should be familiar with adding services to individual hosts.

You should also have at least one hostgroup defined, with at least one host in it; we'll use a group called `webservers`, with the hosts `sparta.naginet` and `athens.naginet` defined in it.

For reference, here is the hostgroup definition and the definitions for the two hosts in it:

```
define hostgroup {
    hostgroup_name   webservers
    alias            Webservers
}
define host {
    use         linux-server
    host_name   athens.naginet
    alias       athens
    address     10.128.0.22
    hostgroups  webservers
}
```

```
define host {
        use           linux-server
        host_name     sparta.naginet
        alias         sparta
        address       10.128.0.21
        hostgroups    webservers
}
```

How to do it...

We can create the service definition for the webservers group as follows:

1. Change to the directory containing the file in which the webservers hostgroup is
    defined, and edit it:

    ```
    # cd /usr/local/nagios/etc/objects
    # vi hostgroups.cfg
    ```

2. Add the following code snippet just after the hostgroup definition. Change the lines in
    bold to suit your own template and hostgroup names:

    ```
    define service {
        use                   generic-service
        hostgroup_name        webservers
        service_description   HTTP
        check_command         check_http
    }
    ```

3. Restart the Nagios Core server:

    ```
    # /etc/init.d/nagios restart
    ```

It's important to note that if we are already monitoring those hosts with a per-host service of
the same name, then we will need to remove those definitions as well; Nagios Core may not
start if a service of the same description is already defined on the same host.

How it works...

Adding a service to a hostgroup works in exactly the same way as adding it to an individual
host, except that it only requires one definition, which is then individually applied to all the
hosts in the group. This means it's a very good way to keep a Nagios Core configuration tidier.
If we have a group of 50 different web servers in it and we need to monitor their HTTP services
on the same basis for each one of them, then we don't need to create 50 service definitions;
we can just create one for their hostgroup, which amounts to a smaller and more easily
updated configuration.

There's more...

Like the `host_name` directive for services, the `hostgroup_name` directive can actually have several hostgroups defined, separated by commas. This means that we can apply the same service to not just one group, but several. For services that we would want to run on several different groups (for example, basic PING monitoring) this can amount to a much more flexible configuration.

See also

- ▶ The *Creating a new service and Creating a new hostgroup* recipe in this chapter
- ▶ The *Using inheritance to simplify configuration* recipe in *Chapter 9, Managing Configuration*

2

Working with Commands and Plugins

In this chapter, we will cover the following recipes:

- ▶ Finding a plugin
- ▶ Installing a plugin
- ▶ Removing a plugin
- ▶ Customizing an existing command
- ▶ Using an alternative check command for a host
- ▶ Writing a new plugin from scratch

Introduction

Nagios Core is perhaps best thought of less as a monitoring tool, and more as a monitoring framework. Its modular design can use any kind of program which returns appropriate values based on some kind of check, such as a `check_command` plugin for a host or service. This is where the concepts of commands and plugins come into play.

For Nagios Core, a **plugin** is any program that can be used to gather information about a host or service. To ensure that a host was responding to PING requests, we'd use a plugin, such as `check_ping`, which when run against a hostname or address—whether by Nagios Core or not—would return a status code to whatever called it, based on whether a response was received to the PING request within a certain period of time. This status code and any accompanying message is what Nagios Core uses to establish what state a host or service is in.

Plugins are generally just like any other program on a Unix-like system; they can be run from the command line, are subject to permissions and owner restrictions, can be written in any programming language, and can take parameters and options to modify how they work. Most importantly, they are entirely separate from Nagios Core itself (even if programmed by the same people), and the way that they're used by the application can be changed.

To allow for additional flexibility in how plugins are used, Nagios Core uses these programs according to the terms of a command definition. A command for a specific plugin defines the way in which that plugin is used, including its location in the filesystem, any parameters it should be passed, and any other options. In particular, parameters and options often include thresholds for WARNING and CRITICAL states.

Nagios Core is usually downloaded and installed along a set of plugins called **Nagios Plugins**, available at http://www.nagiosplugins.org/, which this book assumes you have installed. These plugins were chosen because, as a set, they cover the most common needs for a monitoring infrastructure quite well, including checks for common services, such as web, mail services, and DNS services, as well as more generic checks, such as whether a TCP or UDP port is accessible and open on a server. It's likely that for most of our monitoring needs, we won't need any other plugins; but if we do, Nagios Core makes it possible to use existing plugins in novel ways using custom command definitions, adding third-party plugins written by contributors on the Nagios Exchange website, or even writing custom plugins ourselves from scratch in some special cases.

Finding a plugin

In this recipe, we'll follow a good procedure for finding a plugin appropriate to a specific monitoring task. We'll start by checking to see if an existing plugin is already available to do just what we need. If we can't find one, we'll check to see if we can use another more generic plugin to solve the problem. If we still find that nothing suits, we'll visit Nagios Exchange and search for an appropriate plugin there.

Getting ready

You should have a Nagios Core 3.0 or newer server running with a few hosts and services configured already, and you'll need to have a particular service on one of those hosts, which you're not sure how to monitor.

We'll use a simple problem as an example; we have a server named troy.naginet that runs an rsync process that listens on port 873. We're already monitoring the host's network connectivity via PING, but we'd like to have Nagios Core check whether the rsync server is available and listening at all times, in case it crashes while running or doesn't start up when the system is rebooted.

How to do it...

We can find a new plugin appropriate to any monitoring task as follows:

1. Firstly, since we have the Nagios Core Plugins set installed, we'll check to see if any of the plugins available in it apply directly to our problem. We'll start by visiting `/usr/local/nagios/libexec` on our Nagios Core server, and getting a directory listing:

   ```
   # cd /usr/local/nagios/libexec
   # ls
   check_apt          check_ide_smart      check_nntp        check_simap
   check_breeze       check_ifoperstatus   check_nntps       check_smtp
   check_by_ssh       check_ifstatus       check_nt          check_spop
   ...
   ```

   There's a long list of plugins there, but none of them look like `check_rsync` or `check_backup`, so it doesn't quite seem like there's a plugin in the core to do exactly what we need.

2. However, there is a plugin called `check_tcp`. A web search for its name pulls up its manual page on the Nagios Plugins website as the first result, and a description of what it does:

   "This plugin tests TCP connections with the specified host (or unix socket)."

   We need to do more than just check the port, so this doesn't quite suit us either.

3. A web search for `check_rsync`, which would be an appropriate name for the plugin, turns up a page on the Nagios Exchange website with a plugin named exactly that. We've found an appropriate plugin now:

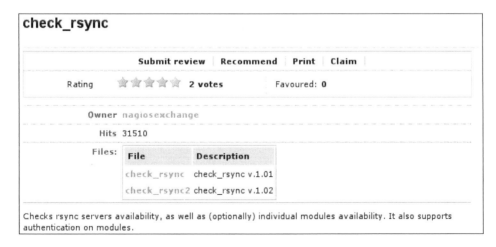

How it works...

If all we needed to do was check that rsync was listening on port 873, and we didn't really need to monitor any of its actual function, then the check_tcp plugin might actually suffice. However, in our case, we might need to find a way to not only check that a port is open, but also check that a specific directory or rsync module is accessible.

Reading the description for check_rsync, it looks like it has the exact functionality we need, checking that a certain rsync module is available on the server. At this point, we could download the plugin and follow its installation instructions.

There's more...

This recipe is intended to highlight that in addition to having a capable set of plugins as a part of the Nagios Core Plugins set, the documentation available online on the Nagios Core Plugins website at http://nagiosplugins.org/ and the other plugins available on Nagios Exchange at http://exchange.nagios.org/ make it relatively straightforward to find an appropriate plugin for the particular monitoring problem we need to solve.

Note that when we download third-party plugins, it's important to check that we trust the plugin to do what we need it to. **Nagios Exchange** is a moderated community with a coding standard, but the plugins are provided at our own risk; if we don't understand what a plugin does, we should be wary of installing it or using it without reading its code, its documentation, and its reviews.

See also

> ▸ The *Installing a plugin*, *Removing a plugin*, and *Writing a new plugin from scratch* recipes in this chapter

Installing a plugin

In this recipe, we'll install a custom plugin that we retrieved from Nagios Exchange onto a Nagios Core server, so that we can use it as a Nagios Core command and hence check a service with it.

Getting ready

You should have a Nagios Core 3.0 or newer server running with a few hosts and services configured already, and have found an appropriate plugin to install, to solve some particular monitoring need. Your Nagios Core server should have internet connectivity to allow you to download the plugin directly from the website.

In this example we'll use `check_rsync`, which is available on the Web at `http://exchange.nagios.org/directory/Plugins/Network-Protocols/Rsync/check_rsync/details`.

This particular plugin is quite simple, consisting of a single Perl script with very basic dependencies. If you want to install this script as an example, then the server will also need to have a Perl interpreter installed; it's installed in `/usr/bin/perl` on many systems.

This example will also include directly testing a server running an `rsync` daemon called `troy.naginet`.

How to do it...

We can download and install a new plugin as follows:

1. Copy the URL for the download link for the most recent version of the `check_rsync` plugin:

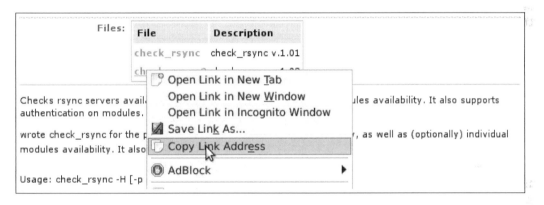

2. Navigate to the plugins directory for the Nagios Core server. The default location is `/usr/local/nagios/libexec`:

    ```
    # cd /usr/local/nagios/libexec
    ```

3. Download the plugin using `wget` into a file called `check_rsync`. It's important to surround the URL in quotes:

    ```
    # wget 'http://exchange.nagios.org/components/com_mtree/
    attachment.php?link_id=307&cf_id=29' -O check_rsync
    ```

4. Make the plugin executable using `chmod` and `chown`:

    ```
    # chown nagios.nagios check_rsync
    ```
    ```
    # chmod 0770 check_rsync
    ```

5. Run the plugin directly with no arguments to check that it runs, and to get usage instructions. It's a good idea to test it as the `nagios` user using `su` or `sudo`:

```
# sudo -s -u nagios
$ ./check_rsync
Usage: check_rsync -H <host> [-p <port>] [-m
<module>[,<user>,<password>] [-m <module>[,<user>,<password>]...]]
```

6. Try running the plugin directly against a host running `rsync`, to see if it works and reports a status:

```
$ ./check_rsync -H troy.naginet
Output normally starts with the status determined, with any extra
information after a colon:
OK: Rsync is up
```

If all of this works, then the plugin is now installed and working correctly.

How it works...

Because Nagios Core plugins are programs in themselves, installing a plugin amounts to saving a program or script into an appropriate directory; in this case, `/usr/local/nagios/libexec`, where all the other plugins live. It's then available to be used the same way as any other plugin.

The next step once the plugin is working is defining a command in the Nagios Core configuration for it, so that it can be used to monitor hosts and/or services. This can be done with the *Creating a new command* recipe in this chapter.

There's more...

If we inspect the Perl script, we can see a little bit of how it works. It works like any other Perl script, except for the fact that its return values are defined in a hash table called `%ERRORS`, and the return values it chooses depend on what happens when it tries to check the `rsync` process. This is the most important part of implementing a plugin for Nagios Core.

Installation procedures for different plugins vary. In particular, many plugins are written in languages such as C, and hence need be compiled. One such plugin is the popular `check_nrpe`. Rather than simply being saved into a directory and made executable, these sorts of plugins often follow the usual pattern of configuration, compilation, and installation:

```
$ ./configure
$ make
# make install
```

For many plugins that are built in this style, the last step in that process will often install the compiled plugin into the appropriate directory for us. In general, if instructions are included with the plugin, then it pays to read them so that we can ensure we install it correctly.

See also

▶   The *Finding a plugin, Removing a plugin*, and *Creating a new command* recipes in this chapter

Removing a plugin

In this recipe, we'll remove a plugin that we no longer need as part of our Nagios Core installation. Perhaps it's not working correctly, the service it monitors is no longer available, or there are security or licensing concerns with its usage.

Getting ready

You should have a Nagios Core 3.0 or newer server running with a few hosts and services configured already, and have a plugin that you would like to remove from the server. In this instance, we'll remove the now unneeded `check_rsync` plugin from our Nagios Core server.

How to do it...

We can remove a plugin from our Nagios Core instance as follows:

1. Remove any part of the configuration that uses the plugin, including hosts or services that use it for `check_command`, and command definitions that refer to the program. As an example, the following definition for a command would no longer work after we removed the `check_rsync` plugin:

    ```
    define command {
        command_name    check_rsync
        command_line    $USER1$/check_rsync -H $HOSTADDRESS$
    }
    ```

    Using a tool such as `grep` can be a good way to find mentions of the command and plugin:

    ```
    # grep -R check_rsync /usr/local/nagios/etc
    ```

2. Change directory on the Nagios Core server to wherever the plugins are kept. The default location is `/usr/local/nagios/libexec`:

    ```
    # cd /usr/local/nagios/libexec
    ```

3. Delete the plugin with the `rm` command:

   ```
   # rm check_rsync
   ```

4. Validate the configuration and restart the Nagios Core server:

   ```
   # /usr/local/nagios/bin/nagios -v /usr/local/nagios/etc/nagios.cfg
   # /etc/init.d/nagios restart
   ```

How it works...

Nagios Core plugins are simply external programs that the server uses to perform checks of hosts and services. If a plugin is no longer wanted, all that needs to be done is to remove references to it in our configuration, if any, and then delete the plugin program from `/usr/local/nagios/libexec`.

There's more...

Usually there's not any harm in leaving the plugin's program on the server even if Nagios Core isn't using it. It doesn't slow anything down or cause any other problems, and it may be needed later. Nagios Core plugins are generally quite small programs, and should not really cause disk space concerns on a modern server.

See also

▸ The *Finding a plugin*, *Installing a plugin*, and *Creating a new command* recipes in this chapter

Creating a new command

In this recipe, we'll create a new command for a plugin that was just installed into the `/usr/local/nagios/libexec` directory on the Nagios Core server. This will define the way in which Nagios Core should use the plugin, and thereby allow it to be used as part of a service definition.

Getting ready

You should have a Nagios Core 3.0 or newer server running with a few hosts and services configured already, and have a plugin installed for which you'd like to define a new command. This will allow you to use it as part of a service definition. In this instance, we'll define a command for an installed `check_rsync` plugin.

How to do it...

We can define a new command in our configuration as follows:

1. Change to the directory containing the objects configuration for Nagios Core. The default location is /usr/local/nagios/etc/objects:

    ```
    # cd /usr/local/nagios/etc/objects
    ```

2. Edit the commands.cfg file:

    ```
    # vi commands.cfg
    ```

3. At the bottom of the file, add the following command definition:

    ```
    define command {
        command_name    check_rsync
        command_line    $USER1$/check_rsync -H $HOSTADDRESS$
    }
    ```

4. Validate the configuration and restart the Nagios Core server:

    ```
    # /usr/local/nagios/bin/nagios -v /usr/local/nagios/etc/nagios.cfg
    # /etc/init.d/nagios restart
    ```

If the validation passes and the server restarts successfully, we should be able to use the check_rsync command in a service definition.

How it works...

The configuration we added to the commands.cfg file defines a new command called check_rsync, which defines a method for using the plugin of the same name to monitor a service. This enables us to use check_rsync as a value for the check_command directive in a service declaration, which might look similar to the following code snippet:

```
define service {
    use                  generic-service
    host_name            troy.naginet
    service_description  RSYNC
    check_command        check_rsync
}
```

Only two directives are required for command definitions, and we've defined both:

► command_name: This defines the unique name with which we can reference the command when we use it in host or service definitions.

► command_line: This defines the command line that should be executed by Nagios Core to make the appropriate check.

This particular command line also uses two macros:

- ▶ $USER1$: This expands to /usr/local/nagios/libexec, the location of the plugin binaries, including check_rsync. It is defined in the sample configuration in the file /usr/local/nagios/etc/resource.cfg.

- ▶ $HOSTADDRESS$: This expands to the address of any host for which this command is used as a host or service definition.

So if we used the command in a service checking the rsync server on troy.naginet, then the completed command might look similar to the following:

```
$ /usr/local/nagios/libexec/check_rsync -H troy.naginet
```

We could run this straight from the command line ourselves as the nagios user to see what kind of results it returns:

```
$ /usr/local/nagios/libexec/check_rsync -H troy.naginet
OK: Rsync is up
```

There's more...

A plugin can be used for more than one command. If we had a particular rsync module to check with the configured name of backup, we could write another command called check_rsync_backup, as follows, to check this module is available:

```
define command {
    command_name   check_rsync_backup
    command_line   $USER1$/check_rsync -H $HOSTADDRESS$ -m backup
}
```

Or if one or more of our rsync servers was running on an alternate port, say port 5873, then we could define a separate command, check_rsync_altport, for that:

```
define command {
    command_name   check_rsync_altport
    command_line   $USER1$/check_rsync -H $HOSTADDRESS$ -p 5873
}
```

Commands can thus be defined as precisely as we need them to be. We explore this in more detail in the *Customizing an existing command* recipe in this chapter.

See also

- ▶ The *Installing a plugin* and *Customizing an existing command* recipes in this chapter

Customizing an existing command

In this recipe, we'll customize an existing command definition. There are a number of reasons why you might want to do this, but a common one is if a check is "overzealous", sending notifications for WARNING or CRITICAL states, which aren't actually terribly worrisome. It can also be useful if a check is too "forgiving" and doesn't detect actual problems with hosts or services.

Another reason is to account for peculiarities in your own network. For example, if you run HTTP daemons on a large number of hosts on the alternative port 8080 that you need to check, it would be convenient to have a check_http_altport command available. We can do this by copying and altering the definition for the vanilla check_http command.

Getting ready

You should have a Nagios Core 3.0 or newer server running with a few hosts and services configured already. You should also already be familiar with the relationship between services, commands, and plugins.

How to do it...

We can customize an existing command definition as follows:

1. Change to the directory containing the objects configuration for Nagios Core. The default location is /usr/local/nagios/etc/objects:

    ```
    # cd /usr/local/nagios/etc/objects
    ```

2. Edit the commands.cfg file, or any file which is at an appropriate location for the check_http command:

    ```
    # vi commands.cfg
    ```

3. Find the definition for the check_http command. In a default Nagios Core configuration, it should look similar to the following:

    ```
    # 'check_http' command_definition
    define command {
        command_name    check_http
        command_line    $USER1$/check_http -H $HOSTADDRESS$ $ARG1$
    }
    ```

4. Copy this definition into a new definition directly below it and alter it to look similar to the following code snippet, renaming the command and adding a new option to its command line:

```
# 'check_http_altport' command_definition
define command {
    command_name    check_http_altport
    command_line    $USER1$/check_http -H $HOSTADDRESS$ -p 8080
$ARG1$
}
```

5. Validate the configuration and restart the Nagios Core server:

```
# /usr/local/nagios/bin/nagios -v /usr/local/nagios/etc/nagios.cfg
```

```
# /etc/init.d/nagios restart
```

If the validation passed and the server restarted successfully, we should now be able to use the check_http_altport command, which is based on the original check_http command, in a service definition.

How it works...

The configuration we added to the commands.cfg file reproduces the command definition for check_http, but changes it in two ways:

- ▸ It renames the command from check_http to check_http_alt, which is necessary to distinguish the commands from one another. Command names in Nagios Core, just like host names, must be unique.

- ▸ It adds the option -p 8080 to the command-line call, specifying the time when the call to check_http is made. The check will be made using TCP port 8080, rather than the default value for TCP port 80.

The check_http_alt command can now be used as a check command in the same way as a check_http command. For example, a service definition that checks whether the sparta.naginet host is running an HTTP daemon on port 8080 might look similar to the following code snippet:

```
define service {
    use                 generic-service
    host_name           sparta.naginet
    service_description HTTP_8080
    check_command       check_http_alt
}
```

There's more...

This recipe's title implies that we should customize the existing commands by editing them in place, and indeed, this works fine if we really do want to do things this way. Instead of copying the command definition, we could just add the `-p 8080` or another customization to the command line and change the original command.

However, this is bad practice in most cases, mostly because it could break the existing monitoring and be potentially confusing to other administrators of the Nagios Core server. If we have a special case for monitoring—in this case, checking a non-standard port for HTTP—then it's wise to create a whole new command based on the existing one with the customizations we need.

There is no limit to the number of commands you can define, so you can be very liberal in defining as many alternative commands as you need. It's a good idea to give them instructive names that say something about what they do, as well as to add explanatory comments to the configuration file. You can add a comment to the file by prefixing it with a # character:

```
#
# 'check_http_altport' command_definition. This is to keep track of
# servers that have panels running on alternative ports.
#
define command {
    command_name   check_http_altport
    command_line   $USER1$/check_http -H $HOSTADDRESS$ -p 8080 $ARG1$
}
```

See also

- ▶ The *Creating a new command* recipe in this chapter
- ▶ The *Creating a new service* recipe in *Chapter 1, Understanding Hosts, Services, and Contacts*

Using an alternative check command for hosts

In this recipe, we'll learn how to deal with a slightly tricky case in network monitoring—monitoring a server that doesn't respond to PING, but still provides some network service that requires checking.

It's good practice to allow PING where you can, as it's one of the stipulations in **RFC 1122** and a very useful diagnostic tool not just for monitoring, but also for troubleshooting. However, sometimes servers that are accessed only by a few people might be configured not to respond to these messages, perhaps for reasons of secrecy. It's quite common for domestic routers to be configured this way.

Another very common reason for this problem, and the example we'll address here, is checking servers that are behind an **IPv4 NAT** firewall. It's not possible to address the host directly via an **RFC1918** address, such as 192.168.1.20, from the public Internet. Pinging the public interface of the router therefore doesn't tell us whether the host for which it is translating addresses is actually working.

However, port 22 for SSH is forwarded from the outside to this server, and it's this service that we need to check for availability.

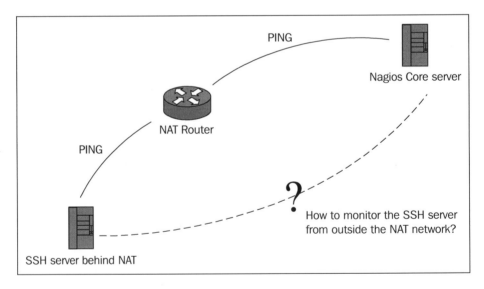

We'll do this by checking whether the host is up through an SSH check, since we can't PING it from the outside as we normally would.

Getting ready

You should have a Nagios Core 3.0 or newer server running with a few hosts and services configured already. You should also already be familiar with the relationship between services, commands, and plugins.

How to do it...

We can specify an alternative check method for a host as follows:

1. Change to the directory containing the objects configuration for Nagios Core. The default location is `/usr/local/nagios/etc/objects`:

   ```
   # cd /usr/local/nagios/etc/objects
   ```

2. Find the file that contains the host definition for the host that won't respond to PING, and edit it. In this example, our `crete.naginet` host is the one we want to edit:

   ```
   # vi crete.naginet.cfg
   ```

3. Change or define the `check_command` parameter of the host to the command that we want to use for the check instead of the usual `check-host-alive` or `check_ping` plugin. In this case, we want to use `check_ssh`. The resulting host definition might look similar to the following code snippet:

   ```
   define host {
        use             linux-server
        host_name       crete.naginet
        alias           crete
        address         10.128.0.23
        check_command   check_ssh
   }
   ```

   Note that defining `check_command` still works even if we're using a host template, such as `generic-host` or `linux-server`. It's a good idea to check that the host will actually respond to our check as we expect it to:

   ```
   # sudo -s -u nagios
   $ /usr/local/nagios/libexec/check_ssh -H 10.128.0.23
   SSH OK - OpenSSH_5.5p1 Debian-6+squeeze1 (protocol 2.0)
   ```

4. Validate the configuration and restart the Nagios Core server:

   ```
   # /usr/local/nagios/bin/nagios -v /usr/local/nagios/etc/nagios.cfg
   # /etc/init.d/nagios restart
   ```

With this done, the next scheduled host check for the `crete.naginet` server should show the host as UP, because it was checked with the `check_ssh` command and not the usual `check-host-alive` command.

How it works

The configuration we added for the `crete.naginet` host uses `check_ssh` to check whether the host is UP, rather than a check that uses PING. This is appropriate because the only public service accessible from `crete.naginet` is its SSH service.

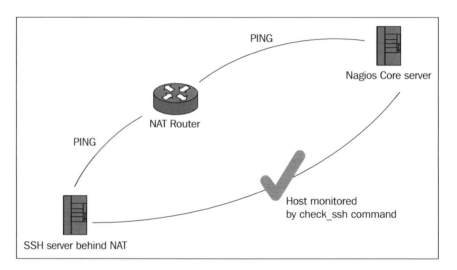

The `check_ssh` command is normally used to check whether a service is available, rather than a host. However, Nagios Core allows us to use it as a host check command as well. Most service commands work this way; you could check a web server behind NAT in the same way with `check_http`.

There's more...

Note that for completeness' sake, it would also be appropriate to monitor the NAT router via PING, or some other check appropriate to its public address. That way, if the host check for the SSH server fails, we can check to see if the NAT router in front of it is still available, which assists in troubleshooting whether the problem is with the server or with the NAT router in front of it. You can make this setup even more useful by making the NAT router a parent host for the SSH server behind it, explained in the *Creating a network host hierarchy* recipe in *Chapter 8, Understanding the Network Layout*.

See also

- ▸ The *Monitoring SSH for any host* and *Checking an alternative SSH port* recipes in *Chapter 5, Monitoring Methods*

- ▸ The *Monitoring local services on a remote machine with NRPE* recipe in *Chapter 6, Enabling Remote Execution*

- ▸ The *Creating a network host hierarchy* and *Establishing a host dependency* recipes in *Chapter 8, Understanding the Network Layout*

Writing a new plugin from scratch

Even given the very useful standard plugins in the Nagios Plugins set, and the large number of custom plugins available on Nagios Exchange, occasionally as our monitoring setup grows more refined, we may find that there is some service or property of a host that we would like to check, but for which there doesn't seem to be any suitable plugin available. Every network is different, and sometimes the plugins that others have generously donated their time to make for the community don't quite cover all your bases. Generally, the more specific your monitoring requirements get, the less likely it is that there's a plugin available that does exactly what you need.

In this example, we'll deal with a very particular problem that we'll assume can't be dealt with effectively by any known Nagios Core plugins, and we'll write one ourselves using Perl. Here's the example problem:

Our Linux security team wants to be able to automatically check whether any of our servers are running kernels that have known exploits. However, they're not worried about every vulnerable kernel, only specific versions. They have provided us with the version numbers of three kernels having small vulnerabilities that they're not particularly worried about but that do need patching, and one they're extremely worried about.

Let's say the minor vulnerabilities are in the kernels with version numbers `2.6.19`, `2.6.24`, and `3.0.1`. The serious vulnerability is in the kernel with version number `2.6.39`. Note that the version numbers in this case are arbitrary and don't necessarily reflect any real kernel vulnerabilities!

The team could log in to all of the servers individually to check them, but the servers are of varying ages and access methods, and managed by different people. They would also have to check manually more than once, because it's possible that a naive administrator could upgrade to a kernel that's known to be vulnerable in an older release, and they also might want to add other vulnerable kernel numbers for checking later on.

So, the team have asked us to solve the problem with Nagios Core monitoring, and we've decided the best way to do it is to write our own plugin, `check_vuln_kernel`, which checks the output of `uname` for a kernel version string, and then does the following:

- If it's one of the slightly vulnerable kernels, then it will return a WARNING state, so that we can let the security team know that they should address it when they're next able to.

- If it's the highly vulnerable kernel version, then it will return a CRITICAL state, so that the security team knows a patched kernel needs to be installed immediately.

- If `uname` gives an error or output we don't understand, then it will return an UNKNOWN state, alerting the team to a bug in the plugin or possibly more serious problems with the server.

- Otherwise, it returns an OK state, confirming that the kernel is not known to be a vulnerable one.

- Finally, they want to be able to see at a glance in the Nagios Core monitoring what the kernel version is, and whether it's vulnerable or not.

For the purposes of this example, we'll only monitor the Nagios Core server itself, but via NRPE we'd be able to install this plugin on the other servers that require this monitoring, where they'll work just as well. You should see the *Monitoring local services on a remote machine with NRPE* recipe in *Chapter 6, Enabling Remote Execution* to learn how to do this.

While this problem is very specific, we'll approach it in a very general way, which you'll be able to adapt to any solution where it's required for a Nagios plugin to:

1. Run a command and pull its output into a variable.
2. Check the output for the presence or absence of certain patterns.
3. Return an appropriate status based on those tests.

All that means is that if you're able to do this, you'll be able to effectively monitor anything on a server from Nagios Core!

Getting ready

You should have a Nagios Core 3.0 or newer server running with a few hosts and services configured already. You should also already be familiar with the relationship between services, commands, and plugins. You should also have Perl installed.

This will be a rather long recipe that ties in a lot of Nagios Core concepts. You should be familiar with all the following concepts:

- Defining new hosts and services, and how they relate to one another
- Defining new commands, and how they relate to the plugins they call

▸ Installing, testing, and using Nagios Core plugins

Some familiarity with Perl would also be helpful, but is not required. We'll include comments to explain what each block of code is doing in the plugin.

How to do it...

We can write, test, and implement our example plugin as follows:

1. Change to the directory containing the plugin binaries for Nagios Core. The default location is /usr/local/nagios/libexec:

   ```
   # cd /usr/local/nagios/libexec
   ```

2. Start editing a new file called check_vuln_kernel:

   ```
   # vi check_vuln_kernel
   ```

3. Include the following code in it; take note of the comments, which explain what each block of code is doing:

   ```perl
   #!/usr/bin/env perl


   #
   # Use strict Perl style and report potential problems to help us write this
   # securely and portably.
   #
   use strict;
   use warnings;


   #
   # Include the Nagios utils.pm file, which includes definitions for the return
   # statuses that are appropriate for each level: OK, WARNING, CRITICAL, and
   # UNKNOWN. These will become available in the %ERRORS hash.
   #
   use lib "/usr/local/nagios/libexec";
   use utils "%ERRORS";
   ```

```perl
#
# Define a pattern that matches any kernel vulnerable enough so
that if we find
# it we should return a CRITICAL status.
#
my $critical_pattern = "^(2\.6\.39)[^\\d]";


#
# Same again, but for kernels that only need a WARNING status.
#
my $warning_pattern = "^(2\.6\.19|2\.6\.24|3\.0\.1)[^\\d]";


#
# Run the command uname with option -r to get the kernel release
version, put
# the output into a scalar $release, and trim any newlines or
whitespace
# around it.
#
chomp(my $release = qx|/bin/uname -r|);


#
# If uname -r exited with an error status, that is, anything
greater than 1,
# then there was a problem and we need to report that as the
UNKNOWN status
# defined by Nagios Core's utils.pm.
#
if ($? != 0) {
    exit $ERRORS{UNKNOWN};
}


#
# Check to see if any of the CRITICAL patterns are matched by the
release
# number. If so, print the version number and exit, returning the
appropriate
```

```
# status.
#
if ($release =~ m/$critical_pattern/) {
    printf "CRITICAL: %s\n", $release;
    exit $ERRORS{CRITICAL};
}


#
# Same again, but for WARNING patterns.
#
if ($release =~ m/$warning_pattern/) {
    printf "WARNING: %s\n", $release;
    exit $ERRORS{WARNING};
}


#
# If we got this far, then uname -r worked and didn't match any of
the
# vulnerable patterns, so we'll print the kernel release and
return an OK
# status.
#
printf "OK: %s\n", $release;
exit $ERRORS{OK};
```

4. Make the plugin owned by the `nagios` user and executable with `chmod`:

```
# chown nagios.nagios check_vuln_kernel
# chmod 0770 check_vuln_kernel
```

Run the plugin directly to test it:

```
# sudo -s -u nagios
$ ./check_vuln_kernel
OK: 2.6.32-5-686
```

We should now be able to use the plugin in a command, and hence in a service check, just like any other command. Note that the code for this plugin is included in the code bundle of this book for your convenience.

How it works...

The code we added in the new plugin file `check_vuln_kernel` is actually quite simple:

1. It runs `uname -r` to get the version number of the kernel.
2. If that didn't work, it exits with a status of UNKNOWN.
3. If the version number matches anything in a pattern containing critical version numbers, it exits with a status of `CRITICAL`.
4. If the version number matches anything in a pattern containing warning version numbers, it exits with a status of `WARNING`.
5. Otherwise, it exits with a status of `OK`.

It also prints the status as a string, along with the kernel version number, if it was able to retrieve one.

We might set up a command definition for this plugin as follows:

```
define command {
    command_name   check_vuln_kernel
    command_line   $USER1$/check_vuln_kernel
}
```

In turn, we might set up a service definition for that command as follows:

```
define service {
    use                  local-service
    host_name            localhost
    service_description  VULN_KERNEL
    check_command        check_vuln_kernel
}
```

If the kernel was not vulnerable, the service's appearance in the web interface might look similar to the following screenshot:

VULN KERNEL OK   06-02-2012 18:00:13 0d 0h 0m 3s   1/4   OK: 2.6.32-5-686

However, if the monitoring server itself happened to be running a vulnerable kernel, then it might look more similar to the following screenshot (and send consequent notifications, if configured to do so):

VULN KERNEL CRITICAL   06-02-2012 18:02:37 0d 0h 0m 8s   1/4   CRITICAL: 2.6.39-5-686

There's more...

This may be a simple plugin, but its structure can be generalized to all sorts of monitoring tasks. If we can figure out the correct logic to return the status we want in an appropriate programming language, then we can write a plugin to do basically anything.

A plugin like this could just as effectively be written in C for improved performance, but we'll assume for simplicity's sake that high performance for the plugin is not required. Instead, we can use a language that's better suited for quick ad hoc scripts like this one; in this case, we use Perl. The file `utils.sh`, also in `/usr/local/nagios/libexec`, allows us to write in shell script if we'd prefer that.

If you write a plugin that you think could be generally useful for the Nagios community at large, then please consider putting it under a free software license and submitting it to the Nagios Exchange, so that others can benefit from your work. Community contribution and support is what has made Nagios Core such a great monitoring platform in such wide use.

Any plugin you publish in this way should conform to the Nagios Plugin Development Guidelines. At the time of writing, these are available at `http://nagiosplug.sourceforge.net/developer-guidelines.html`.

Finally, you should note that the method of including `utils.pm`, used in this example, may be deprecated in future versions of Nagios Core. It is used here for simplicity's sake. The new method of including it in Perl is done with a CPAN module called `Nagios::Plugin`.

See also

- ▶ The *Creating a new command* and *Customizing an existing command* recipes in this chapter
- ▶ The *Creating a new service recipe* in *Chapter 1, Understanding Hosts, Services, and Contacts*
- ▶ The *Monitoring local services on a remote machine with NRPE* recipe in *Chapter 6, Enabling Remote Execution*

3

Working with Checks and States

In this chapter, we will cover the following recipes:

- ▶ Specifying how frequently to check a host or service
- ▶ Changing thresholds for PING RTT and packet loss
- ▶ Changing thresholds for disk usage
- ▶ Scheduling downtime for a host or service
- ▶ Managing brief outages with flapping
- ▶ Adjusting flapping percentage thresholds for a service

Introduction

Once hosts and services are configured in Nagios Core, its behavior is primarily dictated by the checks it makes to ensure that hosts and services are operating as expected, and the state it concludes these hosts and services must be in as a result of those checks.

How often it's appropriate to check hosts and services, and on what basis it's appropriate to flag a host or service as having problems, depends very much on the nature of the service and the importance of it running all the time. If a host on the other side of the world is being checked with PING, and during busy periods its round trip time is over 100ms, then this may not actually be a cause for concern at all, and perhaps not something to even flag a WARNING state over, let alone a CRITICAL one.

However, if the same host were on the local network where it would be appropriate to expect round trip times of less than 10ms, then a round trip time of more than 100ms could well be considered a grave cause for concern, signaling a packet storm or other problem with the local network, and we would want to notify the appropriate administrators immediately. Similarly, for hosts such as web servers, we may not be concerned by a response time of more than a second for a page on a busy budget shared web host for customers. But if the response time for the corporate website or a dedicated colocation customer was getting that bad, it might well be something to notify the web server administrator about.

Hosts and services are therefore not all created equal. Nagios Core provides several ways to define behaviors with more precision, as follows:

- How often a host or service should be checked with its appropriate `check_command` plugin

- How bad a check's results have to be before a WARNING or CRITICAL problem is flagged, if at all

- Defining a downtime period for a host or service, so that Nagios Core knows not to expect it to operate during a specified period of time, often for upgrades or other maintenance

- Whether to automatically tolerate flapping, or hosts and services seeming to go up and down a lot

This chapter will use some common instances of problems with the preceding behaviors to give examples showing how to configure them.

Specifying how frequently to check a host or service

In this recipe, we'll configure a very important host to be checked every three minutes, and if Nagios Core finds it is DOWN as a result of the check failing, it will check again after a minute before it sends a notification about the state to its defined contact. We'll do this by customizing the definition of an existing host.

Getting ready

You should have a Nagios Core 3.0 or newer server with at least one host configured already. We'll use the example of `sparta.naginet`, a host defined in its own file.

You should also understand the basics of commands and plugins, in particular the meaning of the `check_command` directive. These are covered in the recipes in *Chapter 2, Working with Commands and Plugins.*

How to do it...

We can customize the check frequency for a host as follows:

1. Change to the `objects` configuration directory for Nagios Core. The default is `/usr/local/nagios/etc/objects`. If you've put the definition of your host in a different file, then move to its directory instead:

   ```
   # cd /usr/local/nagios/etc/objects
   ```

2. Edit the file containing your host definition, and find the definition within the file:

   ```
   # vi sparta.naginet.cfg
   ```

   The host definition may look similar to the following:

   ```
   define host {
           use                     linux-server
           host_name               sparta.naginet
           alias                   sparta
           address                 10.128.0.21
   }
   ```

3. Add or edit the value of the `check_interval` directive to 3:

   ```
   define host {
           use                     linux-server
           host_name               sparta.naginet
           alias                   sparta
           address                 10.128.0.21
           check_interval          3
   }
   ```

4. Add or edit the value of the `retry_interval` directive to 1:

   ```
   define host {
           use                     linux-server
           host_name               sparta.naginet
           alias                   sparta
           address                 10.128.0.21
           check_interval          3
           retry_interval          1
   }
   ```

5. Add or edit the value of `max_check_attempts` to 2:

```
define host {
      use                 linux-server
      host_name           sparta.naginet
      alias               sparta
      address             10.128.0.21
      check_interval      3
      retry_interval      1
      max_check_attempts  2
}
```

6. Validate the configuration and restart the Nagios Core server:

```
# /usr/local/nagios/bin/nagios -v /usr/local/nagios/etc/nagios.cfg
# /etc/init.d/nagios restart
```

With this done, Nagios Core will run the relevant `check_command` plugin (probably something like `check-host-alive`) against this host every three minutes; if it fails, it will flag the host as down, check again one minute later, and only then send a notification to its defined contact if the second check fails too.

How it works...

The preceding configuration changed three properties of the host object type to effect the changes we needed:

▶ `check_interval`: This defines how long to wait between successive checks of the host under normal conditions. We set this to 3, or three minutes.

▶ `retry_interval`: This defines how long to wait between follow-up checks of the host after first finding problems with it. We set this to 1, or one minute.

▶ `max_check_attempts`: This defines how many checks in total should be run before a notification is sent. We set this to 2 for two checks. This means that after the first failed check is run, Nagios Core will run another check a minute later, and will only send a notification if this check fails as well. If two checks have been run and the host is still in a problem state, it will go from a SOFT state to a HARD state.

Note that setting these directives in a host that derives from a template, as is the case with our example, will override any of the same directives in the template.

There's more...

It's important to note that we can also define the units used by the `check_interval` and `retry_interval` commands. They only use minutes by default, checking the `interval_length` setting that's normally defined in the root configuration file for Nagios Core, by default `/usr/local/nagios/etc/nagios.cfg`:

```
interval_length=60
```

If we wanted to specify these periods in seconds instead, we could set this value to `1` instead of `60`:

```
interval_length=1
```

This would allow us, for example, to set `check_interval` to `15`, to check a host every 15 seconds. Note that if we have a lot of hosts with such a tight checking schedule, it might overburden the Nagios Core process, particularly if the checks take a long time to complete.

Don't forget that changing these properties for a large number of hosts can be tedious, so if it's necessary to set these directives to some common value for more than a few hosts, then it may be appropriate to set the values in a host template and then have these hosts inherit from it. See the *Using inheritance to simplify configuration* recipe in *Chapter 9, Configuration Management* for details on this. Note that the same three directives also work for service declarations, and have the same meaning. We could define the same notification behavior for a service on `sparta.naginet` with a declaration similar to the following:

```
define service {
        use                  generic-service
        host_name            sparta.naginet
        service_description  HTTP
        check_command        check_http
        address              10.128.0.21
        check_interval       3
        retry_interval       1
        max_check_attempts   2
}
```

See also

▸ The *Scheduling downtime for a host* recipe in this chapter

▸ The *Using inheritance to simplify configuration* recipe in *Chapter 9, Configuration Management*

Changing thresholds for PING RTT and packet loss

In this recipe, we'll set up a service for a host that monitors PING, and take a look at how to adjust the thresholds for the WARNING and CRITICAL states, done using command arguments. We'll accomplish this by setting up a service for an existing host that's already being checked with a check_command plugin, such as check-host-alive. Our service will be used to monitor not whether the host is completely DOWN, but whether it's responding to PING requests within a reasonable period of time.

This could be useful to notify and assist in diagnosing problems with the actual connectivity of a service or host.

This recipe will therefore serve as a good demonstration of the concepts of supplying arguments to a command, and adjusting the WARNING and CRITICAL thresholds for a particular service.

Getting ready

You should have a Nagios Core 3.0 or newer server with at least one host configured already, and using a check_command plugin of check-host-alive. We'll use the example of sparta.naginet, a host defined in its own file.

You should also understand the basics of how hosts and services fit together in a Nagios Core configuration, and be familiar with the use of commands and plugins via the check_ command directive.

How to do it...

We can add our PING service to the existing host with custom round trip time and packet loss thresholds as follows:

1. Change to the objects configuration directory for Nagios Core. The default is /usr/ local/nagios/etc/objects. If you've put the definition of your host in a different file, then move to its directory instead:

   ```
   # cd /usr/local/nagios/etc/objects
   ```

2. Edit the file containing your host definition:

   ```
   # vi sparta.naginet.cfg
   ```

3. Add the following definition to the end of the file. Of most interest here is the value for the check_command directive:

   ```
   define service {
       use                 generic-service
   ```

```
    host_name              sparta.naginet
    service_description    PING
    check_command          check_ping!100,20%!200,40%
}
```

4. Validate the configuration and restart the Nagios Core server:

    ```
    # /usr/local/nagios/bin/nagios -v /usr/local/nagios/etc/nagios.cfg
    # /etc/init.d/nagios restart
    ```

With this done, Nagios Core will not only run a host check of `check-host-alive` against your original host to ensure that it's up, but it will also run a more stringent check of the PING responses from the machine as a service to check that it's adequately responsive:

- If the **Round Trip Time** (**RTT**) of the PING response is greater than 100ms (but less than 200ms), Nagios Core will flag a `WARNING` state.

- If the RTT of the PING response is greater than 200ms, Nagios Core will flag a `CRITICAL` state.

- If more than 20 percent (but less than 40 percent) of the PING requests receive no response, Nagios Core will flag a `WARNING` state.

- If more than 40 percent of the PING requests receive no response, Nagios Core will flag a `CRITICAL` state.

In both cases, a notification will be sent to the service's defined contacts if configured to do so.

Otherwise, this service works the same way as any other service, and appears in the web interface.

How it works...

The configuration we added for our existing host creates a new service with a `service_description` of PING. For check_command, we use the `check_ping` command, which uses the plugin of the same name. The interesting part here is what follows the `check_command` definition: the string `!100,20%!200,40%`.

In Nagios Core, a `!` character is used as a separator for arguments that should be passed to the command. In the case of `check_ping`, the first argument defines thresholds, or conditions that, if met, should make Nagios Core flag a `WARNING` state for the service. Similarly, the second argument defines the thresholds for a `CRITICAL` state.

Each of the two arguments are comprised of two comma-separated terms: the first number is the threshold for the RTT of the PING request and its response that should trigger a state, and the second number is the percentage of packet loss that should be tolerated before raising the same state.

This pattern of arguments is specific to `check_ping`; they would not work for other commands such as `check_http`.

There's more...

If we want to look in a bit more detail at how these arguments are applied, we can inspect the command definition for `check_ping`. By default, this is in the `/usr/local/nagios/etc/objects/commands.cfg` file, and looks similar to the following:

```
define command {
      command_name   check_ping
      command_line   $USER1$/check_ping -H $HOSTADDRESS$ -w $ARG1$ -c
$ARG2$ -p 5
}
```

In the value for `command_line`, four macros are used:

- ▶ `$USER1$`: This expands to `/usr/local/nagios/libexec`, or the directory in which the Nagios Core plugins are normally kept, including `check_ping`.

- ▶ `$HOSTADDRESS$`: This expands to the hostname for the host or service definition in which the command is used. In this case, it expands to `10.128.0.21`, the value of the `address` directive for the `sparta.naginet` host.

- ▶ `$ARG1$`: This expands to the value given for the first argument of the command, in our recipe's case, the string `100,20%`.

- ▶ `$ARG2$`: This expands to the value given for the second argument of the command; in our recipe's case, the string `200,40%`.

The complete command-line call for our specific check with all these substitutions made would therefore look similar to the following:

```
/usr/local/nagios/libexec/check_ping -H 10.128.0.21 -w 100,20% -c 200,
40% -p 5
```

This command line makes use of four parameters of the `check_ping` program:

- ▶ `-H`: This specifies the address of the host to check
- ▶ `-w`: This specifies the thresholds for raising a `WARNING` state
- ▶ `-c`: This specifies the thresholds for raising a `CRITICAL` state
- ▶ `-p`: This specifies the number of PING requests to send

We can run this directly from the command line on the Nagios Core server to see what the results of the check might be:

```
# /usr/local/nagios/libexec/check_ping -H 10.128.0.21 -w 100,20% -c
200,40% -p 5
```

The preceding command yields an output including the OK result of the check, and also some performance data, as follows:

```
PING OK - Packet loss = 0%, RTA = 0.17 ms|rta=0.174000
ms;100.000000;200.000000;0.000000 pl=0%;5;10;0
```

The arguments specified in the command are therefore used to customize the behavior of check_command for the particular host or service being edited.

See also

▶ The *Changing thresholds for disk usage* recipe in this chapter

▶ The *Creating a new service* recipe in *Chapter 1, Understanding Hosts, Services, and Contacts*

▶ The *Customizing an existing command* and *Creating a new command* recipes in *Chapter 2, Working with Commands and Plugins*

▶ The *Monitoring PING for any host* recipe in *Chapter 5, Monitoring Methods*

Changing thresholds for disk usage

In this recipe, we'll configure the Nagios Core server to check its own disk usage, and to flag a WARNING or CRITICAL state depending on how little free space is left on the disk. We'll accomplish this by adding a new service to the already defined localhost called DISK, which will run the check_local_disk command to examine the state of mounted volumes on the server.

Because burgeoning disk usage can creep up on any system administrator, and because of the dire effect it can have when a disk suddenly fills completely without any warning, this is amongst the more important things to monitor in any given network.

For simplicity, we'll demonstrate this only for the monitoring server itself, as a host called localhost on 127.0.0.1. This is because the check_disk plugin can't directly check the disk usage of a remote server over a network. However, the principles discussed here could be adapted to running the check on a remote server using check_nrpe. The use of NRPE is discussed in all the recipes in *Chapter 6, Enabling Remote Execution*.

Getting ready

You should have a Nagios Core 3.0 or newer server with a definition for `localhost`, so that the monitoring host is able to check itself. A host definition for `localhost` is included in the sample configuration in `/usr/local/nagios/etc/objects/localhost.cfg`. You should also understand the basics of how hosts and services fit together in a Nagios Core configuration, and be familiar with the use of commands and plugins via the `check_command` directive.

We'll use the example of `olympus.naginet` as our Nagios Core server checking itself, with one block device on one disk, with its device file at `/dev/sda1`.

How to do it...

We can add our `DISK` service to the existing host with custom usage thresholds as follows:

1. Change to the objects configuration directory for Nagios Core. The default is `/usr/local/nagios/etc/objects`. If you've put the definition for your host in a different file, move to its directory instead:

   ```
   # cd /usr/local/nagios/etc/objects
   ```

2. Edit the file containing your host definition:

   ```
   # vi localhost.cfg
   ```

3. Add the following definition to the end of the file. Of most interest here is the value for the `check_command` directive:

   ```
   define service {
       use                    local-service
       host_name              localhost
       service_description    DISK
       check_command          check_local_disk!10%!5%!/dev/sda1
   }
   ```

4. Validate the configuration and restart the Nagios Core server:

   ```
   # /usr/local/nagios/bin/nagios -v /usr/local/nagios/etc/nagios.cfg
   # /etc/init.d/nagios restart
   ```

With this done, a new service is created for `localhost` that checks the disk usage on `/dev/sda1`, and flags a WARNING state for the service if the free space is below 10 percent, and a CRITICAL state if it is below 5 percent.

In both cases, a notification will be sent to the service's defined contacts, if configured to do so.

How it works

The configuration we added for our existing host creates a new service with a `service_description` of DISK. For check_command, we use the `check_local_disk` command, which in turn uses the `check_disk` plugin to check the local machine's disks. The interesting part here is what follows the `check_local_disk` definition: the string `!10%!5%!/dev/sda1`.

In Nagios Core, a `!` character is used as a separator for arguments that should be passed to the command. In the case of `check_local_disk`, the first two arguments define thresholds, or conditions that, if met, should make Nagios Core flag a WARNING state (first argument, 10 percent) or a CRITICAL state (second argument, 5 percent) for the service. The third argument defines the device name of the disk to check, `/dev/sda1`.

There's more...

If we want to look in a bit more detail at how these arguments are applied, we can inspect the command definition for `check_local_disk`. By default, this is in the file `/usr/local/nagios/etc/objects/commands.cfg`, and looks similar to the following:

```
define command {
    command_name    check_local_disk
    command_line    $USER1$/check_disk -w $ARG1$ -c $ARG2$ -p $ARG3$
}
```

In this case, `command_name` and the name of the plugin used in the `command_line` are not the same.

In the value for `command_line`, four macros are used:

▸ `$USER1$`: This expands to `/usr/local/nagios/libexec`, or the directory in which the Nagios Core plugins are normally kept, including `check_disk`.

▸ `$ARG1$`: This expands to the value given for the first argument of the command; in this case, the string `10%`.

▸ `$ARG2$`: This expands to the value given for the second argument of the command; in this case, the string `5%`.

▸ `$ARG3$`: This expands to the value given for the third argument of the command; in this case, the string `/dev/sda1`.

The complete command-line call for our specific check with all these substitutions made would therefore be as follows:

```
/usr/local/nagios/libexec/check_disk -w 10% -c 5% -p /dev/sda1
```

This command line makes use of three parameters of the check_disk program:

- ► -w: This specifies the thresholds for raising a WARNING state
- ► -c: This specifies the thresholds for raising a CRITICAL state
- ► -p: This specifies the device file for the disk to check

We can run this directly from the command line on the Nagios Core server to see what the results of the check might be:

```
# /usr/local/nagios/libexec/check_disk -w 10% -c 5% -p /dev/sda1
```

The output includes both the OK result of the check, and also some performance data:

```
DISK OK - free space: / 2575 MB (71% inode=78%); |
/=1044MB;3432;3051;0;3814
```

See also

- ► The *Changing thresholds for disk usage* recipe in this chapter
- ► The *Creating a new service* recipe in *Chapter 1, Understanding Hosts, Services, and Contacts*
- ► The *Customizing an existing command* and *Creating a new command* recipes in *Chapter 2, Working with Commands and Plugins*
- ► The *Monitoring PING for any host* recipe in *Chapter 5, Monitoring Methods*

Scheduling downtime for a host or service

In this recipe, we'll learn how to schedule downtime for a host or service in Nagios Core. This is useful for elegantly suppressing notifications for some predictable period of time; a very good example is when servers require downtime to be upgraded, or to have their hardware checked.

In this example, we'll demonstrate scheduling downtime for a host named sparta.naginet, and we'll examine the changes it makes in the web interface.

Getting ready

You should have a Nagios Core 3.0 or newer server with a definition for at least one host and at least one service, and some idea of when you would like your downtime to be scheduled. You should also have a working web interface, per the QuickStart installation of Nagios Core 3.0.

You should also have Nagios Core configured to process external commands, and have given your web interface user the permissions to apply them. If you are logging in as the `nagiosadmin` user per the recommended quick start guide, then you can check this is the case with the following directive in `/usr/local/nagios/etc/nagios.cfg`:

```
check_external_commands=1
```

Permissions to submit external commands from the web interface are defined in `/usr/local/nagios/etc/cgi.cfg`; check that your username is included in these directives:

```
authorized_for_all_service_commands=nagiosadmin
authorized_for_all_host_commands=nagiosadmin
```

If you have followed the Nagios Core QuickStart guides, then you will probably find this is already working: `http://nagios.sourceforge.net/docs/3_0/quickstart.html`.

How to do it...

We can set up a fixed period of scheduled downtime for our host and service as follows:

1. Log into the web interface for Nagios Core.
2. Click **Hosts** in the left menu:

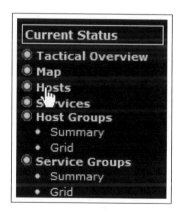

3. Click on the host's name in the table that comes up, to view the details for that host:

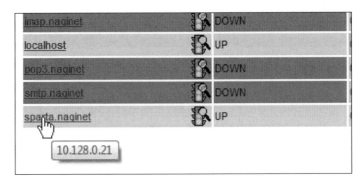

4. Click on **Schedule downtime for this host** in the **Host Commands** menu:

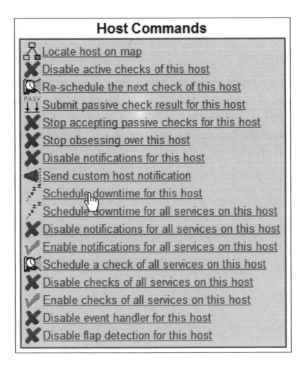

5. Fill out the fields in the resulting form, including the following details:

   ❑ **Host Name**: The name of the host for which you're scheduling downtime. This should have been filled out for you.

   ❑ **Author**: Your name, for records of who scheduled the downtime. This may be greyed out and just say **Nagios Admin**; that's fine.

- ❏ **Comment**: Some comment explaining the reason for the downtime.
- ❏ **Start Time**: The time at which the scheduled downtime should begin, and when the state notifications end.
- ❏ **End Time**: The time at which the scheduled downtime should end, and when the state notifications resume.

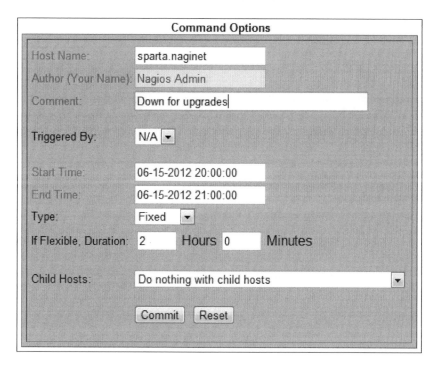

In this case, our downtime will be from 8:00 PM to 9:00 PM on the 15th of June, 2012.

6. Click on **Commit** to submit the downtime definition, and then **Done** in the screen that follows.

With this done, we can safely bring the `sparta.naginet` host down between the nominated times, and any notifications for the host and any of its services will be suppressed until the downtime is over.

Note that restarting Nagios Core is not required for this step, as it usually would be for changes made to Nagios Core's configuration files. The change is done "on the fly".

Note also that comments now appear in the detailed information for both the host and service, defining the downtime and including the reason specified for it.

How it works...

The preceding steps nominate a period of downtime for both the `sparta.naginet` server and all of its services. This accomplishes two things:

- It suppresses all notifications (whether e-mails or anything else) for the host or service for the appropriate time period, including `RECOVERY` notifications. The only exceptions are the `DOWNTIMESTART` and `DOWNTIMEEND` notifications.

- It adds a comment to the host or service showing the scheduled downtime, for the benefit of anyone else who might be using the web interface.

Nagios Core keeps track of any downtime defined for all the hosts and services, and prevents the notifications it would normally send out during that time. Note that it will still run its checks and record the state of both the hosts and services even during downtime. All that is suppressed are the notifications, and not the actual checks.

There's more...

Note that the downtime for individual services can be applied in much the same way, by clicking on **Schedule downtime for this service** in the web interface, under **Service Commands**.

What was defined in this recipe was a method for defining fixed downtime, where we know ahead of time when the host or its services are likely to be unavailable. If we don't actually know what time the unavailability will start, but we do know how long it's likely to last, then we can define a period of flexible downtime. This means that the downtime can start any time within the nominated period, and will last for the length of time we specify from that point.

A notification event is also fired when the host or service begins the downtime, called `DOWNTIMESTART`, and another when the downtime ends, called `DOWNTIMEEND`. This may be a useful notification to send to the relevant contact or contact group if they'd like to be notified when this happens. This can be arranged by ensuring that the host or service is configured to send these messages, by including the s flag in the `notification_options` directive for both hosts and services, and correspondingly in the contact definition:

```
notification_options   d,u,r,f,s
```

See also

- The *Managing brief outages with flapping* and *Adjusting flapping percentage thresholds for a service* recipes in this chapter

- The *Specifying which states to be notified about* and *Tolerating a certain number of failed checks* recipes in *Chapter 4, Configuring Notifications*

- The *Adding comments on hosts or services in web interface* recipe in *Chapter 7, Working with the Web Interface*

Managing brief outages with flapping

In this recipe, we'll learn how to use Nagios Core's state flapping detection and handling to avoid sending excessive notifications when a host or service changes its state too frequently. This is useful in circumstances where a host or service is changing between OK to WARNING to CRITICAL states too frequently within the last 21 checks. If the percentage of state changes is too high, Nagios Core will suppress further notifications and add an icon and comment to the host or service showing that it is flapping.

Flap detection is normally enabled in the QuickStart configuration for Nagios Core, and is part of the sample `generic-host` host template and the `generic-service` service template. It's therefore likely that it's already enabled on most servers, and we only need to check that it's still working.

Getting ready

You should have a Nagios Core 3.0 or newer server with at least one host and one service configured already. You should also have access to a working web interface for the Nagios Core server. It would be helpful if you are monitoring a test service that you can bring up and down to trigger the flap detection to test it; an unused webserver might be good for this.

You should be familiar with the way hosts and services change state as a result of their checks and the different states corresponding to hosts and services in order to understand the basics of how flap detection works.

How to do it...

We can check whether or not flap detection is enabled for our Nagios Core server, our hosts, and our services as follows:

1. Change to the configuration directory for Nagios Core. The default is `/usr/local/nagios/etc`.

   ```
   # cd /usr/local/nagios/etc
   ```

2. Edit the `nagios.cfg` file.

   ```
   # vi nagios.cfg
   ```

3. Look for an existing definition for the `enable_flap_detection` directive, and check that it is set to 1:

   ```
   enable_flap_detection=1
   ```

4. If this was not set to 1, then after we've changed it, we will probably also need to at least temporarily disable the `use_retained_program_state` directive in the same file:

```
use_retained_program_state=0
```

5. Edit the file for our particular hosts and or services. We should check that at least one of the following is the case:

   ❑ The host or service inherits from a template that has the `enable_flap_detection` directive set to 1. For example, both the `generic-host` and `generic-service` templates defined by default in `/usr/local/nagios/etc/objects/templates.cfg` do this.

   ❑ The host or service itself has the `enable_flap_detection` directive set to 1 in its own definition.

   In the latter case, the configuration for the host or service might look similar to the following code snippet:

```
define host {
    . . .
    flap_detection_enabled 1
}
define service {
    . . .
    flap_detection_enabled 1
}
```

6. If any of the preceding configuration was changed, validate the new configuration and restart the Nagios Core server:

```
# /usr/local/nagios/bin/nagios -v /usr/local/nagios/etc/nagios.cfg
# /etc/init.d/nagios restart
```

7. Check that for the hosts or services for which flap detection is wanted, the word **ENABLED** appears in the details for that host or service:

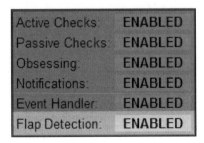

With this done, if a host or service changes its state too frequently within 21 checks, then it will be flagged as flapping, and will appear with a custom icon in views of that host or service:

| sparta.naginet | HTTP | OK | 06-16-2012 16:16:49 |

This service is flapping between states

A comment is also placed on the host or service explaining what has happened for the benefit of anyone viewing the host or service in the web interface, who might perhaps be wondering why notifications have stopped:

Service Comments

↪ Add a new comment 🗑 Delete all comments

Entry Time	Author	Comment	Comment ID	Persistent	Type	Expires	Actions
06-16-2012 16:16:09	(Nagios Process)	Notifications for this service are being suppressed because it was detected as having been flapping between different states (23.0% change >= 20.0% threshold). When the service state stabilizes and the flapping stops, notifications will be re-enabled.	2	No	Flap Detection	N/A	🗑

There will also be an indicator on the details for the host or service defining whether the host or service is flapping:

Is This Service Flapping? **YES** (23.03% state change)

For hosts or services that don't have flap detection enabled, this particular field simply reads **N/A**, and the **Flap Detection** field below it will show as **DISABLED**.

How it works...

The logic behind determining flap detection is actually quite complex. For our purposes, it suffices to explain flap detection as being based on whether a host or service has changed state within its last 21 checks too often—with the thresholds usually expressed as a percentage.

This is discussed in great detail including the formulae that are used to determine flapping state in the Nagios Core 3.0 documentation, available online at the following URL:

```
http://nagios.sourceforge.net/docs/3_0/flapping.html
```

There's more...

A common cause of flapping is that checks are too stringent. As an example, if you are checking a shared web server's response time is less than 50ms while the server is busy, checks might pass and fail without actually giving an accurate reflection of whether the service is doing its job. In this case, it would be appropriate to loosen the thresholds of the service by increasing its percentage thresholds, so that it isn't quite so ready to flag a WARNING or CRITICAL state over things that aren't actually very worrisome. Flap detection can help diagnose these sorts of cases.

We can also enable or disable flap detection for a host via the web interface; in the details screen for both hosts and services, a menu item is available under **Host Commands** labeled **Enable/Disable flap detection for this host**, and under **Service Commands** there's another labeled **Enable/Disable flap detection for this service**.

These may be useful when we want to turn flap detection on or off for a particular host or service temporarily, perhaps because under certain circumstances it is or is not appropriate to use the feature. For permanent setup and for clarity, it would be best to include it explicitly in the configuration as shown in the recipe.

See also

- The *Adjusting flapping percentage thresholds for a service* recipe in this chapter
- The *Tolerating a certain number of failed checks* recipe in *Chapter 4, Configuring Notifications*
- The *Adding comments on hosts or services in web interface* recipe in *Chapter 7, Working with the Web Interface*

Adjusting flapping percentage thresholds for a service

In this recipe, we'll learn how to adjust the percentage thresholds for host or service flap detection. This means that we can adjust how frequently a host or service has to change state within its last 21 checks, before Nagios Core will conclude that it is flapping, and suppress notifications until its state becomes stable again.

Getting ready

You should have a Nagios Core 3.0 or newer server with at least one host and one service configured already. You should also have access to a working web interface for the Nagios Core server.

You should be familiar with the way hosts and services change state as a result of their checks and the different states corresponding to hosts and services, to understand the basics of how flap detection works. Flap detection should also already be enabled and working for the appropriate hosts and services.

How to do it...

We can adjust the thresholds for flap detection for a specific host or service as follows:

1. Change to the `objects` configuration directory for Nagios Core. The default is `/usr/local/nagios/etc/objects`.

   ```
   # cd /usr/local/nagios/etc/objects
   ```

2. Edit the file containing the definition for the host or service for which we want to set the thresholds:

   ```
   # vi sparta.naginet.cfg
   ```

3. Within the host or service definition, set the `low_flap_threshold` and/or `high_flap_threshold` values to appropriate percentages:

   ```
   define host {
       ...
       high_flap_threshold 50.0
       low_flap_threshold 25.0
   }
   define service {
       ...
       high_flap_threshold 45.0
       low_flap_threshold 20.0
   }
   ```

4. Validate the configuration and restart the Nagios Core server:

   ```
   # /usr/local/nagios/bin/nagios -v /usr/local/nagios/etc/nagios.cfg
   # /etc/init.d/nagios restart
   ```

With this done, the flapping thresholds for the host or service should be changed appropriately for future checks.

How it works...

The preceding configuration changes include the following directives:

- `high_flap_threshold`: A host or service that is changing state by a certain percentage of the time must exceed this percentage threshold, before it is determined to be flapping.

- `low_flap_threshold`: If a host or service is already in the flapping state, then its state change percentage must fall below this threshold before the flapping state will end.

For a detailed breakdown of how the state change percentage is calculated, see the Nagios Core 3.0 documentation online at the following URL:

```
http://nagios.sourceforge.net/docs/3_0/flapping.html
```

There's more...

If appropriate, we can also set a global default for hosts and services' flap thresholds with the following directives in `/usr/local/nagios/etc/nagios.cfg`. The following values are examples:

```
high_host_flap_threshold=50.0
low_host_flap_threshold=25.0
high_service_flap_threshold=45.0
low_service_flap_threshold=20.0
```

These values correspond to the percentages of state change, in just the same way that the per-host and per-service configurations do.

Note that there are separate directives for hosts and services in this case. These values are also overridden if you specify thresholds for a particular service or host, as we did in the recipe.

See also

- The *Managing brief outages with flapping* recipe in this chapter

4
Configuring Notifications

In this chapter, we will cover the following recipes:

- ▶ Configuring notification periods
- ▶ Configuring notification for groups
- ▶ Specifying which states to be notified about
- ▶ Tolerating a certain number of failed checks
- ▶ Automating contact rotation
- ▶ Defining an escalation for repeated notifications
- ▶ Defining a custom notification method

Introduction

Notifications in Nagios Core refer to the events fired and the messages generated when hosts or services change state, for the purposes of informing appropriate people or systems.

For example, when connectivity to a host is lost, it leaves the UP state and goes to the DOWN state on the next check. This eventually generates a notification event, and provided the appropriate flags are set and a contact is available, a message about the state change is generated and dealt with in some way as defined in the configuration.

The default text for such notifications goes into some detail about the problem, including the output from the appropriate plugin command:

```
***** Nagios *****
Notification Type: PROBLEM
Host: sparta.naginet
State: DOWN
Address: 10.128.0.21
Info: CRITICAL - Host Unreachable (10.128.0.21)
Date/Time: Sat May 19 16:27:39 NZST 2012
```

So, with this kind of text generated as a result of the event, the next question is what Nagios Core should do with it. A common method of notification that will be familiar to most Nagios Core administrators is sending this text as an e-mail message using the system mailer, but the same generated message can be used in a wide variety of ways. Just as commands can be flexibly defined in terms of the command lines they run, the action appropriate for a particular contact can be defined very flexibly to use the text of any notifications that a contact is configured to receive.

In this chapter, we'll learn how to refine notifications management in Nagios Core, to make sure that the appropriate people or systems are notified about appropriate network events, and not nagged about others which may not matter. We'll also learn how to set up notification methods beyond the simple e-mail message, and how to escalate notifications when problems remain unfixed after a certain period of time.

Configuring notification periods

In this recipe, we'll adjust the configuration for a service that has been bugging us with notifications late at night. We'll arrange to keep checking this host, sparta.naginet, on a 24x7 basis, but we'll prevent it from sending notifications outside of work hours, using two of the predefined time periods in the default Nagios Core configuration.

Getting ready

You should have a Nagios Core 3.0 or newer server with at least one host configured already. We'll use the example of sparta.naginet, a host defined in its own file.

How to do it...

We can define the `check_period` and `notification_period` plugins for our host as follows:

1. Change to the objects configuration directory for Nagios Core. The default is `/usr/local/nagios/etc/objects`. If you've put the definition for your host in a different file, then move to its directory instead.

    ```
    # cd /usr/local/nagios/etc/objects
    ```

2. Edit the file containing your host definition, and find the definition within the file:

    ```
    # vi sparta.naginet.cfg
    ```

    The host definition may look similar to the following code snippet:

    ```
    define host {
        use                 linux-server
        host_name           sparta.naginet
        alias               sparta
        address             10.128.0.21
    }
    ```

3. Add or edit the value for the `check_period` directive to `24x7`:

    ```
    define host {
        use                 linux-server
        host_name           sparta.naginet
        alias               sparta
        address             10.128.0.21
        check_period        24x7
    }
    ```

4. Add or edit the value for the `notification_period` directive to `workhours`:

    ```
    define host {
        use                 linux-server
        host_name           sparta.naginet
        alias               sparta
        address             10.128.0.21
        check_period        24x7
        notification_period workhours
    }
    ```

5. Validate the configuration and restart the Nagios Core server:

```
# /usr/local/nagios/bin/nagios -v /usr/local/nagios/etc/nagios.cfg
# /etc/init.d/nagios restart
```

With this done, Nagios Core will run its check of the host all the time (24 hours a day, 7 days a week), including logging the UP and DOWN states and showing them in the web interface and reporting, but will only send notifications to the nominated contact for the host during work hours, by default from 9 AM to 5 PM, Monday to Friday.

How it works...

The preceding configuration changed two properties of the host object type, to affect the changes we needed:

▸   check_period: This defines the time periods during which the host should be checked; we chose the predefined period 24x7, meaning checks against the host are always to be run, regardless of the time of day or night.

▸   notification_period: This defines the time periods during which the host should send notifications to the appropriate contact; we chose the predefined period workhours, meaning that notifications will only be sent from 9 AM to 5 PM, Monday to Friday.

The same configuration could be applied exactly to a service, rather than a host:

```
define service {
    ...
    check_period          24x7
    notification_period   workhours
}
```

The two time periods to which this new configuration refers are themselves defined in the Nagios Core configuration. The ones we've used, 24x7 and workhours, are standard time periods included in the defaults, kept in the /usr/local/nagios/etc/objects/timeperiods.cfg file. The definition for workhours, for example, looks similar to the following code snippet:

```
define timeperiod {
    timeperiod_name   workhours
    alias             Normal Work Hours
    monday            09:00-17:00
    tuesday           09:00-17:00
    wednesday         09:00-17:00
    thursday          09:00-17:00
    friday            09:00-17:00
}
```

The ones we've used here are just examples of common time periods. We can define time periods ourselves with great precision; see the *Creating a new time period* recipe in *Chapter 1, Understanding Hosts, Services, and Contacts* for some detail on how to do this.

There's more...

The distinction between the two directives is very important. Under most circumstances, we will want a `check_period` directive that corresponds to all times for services that are up day and night, because it means we can retain information about long-term uptime for the service. Keeping a distinct `notification_period` directive simply allows us to control when notifications should be sent, perhaps because they would otherwise go to a pager and wake up a grumpy systems administrator for a relatively unimportant system!

It's valid for Nagios Core configuration to set a `check_period` plugin for a reduced time period, for example `workhours`. However, you shouldn't need to do this unless your host is actually going to be down outside these hours. In most cases, it's appropriate to use the `24x7` time period as a value for `check_period`.

See also

- ▸ The *Configuring notification for groups* recipe in this chapter
- ▸ The *Creating a new time period* recipe in *Chapter 1, Understanding Hosts, Services, and Contacts*
- ▸ The *Specifying how frequently to check a host or service* recipe in *Chapter 3, Working with Checks and States*

Configuring notification for groups

In this recipe, we'll learn how to define a contact group for a host. We'll demonstrate this as part of the general best practice of sending notifications to contact groups, rather than to individual contacts, which allows for more flexibility in assigning individual contacts to the appropriate groups for receiving appropriate notifications.

Getting ready

You should have a Nagios Core 3.0 or newer server with at least one host configured already. We'll use the example of `sparta.naginet`, a host defined in its own file, which we'll configure to send its notifications to an existing contact group called `noc`.

How to do it...

We can configure notifications to be sent to our contact group as follows:

1. Change to the `objects` configuration directory for Nagios Core. The default path is `/usr/local/nagios/etc/objects`. If you've put the definition for your host in a different file, then move to its directory instead.

   ```
   # cd /usr/local/nagios/etc/objects
   ```

2. Ensure that an appropriate `contact_group` definition exists for the group to which you intend to direct your notifications. A valid definition might look something similar to the following code snippet, perhaps kept in `contacts.cfg`:

   ```
   define contactgroup {
        contactgroup_name   noc
        alias               Network Operations
        members             john,jane
   }
   ```

3. If any contacts are referenced for the group, then you should ensure those are also defined. They might look similar to the following code snippet:

   ```
   define contact {
        use             generic-contact
        contact_name    john
        alias           John Smith
        email           john@naginet
   }
   define contact {
        use             generic-contact
        contact_name    jane
        alias           Jane Doe
        email           jane@naginet
   }
   ```

4. Edit the file containing your host definition, and find the definition within the file:

   ```
   # vi sparta.naginet.cfg
   ```

   The host definition may look similar to the following code snippet:

   ```
   define host {
        use                   linux-server
        host_name             sparta.naginet
        alias                 sparta
        address               10.128.0.21
        notification_period   24x7
   }
   ```

Add or edit the value for the `contact_groups` directive to `noc`:

```
define host {
        use                    linux-server
        host_name              sparta.naginet
        alias                  sparta
        address                10.128.0.21
        notification_period    24x7
        contact_groups         noc
}
```

5. If contacts for the host are already defined, then you may wish to remove them, though you don't have to.

6. Validate the configuration and restart the Nagios Core server:

    ```
    # /usr/local/nagios/bin/nagios -v /usr/local/nagios/etc/nagios.cfg
    # /etc/init.d/nagios restart
    ```

With this done, all notifications for this host should be sent to each member of the `noc` group; in our example, the contacts are `jane` and `john`.

How it works...

Defining the contacts that should receive notifications for particular hosts can be done by referring to them individually, or as groups, or both. We could have managed the same result as the preceding one by defining the `contacts` directive for the host as `jane,john`, referring to the individual contacts directly, rather than by their group name.

Almost the same configuration process applies for setting the contact group for services, rather than hosts; we add a value for the `contact_groups` directive to the `service` definition:

```
define service {
    ...
    contact_groups   noc
}
```

When an event takes place for the host or service that prompts a notification, and the valid `notification_option` flags are set for that event, Nagios Core will check the values of both the `contacts` and the `contact_groups` directives for the host, to determine to whom to send the notification. In our case, the server finds the value of `contact_groups` to be `noc`, and so refers to that contact group to identify the individual contacts within it, and then sends the notification to each of them.

There's more...

Which of the two methods to use for defining contacts for hosts or services, whether by individual contact references or groups, is up to you. For large numbers of hosts and services, it tends to be easier to direct notifications to appropriate groups rather than individuals, as it affords us more flexibility in choosing to whom notifications will be sent simply by changing the individuals in the group.

You need to define at least one contact or contact group for a host or service, or have it inherit one through a template, for it to be a valid configuration for Nagios Core.

See also

▶ The *Configuring notification periods*, *Specifying which states to be notified about*, and *Automating contact rotation* recipes in this chapter

▶ The *Creating a new contact* and *Creating a new contact group* recipes in *Chapter 1*, *Understanding Hosts, Services, and Contacts*

Specifying which states to be notified about

In this recipe, we'll learn how to refine which notifications are sent by a host or service, and which notifications should be received by a particular contact. We'll do this by changing both the notification types that hosts and services should generate, and to complement that, the notification types that a contact should be configured to receive.

Getting ready

You should have a Nagios Core 3.0 or newer server, with at least one host configured already. We'll use the example of sparta.naginet, a host defined in its own file, which we'll configure to send only DOWN and RECOVERY notifications, ignoring other notifications such as WARNING and UNKNOWN. It will send notifications to an existing contact called john; we'll ensure that this contact is configured to receive those notifications.

How to do it...

We can configure the notification types for our host as follows:

1. Change to the objects configuration directory for Nagios Core. The default is /usr/local/nagios/etc/objects. If you've put the definition for your host in a different file, then move to its directory instead.

    ```
    # cd /usr/local/nagios/etc/objects
    ```

2. Edit the file containing the definition for your host. It might look similar to the following code snippet:

```
define host {
        use                     linux-server
        host_name               sparta.naginet
        alias                   sparta
        address                 10.128.0.21
        contacts                john
        notification_period     24x7
}
```

3. Add a value for the `notification_options` directive. In our case, we'll use `d,r`, to correspond to notifications for DOWN and RECOVERY states:

```
define host {
        use                     linux-server
        host_name               sparta.naginet
        alias                   sparta
        address                 10.128.0.21
        contacts                john
        notification_period     24x7
        notification_options    d,r
}
```

4. We should also ensure that notifications for this host are enabled, specifically that `notifications_enabled` is set to 1. An easy way to set this and other relevant directives is to have the host inherit from a template such as `linux-server`, as done previously, but we can set it explicitly if we prefer:

```
define host {
        use                     linux-server
        host_name               sparta.naginet
        alias                   sparta
        address                 10.128.0.21
        contacts                john
        notification_period     24x7
        notification_options    d,r
        notifications_enabled   1
}
```

5. Edit the file containing the definition for the host's nominated contacts, or the contacts within its nominated contact group. In this case, we're editing the host's nominated contact `john`. The definition might look similar to the following code snippet:

```
define contact {
    use               generic-contact
    contact_name      john
    alias             John Smith
    email             john@naginet
}
```

6. Edit or set the directive for `host_notification_options`, for each contact, to include the same values that you set for the host. In this case, we set it to d, u, r, which means that `John Smith` can receive the DOWN, UNREACHABLE, and RECOVERY notifications about hosts:

```
define contact {
    use                        generic-contact
    contact_name               john
    alias                      John Smith
    email                      john@naginet
    host_notification_options  d,u,r
}
```

7. Again, you should ensure that the contacts are configured to receive host notifications, using the `host_notifications_enabled` directive being set to 1. We can do this via inheritance from a template such as `generic-contact`, which tends to be easier, or we can set it explicitly:

```
define contact {
    use                        generic-contact
    contact_name               john
    alias                      John Smith
    email                      john@naginet
    host_notification_options  d,r
    host_notifications_enabled 1
}
```

The analogous directive for receiving service notifications is `service_notifications_enabled`.

8. Validate the configuration and restart the Nagios Core server:

```
# /usr/local/nagios/bin/nagios -v /usr/local/nagios/etc/nagios.cfg
# /etc/init.d/nagios restart
```

With this done, notifications sent when the host enters the DOWN state should be sent to the contact, and also when it recovers to the OK state, but no other notifications about the host (such as the UNREACHABLE or DOWNTIMESTART notifications) should be sent about the `sparta.naginet` host to the contact `john`.

How it works...

The kinds of notifications a host should produce is defined in its `notification_options` directive, and the kind of host notifications that a defined contact should receive is configured in its `host_notification_options` directive. Both take the form of comma-separated values.

The valid values for the `notification_options` directive for host objects are:

- ▸ d: Notifications for a host being in the DOWN state
- ▸ u: Notifications for a host being in the UNREACHABLE state
- ▸ r: Notifications for a host recovering from problems (becoming UP)
- ▸ f: Notifications for a host beginning or ending the flapping state
- ▸ s: Notifications for a host beginning or ending scheduled downtime

For example, for a host that should only send notifications when entering the DOWN or UP states, but ignoring notification events for UNREACHABLE or flapping, we might define the following:

```
define host {
    . . .
    notification_options d,r
}
```

The valid directives are slightly different for service objects:

- ▸ w: Notifications for a service being in the WARNING state
- ▸ u: Notifications for a service being in the UNKNOWN state
- ▸ c: Notifications for a service being in the CRITICAL state
- ▸ r: Notifications for a service recovering from problems (becoming OK)
- ▸ f: Notifications for a service beginning or ending a flapping state
- ▸ s: Notifications for a service beginning or ending scheduled downtime

For example, for a host that should send notifications for all of these events except for flapping and scheduled downtime states, we might define the following:

```
define service {
    . . .
    notification_options  w,u,c,r
}
```

All of the preceding values can be used in contact object definitions to restrict the service notifications a particular contact should receive, through the `service_notification_options` directive:

```
define contact {
    . . .
    service_notifications_enabled  1
    service_notification_options   w,u,c,r
}
```

There's more...

Unless we have a specific reason for particular contacts not to accept notifications of a particular kind, it's a good practice to configure contacts to receive all notifications that they are sent, by including all the flags in both the directives for the contact:

```
define contact {
    . . .
    host_notification_options     d,u,r,f,s
    service_notification_options  w,u,c,r,f,s
}
```

This means that the contact will process any notification dispatched to it, and we can instead restrict the kinds of notifications that are sent out by the hosts and services for which this is the delegated contact. With new configurations, it is generally better to start by sending too much information, and then removing unnecessary notification flags if appropriate, rather than potentially missing important messages because they're never sent.

If we intend to do this for all of our contacts, it may be appropriate to include these directives as part of a contact template, and inherit from it using the `use` directive. The `generic-contact` contact template included with the default configuration may be suitable.

If you want to completely disable notifications for a given host, service, or contact, the single value n for `notification_options`, `host_notification_options`, and `service_notification_options` will do this.

▶ The *Configuring notification for groups, Automating contact rotation*, and *Defining a custom notification method* recipes in this chapter

▶ The *Using inheritance to simplify configuration* recipe in *Chapter 9, Configuration Management*

Tolerating a certain number of failed checks

In this recipe, we'll learn how to arrange Nagios Core configuration to only send notifications about problems with a host or service after a check has been repeated a certain number of times and failed each time.

This can be an ideal arrangement for non-critical hosts that occasionally have "blips" or short outages for whatever reason, and only become problematic if they remain down after repeated checks.

Getting ready

You should have a Nagios Core 3.0 or newer server, with at least one host configured already. We'll use the example of `sparta.naginet`, a host defined in its own file. We'll arrange for it to send us notifications only after a total of five failed host checks.

How to do it...

We can configure the number of failed checks to tolerate before sending a notification as follows:

1. Change to the `objects` configuration directory for Nagios Core. The default path is `/usr/local/nagios/etc/objects`. If you've put the definition for your host in a different file, then move to its directory instead.

   ```
   # cd /usr/local/nagios/etc/objects
   ```

2. Edit the file containing your host definition, and find the definition within it. It may look similar to the following code snippet:

   ```
   define host {
       use                 linux-server
       host_name           sparta.naginet
       alias               sparta
       address             10.128.0.21
       notification_period 24x7
   }
   ```

3. Add or edit the value for `max_check_attempts` to 5:

```
define host {
        use                     linux-server
        host_name               sparta.naginet
        alias                   sparta
        address                 10.128.0.21
        notification_period     24x7
        max_check_attempts      5
}
```

4. Validate the configuration and restart the Nagios Core server:

```
# /usr/local/nagios/bin/nagios -v /usr/local/nagios/etc/nagios.cfg

# /etc/init.d/nagios restart
```

With this done, Nagios Core will not send a notification for the host entering the DOWN state until the check has been attempted a total of five times, and has failed each time. In the following screenshot, even though four checks have already taken place and failed, no notification has been sent, and the state is listed as **SOFT**:

Host Status:	**DOWN** (for 0d 0h 0m 1s)
Status Information:	CRITICAL - Host Unreachable (10.128.0.29)
Performance Data:	
Current Attempt:	4/5 (SOFT state)
Last Check Time:	07-24-2012 19:59:02
Check Type:	ACTIVE
Check Latency / Duration:	0.166 / 2.272 seconds
Next Scheduled Active Check:	07-24-2012 19:59:12
Last State Change:	07-24-2012 19:59:11
Last Notification:	N/A (notification 0)
Is This Host Flapping?	**NO** (5.72% state change)
In Scheduled Downtime?	**NO**
Last Update:	07-24-2012 19:59:11 (0d 0h 0m 1s ago)

The SOFT state shows that while Nagios Core has flagged the host as DOWN, it will retry the check until it exhausts `max_check_attempts`. At this point it will flag the host as being in a HARD DOWN state and send a notification.

However, if the host were to come back up before the next check, then the state would change back to **UP**, without ever having sent a notification:

Host Status:	**UP** (for 0d 0h 0m 1s)
Status Information:	PING OK - Packet loss = 0%, RTA = 1.66 ms
Performance Data:	rta=1.665000ms;3000.000000;5000.000000;0.000000 pl=0%;80;100;0
Current Attempt:	1/5 (HARD state)
Last Check Time:	07-24-2012 20:00:49
Check Type:	ACTIVE
Check Latency / Duration:	0.089 / 4.035 seconds
Next Scheduled Active Check:	07-24-2012 20:00:57
Last State Change:	07-24-2012 20:00:56
Last Notification:	N/A (notification 0)
Is This Host Flapping?	**NO** (6.25% state change)
In Scheduled Downtime?	**NO**
Last Update:	07-24-2012 20:00:56 (0d 0h 0m 1s ago)

How it works...

The preceding configuration alters the `max_check_attempts` directive for the host to specify the number of checks that need to have failed before the host will flag a HARD DOWN or UNREACHABLE state, and generate a notification event.

The process for changing the maximum number of attempts before a notification for a service is identical; we add the same directive and value to the definition for the service:

```
define service {
    use                 generic-service
    host_name           sparta.naginet
    service_description HTTP
    check_command       check_http
    max_check_attempts  5
}
```

There's more...

The time between successive retry checks of a host before sending any notification can also be customized with the `retry_interval` directive. By default, the interval is in minutes, so if we wanted to configure a two-minute wait between retry checks, we could add this directive to the host or service:

```
define host {
    ...
    retry_interval  2
}
define service {
    ...
    retry_interval  2
}
```

See also

▶   The *Specifying how frequently to check a host or service* and *Managing brief outages with flapping* recipes in *Chapter 3, Working with Checks and States*

Automating contact rotation

In this recipe, we'll learn how to automatically arrange notifications so that they are only received by certain contacts in a group at certain times.

For companies with more than one person as dedicated network staff, it's a common practice to have an on-call roster, where one member of staff will be the dedicated on-call person for a certain period of time, perhaps a week or two. The kind of setup we'll configure here allows filtering notifications, so that they're only delivered to contacts at appropriate times; notifications are generated by hosts and services and sent to all the contacts in the nominated group, but only one (or perhaps more than one) of the contacts actually receives it.

We'll set this up using two properties of contacts that allow us to restrict the time period within which they should receive notifications: `host_notification_period` and `service_notification_period`.

Getting ready

You should have a Nagios Core 3.0 or newer server, with at least one contact group configured already, with at least two contacts within it. You should be familiar with configuring time periods and understand the basics of notifications as discussed earlier in this chapter.

We'll use the very simple example of three network operators, named as contacts `alan`, `brenden`, and `charlotte`, taking turns with monitoring duty every week. All three are members of the group `ops`, which is specified in the `contact_groups` directive for all of the hosts and services on the network.

How to do it...

We can set up a basic alternating schedule for receiving notifications for our operators as follows:

1. Change to the `objects` configuration directory for Nagios Core. The default path is `/usr/local/nagios/etc/objects`. If you've put the definition for your host in a different file, move to its directory instead.

   ```
   # cd /usr/local/nagios/etc/objects
   ```

2. Check the relevant file or files to ensure your contacts are defined, and that they are members of the appropriate contact group. A good location for such information is in the `contacts.cfg` file. The configuration might look similar to the following code snippet:

   ```
   define contactgroup {
           contactgroup_name   ops
           alias               Network Operations
           members             alan,brenden,charlotte
   }

           define contact {
                use            generic-contact
                contact_name   alan
                alias          Alan Jones
                email          alan@pager.naginet
           }
           define contact {
                use            generic-contact
                contact_name   brenden
                alias          Brenden Peters
                email          brenden@pager.naginet
           }
           define contact {
                use            generic-contact
                contact_name   charlotte
                alias          Charlotte Franks
                email          charlotte@pager.naginet
           }
   ```

3. In this case, all our hosts and services are configured to send messages to the ops contact group:

```
define host {
    ...
    contact_groups  ops
}
define service {
    ...
    contact_groups  ops
}
```

4. Define time periods to correspond to the times during which each of your contacts should be receiving messages. We'll use the special syntax of time period definitions to set up the definitions for this rotation:

```
define timeperiod {
    timeperiod_name  alan-pager
    alias            Alan pager schedule
    2012-06-05 / 21  00:00-24:00
    2012-06-06 / 21  00:00-24:00
    2012-06-07 / 21  00:00-24:00
    2012-06-08 / 21  00:00-24:00
    2012-06-09 / 21  00:00-24:00
    2012-06-10 / 21  00:00-24:00
    2012-06-11 / 21  00:00-24:00
}
define timeperiod {
    timeperiod_name  brenden-pager
    alias            Brenden pager schedule
    2012-06-12 / 21  00:00-24:00
    2012-06-13 / 21  00:00-24:00
    2012-06-14 / 21  00:00-24:00
    2012-06-15 / 21  00:00-24:00
    2012-06-16 / 21  00:00-24:00
    2012-06-17 / 21  00:00-24:00
    2012-06-18 / 21  00:00-24:00
}
define timeperiod {
    timeperiod_name  charlotte-pager
    alias            Charlotte pager schedule
    2012-06-19 / 21  00:00-24:00
    2012-06-20 / 21  00:00-24:00
    2012-06-21 / 21  00:00-24:00
    2012-06-22 / 21  00:00-24:00
```

```
2012-06-23 / 21   00:00-24:00
2012-06-24 / 21   00:00-24:00
2012-06-25 / 21   00:00-24:00
}
```

5. Go back and configure each of your contacts with the `host_notification_period` and `service_notification_period` directives, to filter notifications to only be received during their dedicated time period:

```
define contact {
    use                          generic-contact
    contact_name                 alan
    alias                        Alan Jones
    email                        alan@pager.naginet
    host_notification_period     alan-pager
    service_notification_period  alan-pager
}
define contact {
    use                          generic-contact
    contact_name                 brenden
    alias                        Brenden Peters
    email                        brenden@pager.naginet
    host_notification_period     brenden-pager
    service_notification_period  brenden-pager
}
define contact {
    use                          generic-contact
    contact_name                 charlotte
    alias                        Charlotte Franks
    email                        charlotte@pager.naginet
    host_notification_period     charlotte-pager
    service_notification_period  charlotte-pager
}
```

6. Validate the configuration and restart the Nagios Core server:

```
# /usr/local/nagios/bin/nagios -v /usr/local/nagios/etc/nagios.cfg
# /etc/init.d/nagios restart
```

With this done, the contacts configured should only receive notifications during their dedicated pager time. If these are our only contacts, then all the notifications generated will go to only one person at any given time.

How it works...

The `host_notification_period` and `service_notification_period` directives in the definitions for our contacts are used to limit the times during which these contacts should receive any notifications. Each of our contacts in this example has their own time period defined to correspond to their portion of the pager schedule.

Let's take a look at Alan's example:

```
define timeperiod {
    timeperiod_name   alan-pager
    2012-06-05 / 21   00:00-24:00
    2012-06-06 / 21   00:00-24:00
    2012-06-07 / 21   00:00-24:00
    2012-06-08 / 21   00:00-24:00
    2012-06-09 / 21   00:00-24:00
    2012-06-10 / 21   00:00-24:00
    2012-06-11 / 21   00:00-24:00
}
```

The second line of the directive, `2012-06-05 / 21   00:00-24:00`, can be broken down as follows:

- ▶ Starting from the 5th of June,
- ▶ Every 21 days,
- ▶ From midnight to the following midnight (i.e., the entire day).

The configuration then goes on to do the same for the remaining days of the first week Alan will be on call, and specifies that he will be on call the same day 21 days (3 weeks) later. A similar configuration, but starting one week and two weeks later, is set up for the contacts `brenden` and `charlotte` respectively.

There's more...

Note that there's no reason time periods can't overlap. If it happens to suit us to arrange for more than one contact to receive a notification, we can do that. Similarly, we can leave gaps in the schedule if notifications aren't needed during a certain time period.

Time periods in Nagios Core are highly flexible; to see some examples of the various syntaxes you can use for defining them, take a look at the *Creating a new time period* recipe in *Chapter 1, Understanding Hosts, Services, and Contacts*.

See also

▸ The *Configuring notification for groups* and *Specifying which states to be notified about* recipes in this chapter

▸ The *Creating a new contact*, *Creating a new contact group*, and *Creating a new time period* recipes in *Chapter 1, Understanding Hosts, Services, and Contacts*

Defining an escalation for repeated notifications

In this recipe, we'll learn how to arrange a Nagios Core configuration such that after a certain number of repetitions, notifications for problems on hosts or services are escalated to another contact, instead of (or in addition to) the normally defined contact. This is done by defining a separate object type called a host or service escalation.

This kind of setup could be useful to alert more senior networking staff to an unresolved problem that a less experienced person is struggling to fix, and can also function as a "safety valve" to ensure that problem notifications for hosts eventually do reach someone else if they remain unfixed.

Getting ready

You should have a Nagios Core 3.0 or newer server, with at least one host or service configured already, and at least two contact groups—one for the first few notifications, and one for the escalations. You should understand how notifications are generated and sent to the `contacts` and `contact_groups` for hosts or services.

We'll use the example of a host called `sparta.naginet` which normally sends notifications to a group called `ops`. We'll arrange for all of the notifications after the fourth one to also be sent to a contact group called `emergency`.

How to do it...

We can configure an escalation for our host or service as follows:

1. Change to the objects configuration directory for Nagios Core. The default is `/usr/local/nagios/etc/objects`. If you've put the definition for your host in a different file, then move to its directory instead.

   ```
   # cd /usr/local/nagios/etc/objects
   ```

2. Edit the file containing the definition for the host. The definition might look similar to the following code snippet:

```
define host {
        use                     linux-server
        host_name               sparta.naginet
        alias                   sparta
        address                 10.128.0.21
        contact_groups          ops
        notification_period     24x7
        notification_interval   10
}
```

3. Underneath the host definition, add the configuration for a new hostescalation object:

```
define hostescalation {
        host_name               sparta.naginet
        contact_groups          ops,emergency
        first_notification      5
        last_notification       0
        notification_interval   10
}
```

4. Validate the configuration and restart the Nagios Core server:

```
# /usr/local/nagios/bin/nagios -v /usr/local/nagios/etc/nagios.cfg
# /etc/init.d/nagios restart
```

With this done, when problems are encountered with the host that generate notifications, all the notifications beyond the fifth one will be sent to both the ops contact group and also to the emergency contact group, expanding the number of people or systems contacted, to make it more likely the problem will actually be addressed or fixed. Perhaps someone on the ops team has misplaced their pager.

How it works...

The configuration added in the preceding section is best thought of as a special case or an override for a particular host, in that it specifies a range of notifications that should be sent to a different set of contact groups. It can be broken down as follows:

▸ host_name: This is the same value of host_name given for the host in its definition; we specified sparta.naginet.

▸ contact_groups: This is the contact groups to which notifications meeting this special case should be sent. We specify both the emergency group and the ops group, so that matching notifications go to both. Note that they are comma-separated.

- ▸ `first_notification`: This is the count of the first notification that should match this escalation; we chose the fifth notification.

- ▸ `last_notification`: This is the count of the last notification that should match this escalation. We set this to zero, which means that all notifications after `first_notification` should be sent to the nominated contact or contact groups. The notifications will not stop until they are manually turned off, or the problem is fixed.

- ▸ `notification_interval`: Like the host and service directives of the same name, this specifies how long Nagios Core should wait before sending new notifications if the host remains in a problematic state. Here, we've chosen ten minutes.

Individual contacts can also (or instead) be specified with the `contacts` directive, rather than `contact_groups`.

Service escalations work in much the same way; the difference is that you need to specify the service by its `service_description` directive as well as its host name. Everything else works the same way. A similar escalation for a service check with a `service_description` of `HTTP` running on `sparta.naginet` might look similar to the following code snippet:

```
define serviceescalation {
        host_name               sparta.naginet
        service_description     HTTP
        contact_groups          ops,emergency
        first_notification      5
        last_notification       0
        notification_interval   10
}
```

There's more...

The preceding escalation continues sending notifications both to the original `ops` group and also to the members of the `emergency` group. It's generally a good idea to do it this way rather than sending notifications only to the escalated group, because the point of escalations is to increase the reach of the notifications when a problem is not being dealt with, rather than merely to try contacting a different group of people instead.

This principle applies to stacking escalations, as well; if we had a host group with all of our contacts in it, perhaps named `everyone`, we could define a second escalation so that the tenth notification onwards goes to every single contact:

```
define hostescalation {
        host_name               sparta.naginet
        contact_groups          everyone
        first_notification      10
        last_notification       0
        notification_interval   10
}
```

Just as we can specify multiple host escalations, it's also fine for the ranges of notifications to overlap so that more than one escalation applies.

With a little arithmetic, you can arrange escalations such that they work after a host or service has been in a problematic state for a certain period of time. For example, the escalation we specified in the recipe will apply after the host has been in a problem state for 40 minutes, because `notification_interval` specifies that Nagios Core should wait for 10 minutes between re-sending notifications.

See also

> ► The *Configuring notifications for groups* recipe in this chapter
> ► The *Creating a new contact group* recipe in *Chapter 1, Understanding Hosts, Services, and Contacts*

Defining a custom notification method

In this recipe, we'll learn how to specify an alternative method for a contact to receive notifications about a service. A very typical method for a contact to receive notifications is by sending an e-mail to their contact address; e-mail messages could be sent to an inbox or a paging device.

However, notifications are just text; we can arrange to deal with them via any command we wish, in much the same way as we can configure host or service checks. In this recipe, we'll set up a new contact called `motd`, which when it receives notifications will write them into the server's `/etc/motd` directory to be displayed on login.

Getting ready

You should have a Nagios Core 3.0 or newer server, with at least one host or service configured already. You should understand how notifications are generated and their default behavior in being sent to the `contacts` and `contact_groups` for hosts or services.

We'll use the example of a host called `troy.naginet`, configured to send notifications to the `ops` contact group. We'll add a new contact within this group called `motd`.

How to do it...

We can arrange our custom notification method as follows:

1. Ensure that your /etc/motd file can be written to by Nagios Core, and that it's a static file that your system will not overwrite on boot. If you run your Nagios Core server as the recommended default user and group of nagios, you could do something similar to the following:

    ```
    # chgrp nagios /etc/motd
    # chmod g+w /etc/motd
    ```

2. It would be a good idea to test that the user can write to the file using su or sudo:

    ```
    # sudo -s -u nagios
    $ echo 'test' >>/etc/motd
    ```

3. Change to the objects configuration directory for Nagios Core. The default path is /usr/local/nagios/etc/objects. If you've put the definition for your host in a different file, then move to its directory instead.

    ```
    # cd /usr/local/nagios/etc/objects
    ```

4. Edit the file containing the definitions for your notification commands. By default, this is in the file commands.cfg. Append the following definitions to the file:

    ```
    define command {
        command_name    notify-host-motd
        command_line    /usr/bin/printf "%s\n" "$SHORTDATETIME$:
    $HOSTALIAS$ is $HOSTSTATE$" >>/etc/motd
    }
    define command {
        command_name    notify-service-motd
        command_line    /usr/bin/printf "%s\n" "$SHORTDATETIME$:
    $SERVICEDESC$ on $HOSTALIAS$ is $SERVICESTATE$" >>/etc/motd
    }
    ```

5. Edit the file containing the definitions for your contacts. In the QuickStart configuration, this is in the file contacts.cfg. Append the following definitions to the file:

    ```
    define contact {
        use                             generic-contact
        contact_name                    motd
        contact_groups                  ops
        alias                           MOTD
        host_notification_commands      notify-host-motd
        service_notification_commands   notify-service-motd
    }
    ```

6. Edit the file containing the definitions for your host and/or services, to ensure that they specify ops in their contact_groups directives:

```
define host {
    host_name        troy.naginet
    ...
    contact_groups   ops
}
    define service {
        host_name            troy.naginet
        ...
        contact_groups   ops
    }
```

7. Validate the configuration and restart the Nagios Core server:

```
# /usr/local/nagios/bin/nagios -v /usr/local/nagios/etc/nagios.cfg
# /etc/init.d/nagios restart
```

With this done, the next notifications that go out for the host and services should not only be e-mailed to any contacts in the ops group, but should also be written by the motd contact to /etc/motd, to be presented on login:

```
06-30-2012 17:24:05: troy is DOWN
06-30-2012 17:24:05: HTTP on troy is CRITICAL
06-30-2012 17:25:07: troy is DOWN
06-30-2012 17:25:07: HTTP on troy is CRITICAL
```

How it works...

The first part of the configuration that we added is defining new notification commands. These are actually command definitions, just the same as those used with the check_ command definitions for hosts and services; the difference is that they're used by contacts to send notifications to people (or in this case, write them to files) in the appropriate way.

If you're using the default Nagios Core configuration, the commands already defined in commands.cfg should include notify-host-by-email and notify-service-by-email. I've truncated the complete command line as it's very long:

```
define command {
    command_name    notify-host-by-email
    command_line    /usr/bin/printf "%b" "***** Nagios *****\n\
nNotification...
}
```

```
define command {
    command_name    notify-service-by-email
    command_line    /usr/bin/printf "%b" "***** Nagios *****\n\
nNotification...
}
```

These commands use the system `printf` implementation along with many Nagios Core macros to build an appropriate notification string, which is e-mailed to the appropriate contact using a shell pipe into the system mailer.

If we inspect the `templates.cfg` file where the `generic-contact` template is defined, we can see these methods are referred to in two directives:

```
define contact {
    ...
    service_notification_commands notify-service-by-email
    host_notification_commands notify-host-by-email
}
```

This configuration thus defines a particular notification command to be used for hosts that derive from the `generic-host` template.

Our own command definition does something similar in building a string with a call to `printf`. But instead of writing the output into a pipe to the system mailer, it appends it to the `/etc/motd` file.

The `command_line` directive that we specified for the `motd` contact to process host notifications is as follows:

```
/usr/bin/printf "%s\n" "$SHORTDATETIME$: $HOSTALIAS$ is $HOSTSTATE$" >>/
etc/motd
```

The first thing Nagios Core does when a notification event for this contact is successfully fired is substitute values for its macros, $SHORTDATETIME$, $HOSTALIAS$, and $HOSTSTATE$:

```
/usr/bin/printf "%s\n" "06-30-2012 17:24:05: troy is DOWN" >>/etc/motd
```

The resulting string is then executed as a command by the running Nagios Core user, by default `nagios`, and providing that user has the appropriate permissions, it's appended to the end of the MOTD.

There's more...

Adding messages to the MOTD may not be useful for all network administrators, particularly for larger or more sensitive networks, for which hundreds of notifications could be generated daily. The main thing to take away from this is that Nagios Core can be configured to process notification events in pretty much any way, provided:

  ▶ We can define a command line that will consistently do what is needed with what the results of the macro substitution Nagios Core will perform for us

  ▶ The `nagios` user, or whichever user as which the Nagios Core server is running, has all the relevant permissions it needs to run the command

E-mail notifications, particularly to a mobile paging device, are a very sensible basis for notifications for most administrators. However, if some other means of notification is needed, such as inserting into a database or piping into a Perl script, it is possible to do this as well.

Note that it's safest to specify the full paths to any binaries or file we use in these commands, hence `/usr/bin/printf` rather than merely `printf`. This is to ensure that the program we actually intend to run is run, and avoids having to mess about with the `$PATH` specifications for the `nagios` user.

See also

  ▶ The *Configuring notifications for groups* recipe in this chapter
  ▶ The *Creating a new command* and *Customizing an existing command* recipes in Chapter 2, *Working with Commands and Plugins*

5
Monitoring Methods

In this chapter, we will cover the following recipes:

- ▶ Monitoring PING for any host
- ▶ Monitoring SSH for any host
- ▶ Checking an alternative SSH port
- ▶ Monitoring mail services
- ▶ Monitoring web services
- ▶ Checking that a website returns a given string
- ▶ Monitoring database services
- ▶ Monitoring the output of an SNMP query
- ▶ Monitoring a RAID or other hardware device
- ▶ Creating an SNMP OID to monitor

Introduction

Nagios Core is best thought of as a monitoring framework that uses plugins to perform appropriate checks on hosts and services, and returns results about their states in a format that it understands and can use for sending notifications and keeping track of states on a long-term basis.

The design is quite flexible. As explained in *Chapter 2, Working with Commands and Plugins*, Nagios Core can use as a plugin any command-line application that gives appropriate return values as defined in the Nagios Core header files, Perl library, or shell script. In turn, Nagios Core can be configured to use the same plugin in many different ways, taking advantage of any switch provided by the plugin to adjust its behavior, including providing metadata to it in the form of the values of Nagios Core macros, such as `$HOSTADDRESS$`.

The collection of plugins available on the Nagios Exchange website at `http://exchange.nagios.org/` is fairly large, and documenting all of them is well out of the scope of this book. However, some of the most useful plugins are included as part of the Nagios Plugins set, and are installed as part of the recommended quick start guides for Nagios Core at `http://nagios.sourceforge.net/docs/3_0/quickstart.html`. They include programs to monitor very common network features in typical ways, such as monitoring basic network connectivity, web services, mail servers, and many others. The plugin site itself is at `http://nagiosplugins.org/`.

This chapter will demonstrate the usage of some of the most useful components of this plugin set, which it assumes you have already installed. The focus will be on monitoring tasks that will be relevant to most or even all networks of various sizes, hopefully bringing the reader well past the point of thinking of Nagios Core as merely a process to send PING requests. The last few recipes will show how you can use the **Simple Network Management Protocol** (**SNMP**) as a method for checking any generic network service or system property that may not be covered by the standard Nagios Plugins set.

Monitoring PING for any host

In this recipe, we'll learn how to set up PING monitoring for a host. We'll use the `check_ping` plugin, and its command of the same name, to send `ICMP ECHO` requests to a host. We'll use this as a simple diagnostic check to make sure that the host's network stack is responding in a consistent and timely fashion, in much the same way as an administrator might use the `ping` command interactively to check the same properties.

Getting ready

You should have a Nagios Core 3.0 or newer server with at least one host configured already. We'll use the example of `corinth.naginet`, a host defined in its own file. You should also understand the basics of how hosts and services relate, which is covered in the recipes of *Chapter 1, Understanding Hosts, Services, and Contacts*.

How to do it...

We can add a new PING service check to our existing host as follows:

1. Change to the objects configuration directory for Nagios Core. The default path is `/usr/local/nagios/etc/objects`. If you've put the definition for your host in a different file, then move to its directory instead.

   ```
   # cd /usr/local/nagios/etc/objects
   ```

2. Edit the file containing the definition for the host. The host definition might look similar to the following code snippet:

```
define host {
       use          windows-server
       host_name    corinth.naginet
       alias        corinth
       address      10.128.0.27
}
```

3. Beneath the definition for the host, place a service definition referring to `check_ping`. You may like to use the `generic-service` template, as follows:

```
define service {
       use                   generic-service
       host_name             corinth.naginet
       service_description   PING
       check_command         check_ping!100,20%!200,40%
}
```

4. Validate the configuration and restart the Nagios Core server:

```
# /usr/local/nagios/bin/nagios -v /usr/local/nagios/etc/nagios.cfg
```

```
# /etc/init.d/nagios restart
```

With this done, a new service check will start taking place, with the appropriate contacts and contact groups notified when:

▸ The **Round Trip Time** (**RTT**) of the request and its response exceeds 200ms, or more than 40 percent of the packets are lost during the check; a CRITICAL notification is fired for the service in either case.

▸ If a CRITICAL notification was not fired, and the RTT of the request and its response exceeds 100ms, or more than 20 percent of the packets are lost during the check; in this case, a WARNING notification is fired for the service.

The information about the thresholds is given in the definition for the `check_command` directive, as arguments to the `check_ping` command.

More information about this service will also be visible in the web interface, under the **Services** section.

How it works...

The configuration added in the preceding section defines a new service check on the existing `corinth.naginet` host to check that the RTT and the packet loss for an `ICMP ECHO` request and response are within acceptable limits.

For most network configurations, it may well be the case that the host itself is also being checked by `check_ping`, by way of the command `check-host-alive`. The difference is that the thresholds for the RTT and packet loss are intentionally set very high for this command, because it is intended to establish whether the host is up or down at all, not how responsive it is.

There's more...

In networks where most of the hosts are configured to respond to `ICMP ECHO` requests, it could perhaps be worthwhile to configure service checks on all of the hosts in a configuration. This can be done using the `*` wildcard when defining `host_name` for the service:

```
define service {
    use                   generic-service
    host_name             *
    service_description   PING
    check_command         check_ping!100,20%!200,40%
}
```

This will apply the same check, with a `service_description` directive of PING, to all of the hosts configured in the database. This method will save the hassle of configuring a service separately for all the hosts.

If some of the hosts in a network do not respond to PING, it may be more appropriate to place the ones that do in a hostgroup, perhaps named something such as `icmp`:

```
define hostgroup {
    hostgroup_name   icmp
    alias            ICMP enabled hosts
    members          sparta.naginet,corinth.naginet
}
```

The single service can then be applied to all the hosts in that group, using the hostgroup_ name directive in the `service` definition:

```
define service {
    use                   generic-service
    hostgroup_name        icmp
    service_description   PING
    check_command         check_ping!100,20%!200,40%
}
```

It's generally a good idea to have network hosts respond to ICMP messages wherever possible, in order to comply with the recommendations in RFC1122 and to ease debugging.

Finally, note that the thresholds for the RTT and the packet loss are not fixed; in fact, they're defined in the service definition, in the `check_command` line. For hosts that have higher latency, perhaps due to network load or topology, it may be appropriate to adjust these thresholds, which is covered in the *Changing thresholds for ping RTT and packet loss* recipe in *Chapter 3, Working with Checks and States*.

See also

- ▸ The *Creating a new host, Creating a new service,* and *Creating a new hostgroup* recipes in *Chapter 1, Understanding Hosts, Services, and Contacts*
- ▸ The *Using an alternative check command* recipe in *Chapter 2, Working with Commands and Plugins*
- ▸ The *Changing thresholds for ping RTT and packet loss* recipe in *Chapter 3, Working with Checks and States*

Monitoring SSH for any host

In this recipe, we'll learn how to check that the SSH daemon on a remote host responds to requests, using the `check_ssh` plugin, and the command of the same name. This will allow us to be notified as soon as there are problems connecting to the SSH service.

Getting ready

You should have a Nagios Core 3.0 or newer server with at least one host configured already. We'll use the example of `troy.naginet`, a host defined in its own file. You should also understand the basics of how hosts and services relate, which is covered in the recipes of *Chapter 1, Understanding Hosts, Services, and Contacts*.

It may be a good idea to first verify that the host for which you want to add monitoring is presently running the SSH service that requires checking. This can be done by running the `ssh` client to make a connection to the host:

```
$ ssh troy.naginet
```

We should also check that the plugin itself will return the result required when run against the applicable host, as the `nagios` user:

```
# sudo -s -u nagios
$ /usr/local/nagios/libexec/check_ssh troy.naginet
```

If you're unable to get a positive response from the SSH service on the target machine, even if you're sure it's running, then this could perhaps be a symptom of unrelated connectivity or filtering problems. We may, for example, need to add the monitoring server on which Nagios Core is running to the whitelist for SSH (normally TCP destination port 22) on any applicable firewalls or routers.

How to do it...

We can add a new SSH service check to our existing host as follows:

1. Change to the `objects` configuration directory for Nagios Core. The default path is `/usr/local/nagios/etc/objects`. If you've put the definition for your host in a different file, then move to its directory instead.

    ```
    # cd /usr/local/nagios/etc/objects
    ```

2. Edit the file containing the definition for the host. The host definition might look similar to the following code snippet:

    ```
    define host {
        use          linux-server
        host_name    troy.naginet
        alias        troy
        address      10.128.0.25
    }
    ```

3. Beneath the definition for the host, place a service definition referring to `check_ssh`. It may help to use the `generic-service` template or another suitable template, as follows:

    ```
    define service {
        use                   generic-service
        host_name             troy.naginet
        service_description   SSH
        check_command         check_ssh
    }
    ```

4. Validate the configuration and restart the Nagios Core server:

    ```
    # /usr/local/nagios/bin/nagios -v /usr/local/nagios/etc/nagios.cfg
    # /etc/init.d/nagios restart
    ```

With this done, a new service check will start taking place, with the appropriate contacts and contact groups notified when an attempt to connect to the SSH server fails. The service check will be visible in the web interface, on the **Services** page.

How it works...

The preceding configuration defines a new service with a `service_description` of `SSH` for the existing `troy.naginet` host, using the values in the `generic-service` template and additionally defining a `check_command` directive of `check_ssh`.

This means that in addition to checking whether the host itself is up with `check-host-alive`, as done previously, Nagios Core will also check that the SSH service running on the host is working by attempting to make a connection with it. It will also notify the applicable contacts if there are any problems found with the service after the appropriate number of tests.

For example, if the plugin finds that the host is accessible but not responding to client tests, then it might notify with the following text:

```
Subject: ** PROBLEM Service Alert: troy.naginet/SSH is CRITICAL **

***** Nagios *****

Notification Type: PROBLEM

Service: SSH
Host: troy.naginet
Address: troy.naginet
State: CRITICAL

Date/Time: Wed May 23 13:35:21 NZST 2012

Additional Info:

CRITICAL - Socket timeout after 10 seconds
```

Note that we don't need to actually supply credentials for the SSH check; the plugin simply ensures that the service is running and responding to connection attempts.

There's more...

The definition for the `check_ssh` command warrants some inspection if we're curious as to how the plugin is actually applied as a command, as defined in the QuickStart configuration in `/usr/local/nagios/etc/objects/commands.cfg`:

```
define command {
    command_name   check_ssh
    command_line   $USER1$/check_ssh $ARG1$ $HOSTADDRESS$
}
```

This shows that the `check_ssh` command is configured to run the `check_ssh` binary file in `$USER1$`, a macro that normally expands to `/usr/local/nagios/libexec`, against the host address of the applicable server. It adds in any other arguments beforehand. We haven't used any arguments in this recipe, since we simply want to make a normal check of the SSH service on its default port.

This check should work with most SSH2 compliant servers, most notably including the popular **OpenSSH** server.

Checking SSH accessibility is a common enough thing for servers that you may wish to set up an SSH service check to apply to a hostgroup, rather than merely to an individual host. For example, if you had a group called `ssh-servers` containing several servers that should be checked with a `check_ssh` call, then you could configure them all to be checked with one service definition using the `hostgroup_name` directive:

```
define service {
    use                   generic-service
    hostgroup_name        ssh-servers
    service_description   SSH
    check_command         check_ssh
}
```

This would apply the same service check to each host in the group, which makes the definition easier to update if the check needs to be changed or removed in future.

Note that the `check_ssh` plugin is different from the `check_by_ssh` plugin, which is used to run checks on remote machines, much like NRPE.

See also

- The *Checking an alternative SSH port* recipe in this chapter
- The *Creating a new host*, *Creating a new service*, and *Creating a new hostgroup* recipes in *Chapter 1, Understanding Hosts, Services, and Contacts*
- The *Using check_by_ssh with key authentication instead of NRPE* and *Monitoring local services on a remote machine with NRPE* recipes in *Chapter 6, Enabling Remote Execution*

Checking an alternative SSH port

In this recipe, we'll learn how to deal with the common situation of a machine running an SSH daemon that is listening on an alternative port. So, a service definition that uses `check_ssh`, as used in the *Monitoring SSH for any host* recipe, fails because the plugin defaults to using the standard SSH TCP port number of 22.

This kind of setup is common in situations where an SSH server should not be open to the general public and is often employed as a "security by obscurity" method to reduce automated attacks against the server. The SSH daemon is therefore configured to listen on a different port, usually with a much higher number; administrators who need to use it are told what the port number is.

We'll deal with this situation and monitor the service in Nagios Core, even though it's running on a non-standard port. We'll do this by defining a new command that checks SSH on a specified port number, and creating a service definition that uses that command. The command will accept the port number to check as an argument.

The principles here should generalize well to any other situation where checking an alternative port is necessary, and the Nagios Core plugin being used to make the check supports doing so on an alternative port.

Getting ready

You should have a Nagios Core 3.0 or newer server with at least one host configured already. We'll use the example of `troy.naginet`, a host defined in its own file, and listening on the non-standard SSH port of `5022`. You should also understand the basics of how hosts and services relate, which is covered in the recipes of *Chapter 1, Understanding Hosts, Services, and Contacts*.

A good first step may be to verify that we're able to access the SSH daemon from the monitoring server on the specified port. We can do this from the command line using the `ssh` client, specifying the port number with the `-p` option:

```
$ ssh troy.naginet -p 5022
```

Alternatively, you can run the `check_ssh` plugin directly from the command line:

```
# sudo -s -u nagios
$ /usr/local/nagios/libexec/check_ssh -p 5022 troy.naginet
```

How to do it...

We can set up a service check for SSH on a non-standard port as follows:

1. Change to the `objects` configuration directory for Nagios Core. The default path is `/usr/local/nagios/etc/objects`. If you've put the definition for your host in a different file, then move to its directory instead.

   ```
   # cd /usr/local/nagios/etc/objects
   ```

2. Edit a suitable file containing command definitions, and find the definition for the `check_ssh` command. In the default installation, this file is `commands.cfg`. The `check_ssh` definition looks similar to the following code snippet:

   ```
   define command {
         command_name   check_ssh
         command_line   $USER1$/check_ssh $ARG1$ $HOSTADDRESS$
   }
   ```

3. Beneath the `check_ssh` definition, add a new command definition as follows:

   ```
   define command {
         command_name   check_ssh_altport
         command_line   $USER1$/check_ssh -p $ARG1$ $HOSTADDRESS$
   }
   ```

4. Edit the file containing the definition for the host. The host definition might look similar to the following code snippet:

   ```
   define host {
         use          linux-server
         host_name    troy.naginet
         alias        troy
         address      10.128.0.25
   }
   ```

5. Beneath the definition for the host, place a new service definition using our new command:

   ```
   define service {
         use                   generic-service
         host_name             troy.naginet
         service_description   SSH_5022
         check_command         check_ssh_altport!5022
   }
   ```

6. Validate the configuration and restart the Nagios Core server:

```
# /usr/local/nagios/bin/nagios -v /usr/local/nagios/etc/nagios.cfg
# /etc/init.d/nagios restart
```

With this done, Nagios Core will begin running service checks using the `check_ssh` plugin, but will use the alternative destination port `5022` for its connection attempts for the service, which has a `service_description` of `SSH_5022`.

How it works...

The configuration added in the preceding section has almost exactly the same end result as adding a default `check_ssh` service; the only difference is that a different port is checked in order to make the connection. We use the `check_ssh_altport` command to do this, which we also defined ourselves in a syntax very similar to the `check_ssh` definition.

The difference is that the command accepts an argument which is used as a value for the `-p` option to the `check_ssh` plugin, to check the specified port number; in this case, TCP port `5022`, rather than the default of port `22`.

There's more...

Since arguments in Nagios Core can include spaces, we could also have defined the service check as follows, without having to define an extra command:

```
define service {
    use                  generic-service
    host_name            troy.naginet
    service_description  SSH_5022
    check_command        check_ssh!-p 5022
}
```

This is because the `$ARG1$` macro representing the argument is still used in the original `check_ssh` command, but it needs to have the option included as well as its value. The difference is mainly one of preference, depending on which we feel is clearer and more maintainable. It may help to consider whether a well-named command could assist someone else reading our configuration in understanding what is meant.

See also

▸ The *Monitoring SSH for any host* recipe in this chapter

▸ The *Creating a new host* and *Creating a new service* recipes in *Chapter 1, Understanding Hosts, Services, and Contacts*

▸ The *Creating a new command* recipe in *Chapter 2, Working with Commands and Plugins*

Monitoring mail services

In this recipe, we'll learn how to monitor three common mail services for a nominated host: **SMTP**, **POP**, and **IMAP**. We'll also see how to use the same structure to include additional checks for secure, encrypted versions of each of these services: **SMTPS**, **POPS**, and **IMAPS**.

For simplicity, we'll assume in this recipe that all three of these services are running on the same host, but the procedure will generalize easily for the common case where there are designated servers for one or more of the preceding functions.

Getting ready

You should have a Nagios Core 3.0 or newer server with at least one host configured already. We'll use the example of troy.naginet, a host defined in its own file. You should also understand the basics of how hosts and services relate, which is covered in the recipes of *Chapter 1, Understanding Hosts, Services, and Contacts*.

Checking the connectivity for the required services on the target server is also a good idea, to make sure that the automated connections the monitoring server will be making on the appropriate protocols and ports will actually work as expected. For the plain unencrypted mail services, this could be done via **Telnet** to the appropriate ports. For SMTP:

```
$ telnet marathon.naginet 25
Trying 10.128.0.34...
Connected to marathon.naginet.
Escape character is '^]'.
220 marathon.naginet ESMTP Postfix
```

For POP:

```
$ telnet marathon.naginet 110
Trying 10.128.0.34...
Connected to marathon.naginet.
Escape character is '^]'.
+OK Hello there.
```

And for IMAP:

```
$ telnet marathon.naginet 143
Trying 10.128.0.34...
Connected to marathon.naginet.
Escape character is '^]'.
* OK [CAPABILITY IMAP4rev1 UIDPLUS CHILDREN NAMESPACE...
```

For secure services, one possibility for checking is using the `openssl` client. For SMTPS on its "classic" port number of 465:

```
$ openssl s_client -host marathon.naginet -port 465
CONNECTED(00000003)
...
220 marathon.naginet ESMTP Postfix
```

For POPS:

```
$ openssl s_client -host marathon.naginet -port 995
CONNECTED(00000003)
...
+OK Hello there.
```

And for IMAPS:

```
$ openssl s_client -host marathon.naginet -port 993
CONNECTED(00000003)
...
* OK [CAPABILITY IMAP4rev1 UIDPLUS CHILDREN NAMESPACE...
```

If you prefer, you could instead use a network scanner such as `nmap` to test whether the ports are open and responsive.

Once we've verified the connectivity for the mail services that we need, and also verified whether the host itself is being configured and checked in Nagios Core, we can add the appropriate service checks.

How to do it...

We can add unencrypted mail service checks for SMTP, POP, and IMAP services on our host as follows:

1. Change to the `objects` configuration directory for Nagios Core. The default path is `/usr/local/nagios/etc/objects`. If you've put the definition for your host in a different file, then move to its directory instead.

   ```
   # cd /usr/local/nagios/etc/objects
   ```

2. Edit the file containing the definition for the host. The host definition might look similar to the following code snippet:

   ```
   define host {
       use         linux-server
       host_name   marathon.naginet
       alias       marathon
       address     10.128.0.34
   }
   ```

3. Beneath the definition for the host, place three new service definitions, one for each of the appropriate mail services:

```
define service {
    use                    generic-service
    host_name              marathon.naginet
    service_description    SMTP
    check_command          check_smtp
}
define service {
    use                    generic-service
    host_name              marathon.naginet
    service_description    POP
    check_command          check_pop
}
define service {
    use                    generic-service
    host_name              marathon.naginet
    service_description    IMAP
    check_command          check_imap
}
```

4. Validate the configuration and restart the Nagios Core server:

```
# /usr/local/nagios/bin/nagios -v /usr/local/nagios/etc/nagios.cfg
# /etc/init.d/nagios restart
```

With this done, three new service checks will start taking place, with the appropriate contacts and contact groups notified when an attempt to connect to any of the services fails. Details for these services will also become available in the **Services** section of the web interface.

How it works...

The configuration added in the preceding section adds three new service checks to the existing marathon.naginet host:

▶ SMTP, which uses the check_smtp command to open an SMTP session

▶ POP, which uses the check_pop command to open a POP session

▶ IMAP, which uses the check_imap command to open an IMAP session

In all three cases, the connectivity and responsiveness of the service is checked, and determined to be OK if it returns appropriate values within an acceptable time frame.

It's important to note that the configuration defined here doesn't actually send or receive any e-mail messages; it merely checks the basic connectivity of the service, and whether it answers simple requests. Therefore, just because the status is OK does not necessarily mean that e-mail messages are being correctly delivered; it could just mean that the services are responding.

There's more...

If it's necessary to check the secure SSL/TLS versions of each of these services, then the configuration is very similar but requires a little extra setup beforehand. This is because although plugins to check them are included in the Nagios Plugins setup, they are not configured to be used as commands. Note that this may well change in future versions of Nagios Core.

To add the appropriate commands, the following stanzas could be added to the commands configuration file, normally `/usr/local/nagios/etc/objects/commands.cfg`:

```
define command {
    command_name   check_ssmtp
    command_line   $USER1$/check_ssmtp $ARG1$ -H $HOSTADDRESS$
}
define command {
    command_name   check_spop
    command_line   $USER1$/check_spop $ARG1$ -H $HOSTADDRESS$
}
define command {
    command_name   check_simap
    command_line   $USER1$/check_simap $ARG1$ -H $HOSTADDRESS$
}
```

With this done, the following service definitions can be added to the appropriate host, either replacing or supplementing the checks for the unsecured services. They are just the same as the unsecured versions, except that an s is added to the `service_description` and to `check_command`:

```
define service {
    use                  generic-service
    host_name            marathon.naginet
    service_description  SSMTP
    check_command        check_ssmtp
}
define service {
    use                  generic-service
    host_name            marathon.naginet
    service_description  SPOP
    check_command        check_spop
}
define service {
    use                  generic-service
    host_name            marathon.naginet
    service_description  SIMAP
    check_command        check_simap
}
```

Finally, note that if you are managing more than one mail server running one or more of the preceding services, then it's a good practice to apply the service to a hostgroup containing all the applicable hosts, rather than creating new service definitions for each one. See the *Running a service on all hosts in a group* recipe in *Chapter 1, Understanding Hosts, Services, and Contacts* to learn how to do this.

See also

▸ The *Creating a new host, Creating a new service, Running a service on all hosts in a group*, and *Creating a new hostgroup* recipes in *Chapter 1, Understanding Hosts, Services, and Contacts*

▸ The *Creating a new command* recipe in *Chapter 2, Working with Commands and Plugins*

Monitoring web services

In this recipe, we'll set up a service check to monitor the responsiveness of an HTTP and HTTPS server. We'll use the `check_http` command and the plugin of the same name provided in the Nagios Plugins set to make HTTP and HTTPS requests of a web server, to ensure that it returns an appropriate and timely response. This is useful in situations where it's required to check whether a website is still functioning, particularly if there are times when it comes under heavy load or suffers denial of service attacks.

Getting ready

You should have a Nagios Core 3.0 or newer server with at least one host configured already. We'll use the example of `sparta.naginet`, a host defined in its own file. You should also understand the basics of how hosts and services relate, which is covered in the recipes of *Chapter 1, Understanding Hosts, Services, and Contacts*.

An appropriate first step is making sure that the services we intend to check are accessible from the monitoring server running Nagios Core. This can be done from the command line, using an HTTP client such as `curl` or `wget`:

```
$ wget http://sparta.naginet/
$ curl http://sparta.naginet/
```

The `check_http` plugin binary could also be called directly to test this connectivity; we'd be hoping for an HTTP OK response, with a code of 200:

```
# sudo -s -u nagios
$ /usr/local/nagios/libexec/check_http -I sparta.naginet
HTTP OK: HTTP/1.1 200 OK - 453 bytes in 0.004 second response time
|time=0.004264s;;;0.000000 size=453B;;;0
```

Optionally, we can check HTTPS the same way, adding the `-S` option for the plugin:

```
# sudo -s -u nagios
$ /usr/local/nagios/libexec/check_http -S -I sparta.naginet
HTTP OK: HTTP/1.1 200 OK - 453 bytes in 0.058 second response time
|time=0.057836s;;;0.000000 size=453B;;;0
```

Both may require the installation of a default page to be served by the host, probably something such as `index.html` or `default.asp`, depending on the web server software.

Once the HTTP connectivity to the host from the monitoring server is verified as working with appropriate responses, we can proceed to add our service check.

How to do it...

We can add web service checks for our host as follows:

1. Change to the `objects` configuration directory for Nagios Core. The default path is `/usr/local/nagios/etc/objects`. If you've put the definition for your host in a different file, then move to its directory instead.

   ```
   # cd /usr/local/nagios/etc/objects
   ```

2. Edit the file containing the definition for the host. The host definition might look similar to the following code snippet:

   ```
   define host {
           use         linux-server
           host_name   sparta.naginet
           alias       sparta
           address     10.128.0.21
   }
   ```

3. Beneath the definition for the host, place a new service definition for the HTTP check:

   ```
   define service {
           use                 generic-service
           host_name           sparta.naginet
           service_description HTTP
           check_command       check_http
   }
   ```

4. If an HTTPS check is also needed, add an optional second service definition:

   ```
   define service {
           use                 generic-service
           host_name           sparta.naginet
           service_description HTTPS
           check_command       check_http!-S
   }
   ```

5. Validate the configuration and restart the Nagios Core server:

```
# /usr/local/nagios/bin/nagios -v /usr/local/nagios/etc/nagios.cfg
# /etc/init.d/nagios restart
```

With this done, a new service called HTTP and optionally one called HTTPS will be added to the `sparta.naginet` host, and HTTP requests will be made from the server regularly, reporting if connectivity fails or a response comes back with an unexpected status. These services will both be visible in the **Services** section of the web interface.

How it works...

The configuration added in the preceding section uses `check_http` as a plugin to make scheduled requests of the `sparta.naginet` server. By default, the index page is requested, so the request takes the following form:

```
GET / HTTP/1.0
User-Agent: check_http/v1.4.15 (nagios-plugins 1.4.15)
Connection: close
```

The plugin awaits a response, and then returns a status based on the following criteria:

▶ Whether a well-formed HTTP response was received at all, within acceptable time bounds. If the response was too slow, it might raise a `CRITICAL` state when the plugin times out.

▶ Whether the response code for the HTTP response was `200 Found`, indicating that a document was identified and returned. A response code of `404 Not Found` would prompt a `CRITICAL` state by default.

Inspecting the command definition for the default `check_http` command in `/usr/local/nagios/etc/objects/commands.cfg` gives some insight into how it uses the plugin of the same name:

```
define command {
    command_name    check_http
    command_line    $USER1$/check_http -I $HOSTADDRESS$ $ARG1$
}
```

This uses three Nagios Core macros:

▶ `$USER1$`: This expands to the directory in which the plugin scripts and binaries are kept; usually `/usr/local/nagios/libexec`.

▶ `$HOSTADDRESS$`: This is the value for the `address` directive defined in the service's associated host; in this case `10.0.128.21`.

▶ `$ARG1$`: This is one extra argument, if defined by the command; it allows us to add the `-S` option to the `check_http` call in order to run an HTTPS check.

There's more...

There are a many other great switches available for the `check_http` plugin; a list of them is available by entering the command with no arguments:

```
# ./check_http
check_http: Could not parse arguments
Usage:
 check_http -H <vhost> | -I <IP-address> [-u <uri>] [-p <port>]
       [-w <warn time>] [-c <critical time>] [-t <timeout>] [-L] [-a
auth]
       [-b proxy_auth] [-f <ok|warning|critcal|follow|sticky|stickyport>]
       [-e <expect>] [-s string] [-l] [-r <regex> | -R <case-insensitive
regex>]
       [-P string] [-m <min_pg_size>:<max_pg_size>] [-4|-6] [-N] [-M
<age>]
       [-A string] [-k string] [-S] [--sni] [-C <age>] [-T <content-
type>]
       [-j method]
```

One particularly useful option here is the `-u` option, which allows us to request specific URLs other than the default index document from the server. This can be useful if we're in a situation that requires setting up checks for more than one page on a site, which can be a nice supplement to code unit testing when a site is deployed or updated.

For example, if we wanted to check that three pages were returning `200 Found` responses: `about.php`, `products.php`, and `contact.php`, then we could set up a new command similar to the following to check a specific page:

```
define command {
    command_name   check_http_page
    command_line   $USER1$/check_http -I $HOSTADDRESS$ -u $ARG1$
}
```

This would allow us to make three service checks similar to the following, using the new command:

```
define service {
    use                  generic-service
    host_name            sparta.naginet
    service_description  HTTP-about
    check_command        check_http_page!/about.php
}
```

```
define service {
    use                 generic-service
    host_name           sparta.naginet
    service_description HTTP-products
    check_command       check_http_page!/products.php
}
define service {
    use                 generic-service
    host_name           sparta.naginet
    service_description HTTP-contact
    check_command       check_http_page!/contact.php
}
```

These service checks would run the same way as the one demonstrated in the recipe, except they would each request a specific page. Note the leading slashes on the URLs are required.

Similarly, the -H option allows you to specify hostnames, which is helpful on servers hosting more than one site. This could be done by setting up a command as follows:

```
define command {
    command_name  check_http_host
    command_line  $USER1$/check_http -I $HOSTADDRESS$ -H $ARG1$
}
```

This would allow you to check two sites on the same host, http://www.naginet/ and http://dev.naginet/, in separate service checks:

```
define service {
    use                 generic-service
    host_name           sparta.naginet
    service_description HTTP-www
    check_command       check_http_host!www.naginet
}
define service {
    use                 generic-service
    host_name           sparta.naginet
    service_description HTTP-dev
    check_command       check_http_host!dev.naginet
}
```

It's worth noting that the check_http request will show up in your server logs with its regular requests. If you're concerned about these distorted statistics or the appearance of unwanted values in reports, then it may be easiest to filter these out using its User-Agent header value, which includes the string check_http.

> ▸ The *Checking a website returns a given string* in this chapter
>
> ▸ The *Creating a new host* and *Creating a new service* recipes in *Chapter 1, Understanding Hosts, Services, and Contacts*
>
> ▸ The *Creating a new command* and *Customizing an existing plugin* recipes in *Chapter 2, Working with Commands and Plugins*

Checking that a website returns a given string

In this recipe, we'll build on the basic web service monitoring established in the *Monitoring web services* recipe in this chapter, and learn how to create a command that uses the `check_http` plugin to ensure that a particular string is included as part of an HTTP response.

By default, there's no Nagios Core command defined to use the plugin in this way, so the recipe will include defining a command before using it as part of a service check.

This may be necessary if we're monitoring a website on a server that may not necessarily return a `404 Not Found` or similar error that will flag a `WARNING` or `CRITICAL` state in Nagios; rather than merely checking if a document was found, we can check if it matches a string, to see if it resembles the particular document we expected.

This kind of setup is a nice complement to a suite of code unit tests for a website or web application.

Getting ready

You should have a Nagios Core 3.0 or newer server with at least one host configured already. We'll use the example of `sparta.naginet`, a host defined in its own file, and we'll check that it's returning the simple string, `naginet`, in its responses. You should also understand the basics of how hosts and services relate, which is covered in the recipes of *Chapter 1, Understanding Hosts, Services, and Contacts*.

You should set up basic HTTP monitoring for the host first, as established in the *Checking web services* recipe in this chapter, to make sure that there is connectivity between the monitoring server and the host, and that requests and responses are both working correctly with appropriate error codes.

How to do it...

We can set up a service check that includes an HTTP response content check as follows:

1. Change to the `objects` configuration directory for Nagios Core. The default path is `/usr/local/nagios/etc/objects`. If you've put the definition for your host in a different file, then move to its directory instead.

   ```
   # cd /usr/local/nagios/etc/objects
   ```

2. Edit a suitable file containing command definitions, and find the definition for the `check_http` command. In the QuickStart installation, this file is `commands.cfg`. The `check_http` definition looks similar to the following code snippet:

   ```
   define command {
       command_name    check_http
       command_line    $USER1$/check_http -I $HOSTADDRESS$ $ARG1$
   }
   ```

3. Beneath the `check_http` definition, add a new command definition as follows:

   ```
   define command {
       command_name    check_http_content
       command_line    $USER1$/check_http -I $HOSTADDRESS$ -s $ARG1$
   }
   ```

4. Edit the file containing the definition for the host. The host definition might look similar to the following code snippet:

   ```
   define host {
       use          linux-server
       host_name    sparta.naginet
       alias        sparta
       address      10.128.0.21
   }
   ```

5. Beneath the definition for the host and beneath any other checks that might use `check_http`, place a new service definition using our new command:

   ```
   define service {
       use                  generic-service
       host_name            sparta.naginet
       service_description  HTTP-content
       check_command        check_http_content!naginet
   }
   ```

6. Validate the configuration and restart the Nagios Core server:

   ```
   # /usr/local/nagios/bin/nagios -v /usr/local/nagios/etc/nagios.cfg
   # /etc/init.d/nagios restart
   ```

With this done, Nagios Core should begin making HTTP requests to monitor the service as `check_http` normally does, except that it will only return an OK state if the content of the website includes the string `naginet`. Otherwise, it will generate an alert and flag the service as CRITICAL, with a message similar to the following:

```
HTTP CRITICAL: HTTP/1.1 200 OK - string 'naginet' not found on
'http://10.128.0.21:80/' - 453 bytes in 0.006 second response time
```

How it works...

One of the many options for `check_http` is `-s`, short for `--string`, which takes a single argument specifying a string that must occur in the content for the service check to return an OK state.

When the HTTP response is received, `check_http` examines the text in the response to see if it matches the string specified, on top of its usual behavior of flagging WARNING or CRITICAL states for connectivity or timeout problems.

Note that in order to make this work, it was necessary to define a new command that uses the first argument (in this case the string `naginet`) as the value for the `-s` option to `check_http`. The full command line executed would look similar to the following command:

```
$ /usr/local/nagios/libexec/check_http -H sparta.naginet -s naginet
```

There's more...

The `check_http` plugin allows considerably more than single string checks, if it's necessary to test for the presence of a regular expression in the content. This can be done using the `-r` or `--regex` options. We could define a command to check for regular expressions as follows:

```
define command {
    command_name    check_http_regex
    command_line    $USER1$/check_http -I $HOSTADDRESS$ -r $ARG1$
}
```

If it's necessary to check that a particular regular expression doesn't match the content, this is possible by adding the `--invert-regex` flag:

```
define command {
    command_name    check_http_noregex
    command_line    $USER1$/check_http -I $HOSTADDRESS$ -r $ARG1$
--invert-regex
}
```

A service check using this command would return CRITICAL if the response was found to match the pattern provided as the first argument to a `check_command` directive.

Other similar options include -e or --expect, which allows specifying a comma-separated set of strings, at least one of which must match the first line of the header for the check to pass.

See also

▸ The *Monitoring web services* recipe in this chapter

▸ The *Creating a new host* and *Creating a new service* recipes in *Chapter 1, Understanding Hosts, Services, and Contacts*

▸ The *Creating a new command* and *Customizing an existing plugin* recipes in *Chapter 2, Working with Commands and Plugins*

Monitoring database services

In this recipe, we'll learn how Nagios Core can be used to monitor the status of a database server. We'll demonstrate this with the popular MySQL as an example, using the check_mysql plugin, and we'll discuss running an actual test query and specifying a similar check for PostgreSQL in the *There's more* section of this recipe.

Getting ready

You should have a Nagios Core 3.0 or newer server with at least one host configured already. We'll use the example of delphi.naginet, a host defined in its own file. You should also understand the basics of how hosts and services relate, which is covered in the recipes of *Chapter 1, Understanding Hosts, Services, and Contacts*.

For a check on a remote host to work from the monitoring server, the database server will need to be listening on an appropriate network interface. It's also necessary to make sure that an appropriate database user account exists with which the check_mysql plugin may authenticate. It's a good idea to make this into a dedicated user with no privileges on any database, because the credentials need to be stored in plain text, which could be a security risk if more sensitive credentials were used.

For MySQL, we could create a new user with no privileges with the following command, assuming that the monitoring server olympus.naginet has 10.128.0.11 as an IPv4 address. I've used a randomly generated password here:

```
mysql> CREATE USER 'nagios'@'10.128.0.11' IDENTIFIED BY 'UVocjPHoH0';
```

We can then check the connectivity using the mysql client on the monitoring server:

```
$ mysql --host=delphi.naginet --user=nagios --password=UVocjPHoH0
mysql>
```

Or alternatively, by running the plugin directly from the command line as the `nagios` user:

```
# sudo -s -u nagios
$ /usr/local/nagios/libexec/check_mysql -H delphi.naginet -u nagios -p
UVocjPHoH0
Uptime: 1631  Threads: 1  Questions: 102  Slow queries: 0  Opens: 99
Flush tables: 1  Open tables: 23  Queries per second avg: 0.62
```

If we did not have the MySQL libraries installed when we built the Nagios plugins, we may find that we do not have the `check_mysql` and `check_mysql_query` binaries in `/usr/local/nagios/libexec`. We can fix this by installing the MySQL shared libraries on the monitoring system, and rebuilding and reinstalling the Nagios Plugins package.

By default, it's also necessary to define new commands to actually use these plugins as well, which we'll do in this recipe.

How to do it...

We can set up some basic database monitoring for our MySQL server as follows:

1. Change to the `objects` configuration directory for Nagios Core. The default path is `/usr/local/nagios/etc/objects`. If you've put the definition for your host in a different file, then move to its directory instead.

   ```
   # cd /usr/local/nagios/etc/objects
   ```

2. Edit a suitable file containing command definitions, perhaps `commands.cfg`, and add the following definition:

   ```
   define command {
         command_name   check_mysql
         command_line   $USER1$/check_mysql -H $HOSTADDRESS$ -u $ARG1$
   -p $ARG2$
   }
   ```

3. Edit the file containing the definition for the host. The host definition might look similar to the following code snippet:

   ```
   define host {
         use          linux-server
         host_name    delphi.naginet
         alias        delphi
         address      10.128.0.51
   }
   ```

4. Beneath the definition for the host, place a new service definition for the MySQL check, including the username and password chosen earlier for arguments:

```
define service {
    use                  generic-service
    host_name            delphi.naginet
    service_description  MYSQL
    check_command        check_mysql!nagios!UVocjPHoH0
}
```

5. Validate the configuration and restart the Nagios Core server:

```
# /usr/local/nagios/bin/nagios -v /usr/local/nagios/etc/nagios.cfg
# /etc/init.d/nagios restart
```

With this done, a new service check with description `MYSQL` will be added for the `delphi.naginet` host, which will employ the `check_mysql` plugin to report the status of the MySQL server. The output will also include statistics about its uptime, open tables, and query averages, and like all service output will be visible in the web interface under **Services**.

How it works...

This configuration defines a new command named `check_mysql` to use the plugin of the same name, accepting two arguments; the first is the username of the test Nagios Core user, in this case `nagios`, and the second is the password for that user. The `check_mysql` plugin acts as a MySQL client using the credentials provided to it, and requests diagnostic information from the database, which it returns as part of its check.

If it has problems connecting to or using the MySQL server, it will flag a status of `CRITICAL`, and generate appropriate notifications.

There's more...

We can optionally check access to a specific database using the plugin by supplying a value to the `-d` parameter. This should be a database to which the `nagios` user has been given access, otherwise the check would fail.

If we want to check whether we can actually run a query after connecting, we could extend this even further to use the `check_mysql_query` plugin:

```
define command {
    command_name  check_mysql_query
    command_line  $USER1$/check_mysql_query -H $HOSTADDRESS$ -u $ARG1$
-p $ARG2$ -d $ARG3$ -q $ARG4$
}
define service {
    use                  generic-service
    host_name            delphi.naginet
```

```
    service_description   MYSQL_QUERY
    check_command         check_mysql_query!nagios!UVocjPHoHO!exampledb
!"SELECT COUNT(1) FROM exampletbl"
}
```

The preceding code snippet would attempt to run the SELECT COUNT (1) FROM exampletbl query on the exampledb database. Note that it is important to wrap the query in quotes so that it gets processed as one argument, rather than several.

A similar service check to the one specified in this recipe could be configured for PostgreSQL database servers, using the check_pgsql plugin, also part of the standard Nagios Plugins set. The command and service check definitions might look similar to the following code snippet:

```
define command {
    command_name   check_pgsql
    command_line   $USER1$/check_pgsql -H $HOSTADDRESS$ -p $ARG1$
}
define service {
    use                   generic-service
    host_name             delphi.naginet
    service_description   PGSQL
    check_command         check_pgsql!N4Nw8o8X
}
```

In the preceding example, an access would need to be granted on the PostgreSQL server for the monitoring server's IP address in pg_hba.conf, with access to the default standard template1 database.

In production environments, it's often the case that for security or programming policy reasons, database servers are not actually configured to accept direct connections over network interfaces, even on secure interfaces. Packaged MySQL and PostgreSQL servers on many systems will in fact default to listening only on the localhost interface on 127.0.0.1.

This can complicate the monitoring setup a little, but it can usually be addressed by installing a remote Nagios plugin execution agent on the database server, such as NRPE or NSclient++. NRPE usage is addressed in *Chapter 6, Enabling Remote Execution*, and uses a MySQL server configured in this way as its demonstration of the concept.

See also

▶ The *Creating a new host* and *Creating a new service* recipes in *Chapter 1, Understanding Hosts, Services, and Contacts*

▶ The *Creating a new command* recipe in *Chapter 2, Working with Commands and Plugins*

▶ The *Monitoring local services on a remote machine with NRPE* recipe in *Chapter 6, Enabling Remote Execution*

Monitoring the output of an SNMP query

In this recipe, we'll learn how to use the `check_snmp` plugin to monitor the output given by **Simple Network Management Protocol** (**SNMP**) requests.

Despite its name, SNMP is not really a very simple protocol, but it's a very common method for accessing information on many kinds of networked devices, including monitoring boards, usage meters, and storage appliances, as well as workstations, servers, and routing equipment.

Because SNMP is so widely supported and typically able to produce such a large volume of information to trusted hosts, it's an excellent way to gather information from hosts that's not otherwise retrievable from network services. For example, while checking for a PING response from a large router is simple enough, there may not be an easy way to check properties, such as the state of each of its interfaces, or the presence of a certain route in its routing tables.

Using `check_snmp` in Nagios Core allows automated retrieval of this information from the devices, and generating alerts appropriately. While its setup is somewhat complex, it is worth learning how to use it, as it is among the most powerful plugins in Nagios Core for network administrators, and it is quite typical to see dozens of commands defined for its use in a typical configuration for a large network. It can often be used to complement or even replace remote plugin execution daemons such as NRPE or NSclient++.

Getting ready

You should have a Nagios Core 3.0 or newer server with at least one host configured already. You should also understand the basics of how hosts and services relate, which is covered in the recipes of *Chapter 1, Understanding Hosts, Services, and Contacts*.

This recipe assumes a basic knowledge of SNMP, including its general intended purpose, the concept of an SNMP community, and what SNMP MIBs and OIDs are. In particular, if you're looking to monitor some property of a network device that's available to you via SNMP, you should know what the OID for that data is. This information is often available in the documentation for network devices, or can be deduced by running an appropriate `snmpwalk` command against the host to view the output for all its OIDs.

You should check that an SNMP daemon is running on the target host, and also that the `check_snmp` plugin is available on the monitoring host. It is included as part of the standard Nagios Plugins, so provided the Net-SNMP libraries were available on the system when these were compiled, the plugin should be available. If it is not, you may need to install the Net-SNMP libraries on your monitoring system and recompile the plugins.

We'll use the example of retrieving the total process count from a Linux server with hostname `ithaca.naginet`, and flagging WARNING and CRITICAL states at appropriate high ranges. We'll also discuss how to test for the presence or absence of strings, rather than numeric thresholds.

It's a good idea to test that the host will respond to SNMP queries in the expected form. We can test this with `snmpget`. Assuming a community name of `public`, we could write:

```
$ snmpget -v1 -c public ithaca.naginet .1.3.6.1.2.1.25.1.6.0
iso.3.6.1.2.1.25.1.6.0 = Gauge32: 81
```

We can also test the plugin by running it directly as the `nagios` user:

```
# sudo -s -u nagios
$ /usr/local/nagios/libexec/check_snmp -H ithaca.naginet -C public -o
.1.3.6.1.2.1.25.1.6.0
SNMP OK - 81 | iso.3.6.1.2.1.25.1.6.0=81
```

How to do it...

We can define a command and service check for the Linux process count OID as follows:

1. Change to the `objects` configuration directory for Nagios Core. The default path is `/usr/local/nagios/etc/objects`. If you've put the definition for your host in a different file, then move to its directory instead.

   ```
   # cd /usr/local/nagios/etc/objects
   ```

2. Edit a suitable file containing command definitions, perhaps `commands.cfg`, and add the following definition to the end of the file.

   ```
   define command {
       command_name    check_snmp_linux_procs
       command_line    $USER1$/check_snmp -H $HOSTADDRESS$ -C $ARG1$ -o
   .1.3.6.1.2.1.25.1.6.0 -w 100 -c 200
   }
   ```

3. Edit the file containing the definition for the host. The host definition might look similar to the following code snippet:

   ```
   define host {
       use         linux-server
       host_name   ithaca.naginet
       alias       ithaca
       address     10.128.0.61
   }
   ```

4. Beneath the definition for the host, place a new service definition using our new command. Replace `public` with the name of your SNMP community if it differs:

```
define service {
    use                   generic-service
    host_name             ithaca.naginet
    service_description   SNMP_PROCS
    check_command         check_snmp_linux_procs!public
}
```

5. Validate the configuration and restart the Nagios Core server:

```
# /usr/local/nagios/bin/nagios -v /usr/local/nagios/etc/nagios.cfg
# /etc/init.d/nagios restart
```

With this done, a new service check with a description of SNMP_PROCS will be added to the ithaca.naginet host, and the check_snmp plugin will issue a request for the value of the specified OID as its regular check. It will flag a WARNING state if the count is greater than 100, and a CRITICAL state if greater than 200, notifying accordingly. All this appears in the web interface the same way as any other service, under the **Services** menu item.

How it works...

The preceding configuration defines both a new command based around the check_snmp plugin, and in turn, a new service check using that command for the ithaca.naginet server. The community name for the SNMP request, public, is passed into the command as an argument; everything else, including the OID to be requested, is fixed into the check_snmp_linux_procs command definition.

A part of the command line defined includes the -w and -c options. For numeric outputs like ours, these are used to define the limits for the value beyond which a WARNING or CRITICAL state is raised, respectively. In this case, we define a WARNING threshold of 100 processes, and a CRITICAL threshold of 200 processes.

Similarly, if the SNMP check fails completely due to connectivity problems or syntax errors, an UNKNOWN state will be reported.

There's more...

It's also possible to test the output of SNMP checks to see if they match a particular string or pattern to determine whether the check succeeded. If we needed to check that the system's hostname was ithaca.naginet, for example (perhaps as a simple test SNMP query that should always succeed), then we might set up a command definition as follows:

```
define command {
    command_name   check_snmp_hostname
    command_line   $USER1$/check_snmp -H $HOSTADDRESS$ -C $ARG1$ -o
.1.3.6.1.2.1.1.5.0 -r $ARG2$
}
```

With a corresponding service check as follows:

```
define service {
    use                   generic-service
    host_name             ithaca.naginet
    service_description   SNMP_HOSTNAME
    check_command         check_snmp_hostname!public!ithaca
}
```

This particular check would only succeed if the SNMP query succeeds and returns a string matching the string ithaca, as specified in the second argument.

See also

▶ The *Creating an SNMP OID to monitor* in this chapter

▶ The *Creating a new host* and *Creating a new service* recipes in *Chapter 1, Understanding Hosts, Services, and Contacts*

▶ The *Creating a new command* recipe in *Chapter 2, Working with Commands and Plugins*

Monitoring a RAID or other hardware device

In this recipe, we'll learn a general strategy for monitoring the properties of hardware devices. Because of the different ways that vendors implement their hardware, this tends to be less straightforward than monitoring standard network services.

There are at least four general approaches to this problem.

Getting ready

You will need to know some specifics about the hardware that you want to monitor, including the model number. You should preferably also have a Nagios Core 3.0 server that was compiled with Net-SNMP libraries available to build the check_snmp plugin, part of the Nagios Plugins set.

How to do it...

We can find a way to monitor an arbitrary hardware device on a local or remote machine as follows:

1. Check if official or unofficial Nagios Core plugins already exist for polling the particular device. The best place to start is with Nagios Exchange at *http://exchange.nagios.org/*; just search for the make of hardware, and see if a plugin already exists, per the *Finding a plugin* recipe in *Chapter 2, Working with Commands and Plugins*. You can then install it by following the *Installing a plugin* recipe in the same chapter.

2. Check if any of the values you need from the hardware are or can be exported as SNMP OIDs, to be checked with the *Monitoring the output of an SNMP query* recipe in this chapter.

3. If they aren't, but there's a command-line diagnostic tool with output, or a return value that can be used as the check, you could consider exporting it as a custom OID in an SNMP server, by using the *Creating a new SNMP OID to monitor* recipe in this chapter.

4. Finally, we may have to resort to writing our own plugin. This is not actually as difficult as it may seem; it is discussed in the *Writing a new plugin from scratch* recipe in *Chapter 2, Working with Commands and Plugins*. This may be the only option for custom or very uncommon hardware.

How it works...

If we find an appropriate plugin for the hardware online, the main snag here is that we will need to not only be sure that the plugin works, by testing it against the hardware in both an OK and a CRITICAL state (which might be hard to do), but we will also need to make sure that the plugin is safe to run. The plugins on Nagios Exchange are reviewed before they are added, but the code for plugins that you find on any other website might not be safe to run.

Using SNMP for these kinds of checks wherever possible has two advantages, in that the values can be checked using a standard Nagios plugin, check_snmp, and the values can also be read over the network, meaning that we may not need to rely on remote execution daemons such as NRPE or NSclient++ to get this information.

See also

▸ The *Monitoring the output of an SNMP query* and *Creating a new SNMP OID to monitor* recipes in this chapter

▸ The *Finding a plugin, Installing a plugin*, and *Writing a new plugin from scratch* recipes in *Chapter 2, Working with Commands and Plugins*

Creating an SNMP OID to monitor

In this recipe, we'll learn how to configure a Net-SNMP snmpd server on a Linux server to return the output of a command in an SNMP OID. This can be useful as an alternative to NRPE monitoring for information that is not otherwise available in a checkable network service, so that Nagios Core can check it via its standard check_snmp method.

As an example, this can be a very good way of monitoring hardware devices, such as **RAID** arrays on remote servers, where command-line diagnostic tools are available to report a status as a number or string, but they only work locally and don't otherwise include any information in an SNMP MIB tree.

Getting ready

The host we intend to check should be running a Net-SNMP snmpd server that allows full read access to the MIB tree for a specified community string, such as public. This SNMP server should be capable of using the exec directive in its configuration to return the output of a command as the value of an SNMP OID when requested by an SNMP client. As such, you will need to know the basics of SNMP.

You will also need a Nagios Core 3.0 or newer server with SNMP enabled in order to actually monitor the OID, which is explained in the *Monitoring the output of an SNMP query* recipe.

In this example, we'll deal with a simple script running on a target host ithaca.naginet called /usr/local/bin/raidstat that returns an integer: zero for the RAID being in a good state, and non-zero to signal any problems. We'll assume this tool can be run as any user and does not require root privileges.

How to do it...

We can set up our custom SNMP OID as follows:

1. Add the following line to the snmpd.conf file on the target host, substituting in the path of the command that generates the needed output:

    ```
    exec raidstat /usr/local/bin/raidstat
    ```

2. Restart the snmpd server on the target host, which might be done as follows, depending on the system:

    ```
    # /etc/init.d/snmpd restart
    ```

3. Back on the monitoring server, we can walk the `.1.3.6.1.4.1.2021` OID, and find our `raidstat` OID and its value in the output:

```
$ snmpwalk -v1 -c public ithaca.naginet .1.3.6.1.4.1.2021 | less
...
iso.3.6.1.4.1.2021.8.1.2.1 = STRING: "raidstat"
iso.3.6.1.4.1.2021.8.1.3.1 = STRING: "/usr/local/bin/raidstat"
iso.3.6.1.4.1.2021.8.1.100.1 = INTEGER: 0
iso.3.6.1.4.1.2021.8.1.101.1 = STRING: "GOOD"
...
```

4. We now know which OID we can query for a check using the *Monitoring the output of an SNMP query* recipe in this chapter, and can test retrieving it directly with `snmpget`:

```
$ snmpget -v1 -c public ithaca.naginet .1.3.6.1.4.1.2021.8.1.100.1
```

How it works...

The `exec` call in the `snmpd` configuration defines a program that should be run to return a new value in the OID tree. The four OIDs we found in the output are as follows:

▶ `1.3.6.1.4.1.2021.8.1.2.1`: This is the name of the OID we've assigned, `raidstat`

▶ `1.3.6.1.4.1.2021.8.1.3.1`: This is the full path to the script that was called, `/usr/local/bin/raidstat`

▶ `1.3.6.1.4.1.2021.8.1.100.1`: This is the return value from the call, expressed as an integer

▶ `1.3.6.1.4.1.2021.8.1.101.1`: This is any output from the call, expressed as a string

This setup can therefore be used to check the return value and character output of any command that the `snmpd` user is able to execute, a good method for ad hoc monitoring for very specific cases like this.

There's more...

More than one `exec` command can be added to the server configuration if required. For example, if we needed to check the state of the CPU temperature with a command `tempstat`, then we might define:

```
exec raidstat /usr/local/bin/raidstat
exec tempstat /usr/local/bin/tempstat
```

The return values and output for both would then show up in the SNMP output, in separate OIDs.

If necessary, the command definitions can also be followed by arguments:

```
exec tempstat /usr/local/bin/tempstat --cpu=0
```

A full discussion of how `exec` and the similar `pass` configuration for Net-SNMP works is outside the scope of this book, but is discussed extensively in its documentation available at the time of writing at `http://www.net-snmp.org/docs/readmefiles.html`.

Note that if exporting values via SNMP is unsuitable, an alternative for remote monitoring is to use **Nagios Remote Plugin Executor** (**NRPE**) to run a check on the target server and return the result to the monitoring server. This is discussed in the recipes of *Chapter 6, Enabling Remote Execution*.

See also

- ► The *Creating an SNMP OID to monitor* recipe in this chapter
- ► The *Creating a new host* and *Creating a new service* recipes in *Chapter 1, Understanding Hosts, Services, and Contacts*
- ► The *Creating a new command* recipe in *Chapter 2, Working with Commands and Plugins*
- ► The *Monitoring local services on a remote machine with NRPE* recipes in *Chapter 6, Enabling Remote Execution*

6
Enabling Remote Execution

In this chapter, we will cover the following recipes:

- ▸ Monitoring local services on a remote machine with NRPE
- ▸ Setting the listening address for NRPE
- ▸ Setting allowed client hosts for NRPE
- ▸ Creating new NRPE command definitions securely
- ▸ Giving limited sudo privileges to NRPE
- ▸ Using check_by_ssh with key authentication instead of NRPE

Introduction

For a dedicated Nagios Core server with access to all the relevant parts of the network, making checks is relatively simple using commands and plugins that make ICMP, TCP, and UDP connections to network hosts and services, in order to determine their operating state. These can be used to check any sort of network service, without requiring anything to be installed on the target machine. As an example, when the check_http plugin is used to check a web server, it works in the same way as if a browser was making the request.

However, monitoring a network thoroughly usually has more to it than simply checking network connectivity and availability. It's also a good idea to check properties of the network that don't directly correspond to a network service, and hence can't be directly checked over a network connection.

These are often properties of hardware or the underlying system, such as disk space or system load average, or processes that are configured only to listen locally, commonly done for database servers.

We could install Nagios Core on all of the systems, perhaps, but this would make maintenance difficult. It would be much better to have some means of remote execution of diagnostic programs, so that they are run directly on the target host to retrieve the information they need, and the results are returned to a single Nagios Core server via a dedicated network service.

There are three general approaches to managing this problem:

▸ Use `check_nrpe` to run a standard Nagios Core plugin on the target machine and return its results transparently to the monitoring server.

▸ Use `check_by_ssh` to run an arbitrary command on the target machine from the monitoring server by first connecting to it with SSH.

▸ Use `check_snmp` to check an SNMP OID that's configured to provide the return value and output of some command on the target host.

This chapter covers the first two solutions, focusing on the more commonly used **Nagios Remote Plugin Executor** (**NRPE**), and explaining how it differs from the `check_by_ssh` solution. For some information on configuring SNMP, see the *Monitoring the output of an SNMP query* and *Creating an SNMP OID to monitor* recipes in *Chapter 5, Monitoring Methods*.

Monitoring local services on a remote machine with NRPE

In this recipe, we'll learn how to install and run an NRPE server on a target host, `roma.naginet`. We'll use this to check the load average on that host with the `check_load` plugin.

The plugins for these checks will be executed on the target server by the NRPE daemon, but the results will be returned to our Nagios Core monitoring server `olympus.naginet`. This requires installing the `check_nrpe` plugin on the monitoring server, and the full Nagios Plugins set (but not Nagios Core itself) on the target server.

This is a reasonably long and in-depth recipe as it involves installing a total of three software packages on two servers.

Getting ready

You will need a monitoring server with Nagios Core 3.0 or newer installed. You should also have a UNIX-like target host that you intend to monitor that can run the NRPE daemon. Most modern UNIX-like systems including Linux and BSD should be able to do this. Both the monitoring server and the target host will need internet connectivity, and you should already be monitoring the target host itself with a host definition, to which we'll be adding service checks.

If your servers don't have a direct gateway to the Internet, then you can work around this by uploading the relevant files after downloading them onto a workstation, or another machine with Internet access.

You should understand the basics of configuring, compiling, and installing software from source. In most cases, the usual `./configure`, `make`, and `make install` process will be all that's necessary, and the recipe will walk you through this. You will need to have `make` installed, along with any other tools needed for the configure and build processes, including a C compiler such as `gcc`.

You should also have a good grasp of how hosts and services interrelate in Nagios Core, which is discussed in the recipes of *Chapter 1*, and how Nagios Core uses commands and plugins, discussed in *Chapter 2*. You should not need an in-depth understanding of the use of any particular plugin; the recipe will demonstrate the usage of the plugins to which it refers.

Finally, you should be able to configure any firewalls to allow connectivity from the Nagios Core server to the server being monitored with TCP destination port `5666`.

How to do it...

This first part of the recipe is done on the target server:

1. Download and install the latest Nagios Plugins package. At the time of writing, the link is available at `http://nagiosplugins.org/download/`.

   ```
   $ wget http://downloads.sourceforge.net/project/nagiosplug/
   nagiosplug/1.4.16/nagios-plugins-1.4.16.tar.gz
   $ tar -xzf nagios-plugins-1.4.16.tar.gz
   ```

2. Configure, compile, and install the plugins, the same way you would on a new monitoring server. You will need to have `root` privileges for the `make install` call.

   ```
   $ cd nagios-plugins-1.4.16
   $ ./configure
   $ make
   # make install
   ```

   You may need to install some shared libraries and headers on the system to do this for certain plugins, such as a `libssl` implementation. The output of the `./configure` script should alert you to any such problems.

3. Download and install the latest version of NRPE from the Nagios Exchange website. At the time of writing, the link is available at `http://exchange.nagios.org/directory/Addons/Monitoring-Agents/NRPE--2D-Nagios-Remote-Plugin-Executor/details`.

   ```
   $ wget http://prdownloads.sourceforge.net/sourceforge/nagios/nrpe-
   2.13.tar.gz
   $ tar -xzf nrpe-2.13.tar.gz
   ```

4. Enter the `nrpe-2.13` source directory, and configure, compile, and install the daemon and a stock configuration for it. You will need to have `root` privileges for both the `make install-daemon` and the `make install-daemon-config` calls:

```
$ cd nrpe-2.13
$ ./configure
$ make all
# make install-daemon
# make install-daemon-config
```

If you do not already have a `nagios` user on the target host, you may need to create one before the daemon will install properly:

```
# groupadd nagios
# useradd -r -g nagios nagios
```

5. Edit the newly installed file at `/usr/local/nagios/etc/nrpe.cfg` and find the line beginning with `allowed_hosts`. Add a comma and the IP address of your monitoring server to this line. In this case, we've added the IP address `10.128.0.11`:

```
allowed_hosts=127.0.0.1,10.128.0.11
```

6. Start the `nrpe` daemon, and check that it is running by searching the process table with `pgrep` or `ps`:

```
# /usr/local/nagios/bin/nrpe -c /usr/local/nagios/etc/nrpe.cfg -d
# pgrep nrpe
18593
# ps -e | grep [n]rpe
nagios 18593 1 0 21:55 ? 00:00:01 nrpe
```

7. If you would like the `nrpe` daemon to start on boot, add an `init` script appropriate to your system. An example `init-script` is generated at `./configure` time in the source directory. Versions are also generated for Debian-derived systems and SUSE systems in `init-script.debian` and `init-script.suse`. Exactly how this should be done will depend on your particular system, for which you may need to consult its documentation.

This next part of the recipe is done on the monitoring server.

1. Again, download the latest version of NRPE, the same way as done for the target server:

```
$ wget http://prdownloads.sourceforge.net/sourceforge/nagios/nrpe-2.13.tar.gz
$ tar -xzf nrpe-2.13.tar.gz
```

2. Again, configure and build the software. However, note that this time the install line is different, as we're installing the `check_nrpe` plugin rather than the `nrpe` daemon:

```
$ cd nrpe-2.13.tar.gz
$ ./configure
$ make all
# make install-plugin
```

3. Check that the plugin is installed correctly. It should be saved at `/usr/local/nagios/libexec/check_nrpe`:

```
$ ls /usr/local/nagios/libexec/check_nrpe
/usr/local/nagios/libexec/check_nrpe
```

4. Move to the directory containing the Nagios Core object configuration. By default, this is `/usr/local/nagios/etc/objects`:

```
$ cd /usr/local/nagios/etc/objects
```

5. Edit an appropriate file for defining new commands. For the default installation, `/usr/local/nagios/etc/objects/commands.cfg` is a good choice. Add the following definition to the end of this file:

```
define command {
    command_name   check_nrpe
    command_line   $USER1$/check_nrpe -H $HOSTADDRESS$ -c $ARG1$
}
```

6. Edit the file defining the target host as an object. The definition might look something similar to the following code snippet:

```
define host {
    use         linux-server
    host_name   roma.naginet
    alias       roma
    address     10.128.0.61
}
```

7. Beneath the definition for the host, after any other services defined for it, add the following service definition:

```
define service {
    use                   generic-service
    host_name             roma.naginet
    service_description   LOAD
    check_command         check_nrpe!check_load
}
```

8. Validate the configuration and restart the Nagios Core server:

```
# /usr/local/nagios/bin/nagios -v /usr/local/nagios/etc/nagios.cfg
# /etc/init.d/nagios restart
```

With this done, a new service with the description LOAD will appear in the web interface ready to be checked, and will come up with an appropriate status, including the load average as read from the nrpe daemon on the target host:

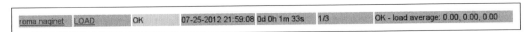

We can see more detail about how the check was performed and its results in the details page for the service:

Current Status:	**OK** (for 0d 0h 0m 31s)
Status Information:	OK - load average: 0.00, 0.00, 0.01
Performance Data:	load1=0.000;15.000;30.000;0; load5=0.000;10.000;25.000;0; load15=0.010;5.000;20.000;0;
Current Attempt:	1/3 (HARD state)
Last Check Time:	07-25-2012 21:58:12
Check Type:	ACTIVE
Check Latency / Duration:	0.067 / 0.087 seconds
Next Scheduled Check:	07-25-2012 21:58:18
Last State Change:	07-25-2012 21:57:48
Last Notification:	N/A (notification 0)
Is This Service Flapping?	**NO** (0.00% state change)
In Scheduled Downtime?	**NO**
Last Update:	07-25-2012 21:58:18 (0d 0h 0m 1s ago)

If the load average on roma.naginet exceeds the limits defined for the check_load command in /usr/local/nagios/etc/nrpe.cfg on the target host, the service will enter WARNING or CRITICAL states, and will send notifications if configured to do so, all in the same manner as a non-NRPE service.

How it works...

The NRPE plugin and daemon are used to run Nagios Core plugins on the target host, rather than on the monitoring server itself. The results of the check are then passed back to the monitoring server, and recorded and analyzed by Nagios Core the same way as if the service was running a plugin on the monitoring server, for example check_http or check_ssh.

The recipe we followed does four main things:

▸ We installed the latest Nagios Plugins package to the target host, including the check_load plugin. This is necessary because the plugin is actually run on the target host and not on the monitoring server, as is the case with the plugins that check network services.

▸ We installed the nrpe daemon to the target host, along with a stock configuration file nrpe.cfg. This is the network service through which the check_nrpe plugin will request commands to be run on the target host. The plugins will be run by this process, typically as the nagios user.

▸ We installed the check_nrpe plugin to the monitoring host, and defined a command of the same name to use it. The command accepts one argument in the $ARG1$ macro; its value is the command that should be run on the target host. In this case, we supplied check_load for this argument.

▸ We set up a service to monitor the output of the standard check_load plugin, via check_nrpe.

Like other Nagios Core plugins, the check_nrpe program can be run directly from the command line. If we wanted to test the response of the configuration that we arranged in the previous section, then we might run the following command:

```
$ /usr/local/nagios/libexec/check_nrpe -H roma.naginet -c check_load
OK - load average: 0.00, 0.00, 0.00|load1=0.000;15.000;30.000;0;
load5=0.000;10.000;25.000;0; load15=0.000;5.000;20.000;0;
```

In this case, the state of OK and the load average values, as retrieved by check_load, were returned by the nrpe daemon as the result of the check_nrpe call.

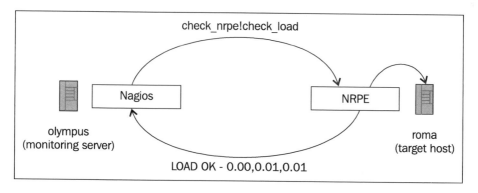

It's very important to note that this simple configuration of NRPE is not completely secure by default. The recipes listed under the *See also* section for this recipe provide some basic means to secure NRPE instances from abuse. These should be used in concert with a sensible firewall policy.

There's more...

Of course, `check_load` is not the only plugin that can be run on the target server this way. If we inspect the `/usr/local/nagios/etc/nrpe.cfg` file `/usr/local/nagios/etc/nrpe.cfg` on the target host, near the end of the file, we find some other example definitions of commands that `check_nrpe` will run upon requests issued from the monitoring server:

```
command[check_users]=/usr/local/nagios/libexec/check_users -w 5 -c 10
command[check_load]=/usr/local/nagios/libexec/check_load -w 15,10,5 -c
30,25,20
command[check_hda1]=/usr/local/nagios/libexec/check_disk -w 20% -c 10% -p
/dev/hda1
command[check_zombie_procs]=/usr/local/nagios/libexec/check_procs -w 5 -c
10 -s Z
command[check_total_procs]=/usr/local/nagios/libexec/check_procs -w 150
-c 200
```

We recognize `check_load` as the second of these. Note that it already includes some thresholds for WARNING and CRITICAL alerts in its `-w` and `-c` parameters.

If we also wanted to check the number of processes on this server, we could add a service check for `roma.naginet`, defined as follows:

```
define service {
    use                  generic-service
    host_name            roma.naginet
    service_description  PROCS
    check_command        check_nrpe!check_total_procs
}
```

This service will generate a WARNING alert if the number of processes exceeds 150, and a CRITICAL alert if it exceeds 200. Again, the plugin is run on the target server, and not on the monitoring server.

Another useful and common application of `check_nrpe` is to make remote checks on database servers, with plugins such as `check_mysql` and `check_pgsql`, in the case where servers do not listen on network interfaces for security reasons. Instead, they listen only on `localhost` or UNIX sockets, and are hence inaccessible to the monitoring server. To work around this problem, we could add a new command definition to the end of `nrpe.cfg` on the target server as follows:

```
command[check_mysql]=/usr/local/nagios/libexec/check_mysql -u nagios -d
nagios -p wGG7H233bq
```

A corresponding check that uses the `check_mysql` command can then be made on the monitoring server:

```
define service {
    use                  generic-service
    host_name            roma.naginet
    service_description  MYSQL
    check_command        check_nrpe!check_mysql
}
```

See the *Monitoring database services* recipe in *Chapter 5, Monitoring Methods*, for some detail on how to use the `check_mysql` and `check_pgsql` plugins.

NRPE is thus useful not only for making checks of system properties or hardware, but also for any plugin that needs to be run on the target host rather than the monitoring host.

Finally, it's important to note that the command definitions included in the default `nrpe.cfg` file are intended as examples; you will probably want to fine-tune the parameters for some of them, and remove the ones you don't use, along with adding your own.

See also

▸ The *Setting the listening address for NRPE, Setting allowed client hosts for NRPE, Creating new NRPE command definitions securely*, and *Giving limited sudo privileges to NRPE* recipes in this chapter

▸ The *Monitoring database services* recipe in *Chapter 5, Monitoring Methods*

Setting the listening address for NRPE

In this recipe, we'll learn how to make NRPE listen on a specific IP address on a target host. This might be done on hosts with multiple interfaces in order to prevent spurious requests made to the `nrpe` daemon from untrusted interfaces, perhaps the public Internet. It could also be appropriate for configuring the daemon only to listen on a trusted VPN interface.

This setup can be particularly useful when the server has an interface into a dedicated management network to which the monitoring server also has access, preventing the `nrpe` daemon from responding to requests on other interfaces unnecessarily, and thereby closing a possible security hole.

Getting ready

You should have a target host configured for checking in a Nagios Core 3.0 or later monitoring server. The target host should be running the `nrpe` daemon, and listening on all interfaces (which we'll fix). You can verify that `nrpe` is running with `pgrep` or `ps`:

```
# pgrep nrpe
29964
# ps -e | grep [n]rpe
nagios 29964 1 0 21:55 ? 00:00:01 nrpe
```

You can check whether the `nrpe` daemon is listening on all interfaces by checking the output of `netstat`:

```
# netstat -plnt | grep nrpe
tcp 0 0 0.0.0.0:5666 0.0.0.0:* LISTEN 29964/nrpe
```

The address of `0.0.0.0` shows that `nrpe` is listening on all interfaces, which is what we'd like to correct.

How to do it...

We can configure the `nrpe` daemon only to listen on one address as follows:

1. Edit the `nrpe` daemon's configuration file. The default location is `/usr/local/nagios/etc/nrpe.cfg`. Look for the line beginning with `server_address`, which is normally commented out by default:

    ```
    #server_address=127.0.0.1
    ```

    If you don't have such a line, then you can add it at the end of the file.

2. Uncomment the line if it's commented by removing the leading # character, and change the `127.0.0.1` address to the address to which you want to restrict the `nrpe` process listening:

    ```
    server_address=10.128.0.61
    ```

3. Restart the `nrpe` daemon. If you have installed an `init` script for it, you may be able to do this with the following:

    ```
    # /etc/init.d/nrpe restart
    ```

    If not, you can restart the process by sending it a `HUP` signal with the `kill` command, which will prompt it to re-read its configuration file and resume running:

    ```
    # pgrep nrpe
    29964
    # kill -HUP 29964
    ```

With this done, the `nrpe` daemon should now only be listening on the specified address. We can verify this using `netstat`:

```
# netstat -plnt | grep nrpe
tcp 0 0 10.128.0.61:5666 0.0.0.0:* LISTEN 29964/nrpe
```

How it works...

The configuration we adjusted in the preceding section defines an address on which the `nrpe` daemon should listen, and implies that it should not respond to requests on any others.

Because the `nrpe` server is explicitly designed to run commands at the request of remote servers, it's very important to take steps like these wherever appropriate to prevent attackers from exploiting the service.

See also

 ▶ The *Monitoring local services on a remote machine with NRPE* recipe in this chapter.

Setting allowed client hosts for NRPE

In this recipe, we'll learn how to configure the NRPE daemon to answer requests from a particular IP address, typically the designated Nagios Core server or servers monitoring your network. This means that `nrpe` will not run plugins or return results for any `check _nrpe` request made from IP addresses not in this list.

This is an elementary security step in running an NRPE server. This should be done in concert with a hardware or software firewall and security policy. If your target host has interfaces or routes into untrusted networks, there is a risk of attackers making spurious requests for information about the system, clogging up your disk with logs from excessive check requests, or even possibly exploiting the `nrpe` daemon or the Nagios Plugins.

Getting ready

You should have a target host configured for checking in a Nagios Core 3.0 or later monitoring server. The target host should be running the `nrpe` daemon. You can verify that `nrpe` is running with `pgrep` or `ps`:

```
# pgrep nrpe
29964
# ps -e | grep [n]rpe
nagios 29964 1 0 21:55 ? 00:00:01 nrpe
```

We can verify that the target host is not configured to respond to a particular IP address by attempting to open a `telnet` or `netcat` connection to it. If we are not one of the allowed hosts, `nrpe` will close the session immediately without waiting for any input:

```
$ telnet roma.naginet 5666
Trying 10.128.0.61...
Connected to 10.128.0.61.
Escape character is '^]'.
Connection closed by foreign host.
```

This assumes that NRPE is listening on its default port number `5666`. In this example, we'll add the IP address `10.128.0.12` to the list of hosts allowed to request information from NRPE.

How to do it...

We can configure the `nrpe` daemon to respond to a new address as follows:

1. Edit the `nrpe` daemon's configuration file. The default location is `/usr/local/nagios/etc/nrpe.cfg`. Look for the line beginning with `allowed_hosts`. It may look similar to the following code snippet:

   ```
   allowed_hosts=127.0.0.1,10.128.0.11
   ```

2. Add or remove IP addresses from the line, separating them with commas. For this example, we're adding one more address:

   ```
   allowed_hosts=127.0.0.1,10.128.0.11,10.128.0.12
   ```

3. Restart the `nrpe` daemon. If you have installed an `init` script for it, you may be able to this with something similar to the following:

   ```
   # /etc/init.d/nrpe restart
   ```

   If not, you can restart the process by sending it a `HUP` signal with the `kill` command, which will prompt it to re-read its configuration file and resume running:

   ```
   # pgrep nrpe
   29964
   # kill -HUP 29964
   ```

With this done, the `nrpe` daemon should now respond only to the nominated hosts making `check_nrpe` requests, immediately closing the connection otherwise. We can verify whether our new host is allowed to talk to the `nrpe` service on `roma.naginet` with another `telnet` test:

```
$ telnet roma.naginet 5666
```

Note that the `nrpe` daemon is now waiting for input, rather than closing the connection immediately as it was doing before. This implies that we can now run `check_nrpe` checks from `10.128.0.12`, if we need to.

How it works...

The configuration we adjusted above defines a set of addresses to which the `nrpe` daemon should respond if a request is made, and implies that it should refuse to answer requests made by any other address.

The `nrpe` daemon inspects the IP address of incoming connections, and if the `allowed_hosts` directive is defined, checks that the address features in that list. If it does not, it closes the connection and refuses to run any plugins, much less return any output from them.

There's more...

The `allowed_hosts` directive is actually optional; if we wished, we could set the `nrpe` server up to respond to requests from any IP address. The default installation and example configuration, however, enables it by default, allowing both requests from the localhost IP `127.0.0.1`, and any network addresses the host had at the time `./configure` was run.

This is a sensible policy because Nagios Core plugins are designed by third parties in an open source community, for monitoring purposes in trusted networks, and may not necessarily be very secure. A plugin doesn't actually have to have a security hole to cause such problems; if the check it makes is very resource-intensive, for example opening a lot of TCP connections or querying a large database, an attacker could cause problems on the target host, if allowed, simply by making a large number of such `check_nrpe` requests in a short period of time.

See also

 ▸ The *Monitoring local services on a remote machine with NRPE* recipe in this chapter

Creating new NRPE command definitions securely

In this recipe, we'll learn how to securely create new command definitions for `nrpe` to run upon request by a monitoring server. We need to do this because even if we have a huge set of plugins installed on our target host running `nrpe`, the daemon will only run commands defined in its configuration file.

We'll also learn how arguments can be passed to these commands if strictly necessary, and about the potentially negative security consequences of this.

Getting ready

You should have a target host configured for checking in a Nagios Core 3.0 or later monitoring server. The target host should be running the `nrpe` daemon. You can verify that `nrpe` is running with `pgrep` or `ps`:

```
# pgrep nrpe
29964
# ps -e | grep [n]rpe
nagios 29964 1 0 21:55 ? 00:00:01 nrpe
```

We can inspect the list of commands that `nrpe` is already configured to run by looking for `command` directives in its configuration file. By default, this file is `/usr/local/nagios/etc/nrpe.cfg`, and the default command definitions are near the end of the file:

```
command[check_users]=/usr/local/nagios/libexec/check_users -w 5 -c 10
command[check_load]=/usr/local/nagios/libexec/check_load -w 15,10,5 -c
30,25,20
command[check_hda1]=/usr/local/nagios/libexec/check_disk -w 20% -c 10% -p
/dev/hda1
command[check_zombie_procs]=/usr/local/nagios/libexec/check_procs -w 5 -c
10 -s Z
command[check_total_procs]=/usr/local/nagios/libexec/check_procs -w 150
-c 200
```

We'll add another command to this set to check whether the swap space available is above a specific threshold, using the standard Nagios Core plugin `check_swap`. We can test whether it is working first by running it on the target host:

```
$ /usr/local/nagios/libexec/check_swap -w 10% -c 5%
SWAP OK - 100% free (216 MB out of 217 MB) |swap=216MB;21;10;0;217
```

For completeness, we'll also show how to define a service check using this new plugin on the Nagios Core monitoring server.

How to do it...

We can add a new command definition to an `nrpe` configuration as follows:

1. Edit the `nrpe` daemon's configuration file. The default location is `/usr/local/nagios/etc/nrpe.cfg`. Look for lines beginning with `command`, which are near the end of the file by default.

2. Add the following line to the end of the file:

```
command[check_swap]=/usr/local/nagios/libexec/check_swap -w 10% -c
5%
```

3. Restart the `nrpe` daemon. If you have installed an `init` script for it, you may be able to do this with something similar to the following command:

```
# /etc/init.d/nrpe restart
```

If not, you can restart the process by sending it a HUP signal with the `kill` command, which will prompt it to re-read its configuration file and resume running:

```
# pgrep nrpe

29964

# kill -HUP 29964
```

With this done, assuming that our monitoring server is part of the `allowed_hosts` directive and can contact the target host, a call to `check_nrpe` on the monitoring host should return the status and output of the `check_swap` plugin on the target host:

```
$ /usr/local/nagios/libexec/check_nrpe -H roma.naginet -c check_swap
SWAP OK - 100% free (216 MB out of 217 MB) |swap=216MB;21;10;0;217
```

In turn, this allows us to use the check in a service definition on the monitoring server, with a `check_nrpe` command:

```
define service {
        use                  generic-service
        host_name            roma.naginet
        service_description  SWAP
        check_command        check_nrpe!check_swap
}
```

How it works...

The configuration added in the preceding section defines a new command in `nrpe.cfg` called `check_swap`. The definition of new commands in `nrpe.cfg` takes the following general form:

```
command[command_name] = command_line
```

We defined a command `check_swap` for NRPE. It doesn't accept any arguments, where the actual `check_swap` plugin requires them; instead, the arguments are hard-coded into the command definition, with the two options `-w 10%` and `-c 5%` setting the thresholds for free swap space.

Besides checking system properties, such as the load average or the swap space, which might not otherwise be directly retrievable except via systems such as SNMP, another common use for NRPE is to report on the state of network services that only listen locally, or are otherwise unreachable by the monitoring host. Database server monitoring is a good example. We could define the following command in `nrpe.cfg`:

```
command[check_mysql] = /usr/local/nagios/libexec/check_mysql -u nagios -d
nagios -p NFmxenQ5
```

Assuming that the `check_mysql` plugin is installed on this target host, which it ought to be if the MySQL client library and headers were available at compile time, this command would then enable this check to be run from the monitoring host:

```
$ /usr/local/nagios/libexec/check_nrpe -H roma.naginet -c check_mysql
Uptime: 420865  Threads: 1  Questions: 172  Slow queries: 0  Opens: 99
Flush tables: 1  Open tables: 23  Queries per second avg: 0.0
```

This can be configured as a service check using an appropriate command definition for `check_nrpe` as follows:

```
define service {
    use                     generic-service
    host_name               roma.naginet
    service_description     MYSQL
    check_command           check_nrpe!check_mysql
}
```

Thus we're able to get the status of the MySQL server on the remote host `roma.naginet` without actually connecting directly to the MySQL server itself; we arrange for the NRPE service on the target host to do it on the monitoring server's behalf.

This is not just useful for network services running on the target host. It can be used to delegate any kind of check that a remote host can perform where the monitoring server cannot. Using NRPE is thus also a way to work around the addressability problems of NAT, because a service running on an address such as `192.168.1.1` would not be addressable from outside the network. If NRPE were running on the NAT gateway, we could use that to address the appropriate systems by their local addresses.

There's more...

Also, near the bottom of `nrpe.cfg`, you'll find some information on providing arguments to NRPE commands as part of the `check_nrpe` request, as opposed to hard-coding them. The comment included in the file makes it quite clear that this carries some risks:

The following examples allow user-supplied arguments and can only be used if the NRPE daemon was compiled with support for command arguments AND the dont_ blame_nrpe directive in this config file is set to '1'. This poses a potential security risk, so make sure you read the SECURITY file before doing this.

It's important to understand that, when running NRPE on a target host, you are running a service that is designed to allow network machines to run commands on the target machine with no strong authentication, which is why keeping NRPE secure is so important. If you allow passing arguments to commands, you need to be aware of the full ramifications and risks of doing so, and the recommended SECURITY file explains these well.

If you really want to use it, it requires reconfiguring and recompiling the nrpe daemon with the --enable-command-args switch:

```
$ ./configure --enable-command-args
$ make all
# make install-daemon
```

Then set the dont_blame_nrpe in nrpe.cfg parameter to 1, where it otherwise defaults to 0:

```
dont_blame_nrpe=1
```

After restarting nrpe (if you have rebuilt it, you will need to restart it completely this time, and not simply send the process a HUP signal), this allows us to use command definitions similar to the following:

```
command[check_mysql_args]=/usr/local/nagios/libexec/check_mysql -H
localhost -u $ARG1$ -d $ARG2$ -p $ARG3$
```

This command in turn allows checks from the monitoring servers like this, using the -a option of check_nrpe:

```
# /usr/local/nagios/libexec/check_nrpe -H roma.naginet -c check_mysql_
args -a nagios nagios NFmxenQ5
```

Because of the security concerns, I would recommend you avoid using command arguments if at all possible. If you do absolutely need to use them, it's also important to make sure that the traffic is encrypted, especially if it contains usernames and passwords. Advice on how to manage this is included in the SECURITY document for the nrpe daemon.

See also

▸ The *Monitoring local services on a remote machine with NRPE* and *Giving limited sudo privileges to NRPE* recipes in this chapter

▸ The *Monitoring database services* recipe in *Chapter 5, Monitoring Methods*

Giving limited sudo privileges to NRPE

In this recipe, we'll learn how to deal with the difficulty of execution permissions for NRPE. The majority of the standard Nagios plugins don't require special privileges to run, although this depends on how stringent your system's security restrictions are. However, some of the plugins require being run as `root`, or perhaps as a user other than `nrpe`. This is sometimes the case with plugins that need to make requests of system-level resources, such as checking the integrity of `RAID` arrays.

There are four general approaches to fixing this:

- **Bad**: One method is to change the plugins to `setuid`, meaning that they will always be run as the user who owns them, no matter who executes them. The problem with this is that setting this bit allows anyone to run the program as `root`, not just `nrpe`, a very common vector for exploits.

- **Worse**: Another method is to run `nrpe` as `root`, or as the appropriate user. This is done by changing the `nrpe_user` and `nrpe_group` properties in `nrpe.cfg`. This is even more dangerous, and completely inconsistent with the principle of least privilege; we should confer a user as little permission as possible to allow it to do its job. Never do this!

- **Better**: A third method is to use `command_prefix` in `nrpe.cfg` to prepend `/usr/bin/sudo` to all commands, and gives `nrpe` full `sudo` privileges to run only the plugins in `/usr/local/nagios/libexec`. This is a bit better, but still quite risky as we probably don't need every single command to be run as `root`, only one or two.

- **Best**: The best method is to use `sudo` to assign the `nrpe` user limited privileges for a subset of commands, only the ones it needs to run, and only as the user by which it needs to be run.

The last solution is the most likely to be secure, so we'll examine an example here. We'll run the `check_procs` plugin as `root`, to get a process count. In most cases, you wouldn't need `root` privileges to get a complete count of all processes, but it might be needed on a system with a very locked-down `grsecurity` patch installed.

Getting ready

You should have a target host configured for checking in a Nagios Core 3.0 or later monitoring server. The target host should be running the `nrpe` daemon, and listening on all interfaces. You can verify that `nrpe` is running with `pgrep` or `ps`:

```
# pgrep nrpe
29964
# ps -e | grep [n]rpe
nagios 29964 1 0 21:55 ? 00:00:01 nrpe
```

You should also have `sudo` installed and working on the target system, and understand what it does. We'll be editing the `/etc/sudoers` file to confer `root` privileges to our `nrpe` user, for one program only. This recipe will assume that the `nrpe` daemon is running as the `nagios` user in the `nagios` group.

How to do it...

We can confer limited `root` privileges for one command to our `nrpe` user as follows:

1. Edit the `/etc/sudoers` file. The safest way to do this is generally with a call to `visudo`, which will make a temporary copy of the file and verify its syntax is correct before installing it:

   ```
   # visudo
   ```

2. Add the following line to the file, and save it:

   ```
   nagios ALL=(ALL) NOPASSWD: /usr/local/nagios/libexec/check_procs
   ```

   Note that if the `requiretty` directive appears anywhere in your `/etc/sudoers` file, you may need to remove it to make this work.

3. Become the `nagios` user with `sudo`, and test whether running the command runs as `root`, with no password prompt:

   ```
   # sudo -s -u nagios
   $ sudo /usr/local/nagios/libexec/check_procs
   PROCS OK: 89 processes
   ```

4. Edit the `nrpe` daemon's configuration file. The default location is `/usr/local/nagios/etc/nrpe.cfg`. Look for the command definition for `check_total_procs`, and if there isn't one, create it. Note that `/usr/bin/sudo` has been added to the start of the command:

   ```
   command[check_total_procs]=/usr/bin/sudo /usr/local/nagios/libexec/check_procs -w 150 -c 200
   ```

5. Restart the `nrpe` daemon. If you have installed an `init` script for it, you may be able to do this with something similar to the following:

   ```
   # /etc/init.d/nrpe restart
   ```

   If not, you can restart the process by sending it a HUP signal with the `kill` command, which will prompt it to re-read its configuration file and resume running:

   ```
   # pgrep nrpe
   29964
   # kill -HUP 29964
   ```

With this done, we should now be able to run a `check_nrpe` call from the monitoring server, and get a successful response:

```
$ /usr/local/nagios/libexec/check_nrpe -H roma.naginet -c check_total_
procs
PROCS OK: 89 processes
```

How it works...

The preceding configuration does not change the behavior of `nrpe` very much; most of the configuration is actually done on its host system. All we changed was the command definition for `check_total_procs` to run it from within `sudo`.

To make this work without a password, we defined it in the `/etc/sudoers` file so that no password was required to execute this particular program as `root` for the `nagios` user. Because `nrpe` runs as the `nagios` user, it is therefore able to use `sudo` with no password for this command only.

This means that when we call the `check_total_procs` command from the monitoring server, it returns us the full output of the plugin as it was run with `root` privileges, but the `nagios` user doesn't have `root` privileges to run anything else potentially dangerous, such as `rm` or `halt`.

There's more...

While this is a much more secure way of allowing privileges as another user for `nrpe`, it still requires trusting that the plugin that is being run with `root` privileges is secure and can't easily be exploited. Be very careful before running this with custom code or with stray plugins you find on the Web!

If you intend to allow the `nagios` user to run more than a couple of distinct programs, it may look a little tidier to define them in `/etc/sudoers` with `Cmnd_Alias`:

```
Cmnd_Alias NAGIOS = /usr/local/nagios/libexec/check_procs, /usr/local/
nagios/libexec/check_load
nagios ALL=(ALL) NOPASSWD: NAGIOS
```

See also

> ▸ The *Monitoring local services on a remote machine with NRPE* and *Using check_by_ssh with key authentication instead of NRPE* recipes in this chapter

Using check_by_ssh with key authentication instead of NRPE

While all of the previous recipes in this chapter show that NRPE can be very effectively tied down and secured, it may be that we require some means of authentication to a target host in order to run the appropriate Nagios plugins on it. The nrpe daemon does not require any authentication to return information about the host's state; as long as the IP addresses all match, and the command is defined for running, it will return information.

If you already use SSH keys for a public key infrastructure in your network, then you may find it preferable to use the check_by_ssh plugin instead, which allows you to use public keys to authenticate with a target host before running any commands. This is only suitable if the target host runs an ssh daemon.

In this recipe, we'll repeat the setup for the check_load plugin as done in the first recipe in this chapter, *Monitoring local services on a remote machine with NRPE*, but we'll use the check_by_ssh plugin instead.

Getting ready

You should have a Nagios Core 3.0 or newer server ready, with the ssh client software installed, and a target host running sshd. The OpenSSH implementations should work fine.

The target host should have all of the Nagios Plugins installed; in this case, we're using check_load.

You should be familiar with public key authentication and its advantages and disadvantages. Wikipedia has an excellent article about public key cryptography and authentication at http://en.wikipedia.org/wiki/Public-key_cryptography.

There is a popular introduction to SSH authentication with a key infrastructure at http://support.suso.com/supki/SSH_Tutorial_for_Linux.

We will be running through a sensible key infrastructure setup, but it would pay to have an understanding of how it works in case this setup does not suit your configuration.

How to do it...

We can arrange to get the output of `check_load` from our remote host by way of `check_by_ssh` as follows:

1. On the monitoring server, decide on a location for the private and public keys for the `nagios` user. I recommend placing them in `/usr/local/nagios/keys`. Create this directory and make it owned by the `nagios` user, and only readable by that user:

   ```
   # KEYSDIR=/usr/local/nagios/keys
   # mkdir -p $KEYSDIR
   # chown nagios.nagios $KEYSDIR
   # chmod 0700 $KEYSDIR
   ```

2. Become the `nagios` user using `su` or `sudo`:

   ```
   # su nagios
   # sudo -s -u nagios
   ```

3. Generate a pair of private and public SSH keys using `ssh-keygen`. Here we've used 2048-bit RSA; use whichever key length and cipher is appropriate for your network setup.

   ```
   $ ssh-keygen -b 2048 -t rsa -f /usr/local/nagios/keys/id_rsa
   ```

   When prompted for a passphrase, simply press *Enter* to signal that you don't want one.

   This should create two files in `/usr/local/nagios/keys`, called `id_rsa` and `id_rsa.pub`. The first one is the **private key**, and should be kept secret at all times. The second, the **public key**, is safe to distribute and to install on other machines.

4. Decide on a location for the `authorized_keys` file on the target host. The easiest way to do this is probably to specify a `$HOME` directory for the `nagios` user, and to create it if appropriate:

   ```
   # NAGIOSHOME=/home/nagios
   # usermod -d $NAGIOSHOME nagios
   # mkdir -p $NAGIOSHOME/.ssh
   # chown -R nagios.nagios $NAGIOSHOME
   # chmod 0700 $NAGIOSHOME/.ssh
   ```

5. Copy the `/usr/local/nagios/keys/id_rsa.pub` file from the monitoring server to `/home/nagios/.ssh/authorized_keys` on the target machine. The best way to do this varies. One possible method is to use `scp`:

   ```
   $ whoami
   nagios
   ```

```
$ scp /usr/local/nagios/keys/id_rsa.pub roma.naginet:.ssh/
authorized_keys
```

You may have to set a password temporarily for the `nagios` user on the target host to do this:

```
# passwd nagios
Enter new UNIX password:
Retype new UNIX password:
passwd: password updated successfully.
```

6. Check that you can now log in from the monitoring server to the target server as the `nagios` user with no password:

```
$ whoami
nagios
$ ssh -i /usr/local/nagios/keys/id_rsa roma.naginet
Linux roma 2.6.32-5-686 #1 SMP Mon Oct 3 04:15:24 UTC 2011 i686
Lost login: Sun Jul 29 18:23:14 2012 from olympus.naginet
```

7. Back on the monitoring server, check that you're able to run the `check_by_ssh` plugin to call one of the installed plugins on the remote server; in this example, we're calling `check_load`:

```
$ whoami
nagios
$ /usr/local/nagios/libexec/check_by_ssh \
    -H roma.naginet \
    -i /usr/local/nagios/keys/id_rsa \
    -C '/usr/local/nagios/libexec/check_load -w 15,10,5 -c
30,24,20'
OK - load average: 0.00, 0.00, 0.00|load1=0.000;15.000;30.000;0;
load5=0.000;10.000;24.000;0;  load15=0.000;5.000;20.000;0;
```

Note that the value for the `-C` option needs to be surrounded with quotes.

8. Now that we've verified that `check_by_ssh` works with our infrastructure, we can define a command to use it in `/usr/local/nagios/etc/objects /commands.cfg`:

```
define command {
    command_name   check_by_ssh
    command_line   $USER1$/check_by_ssh -H $HOSTADDRESS$ -i /usr/
local/nagios/keys/id_rsa -C '$ARG1$'
}
```

9. We can apply that command to a new service check for `roma.naginet` as follows, preferably placed beneath the host definition:

```
define service {
    use                   generic-service
    host_name             roma.naginet
    service_description   LOAD_BY_SSH
    check_command         check_by_ssh!/usr/local/nagios/libexec/
check_load -w 15,10,5 -c 30,25,20
    }
```

10. Validate the configuration and restart the Nagios Core server:

`# /usr/local/nagios/bin/nagios -v /usr/local/nagios/etc/nagios.cfg`

`# /etc/init.d/nagios restart`

With this done, a new service with the description LOAD_BY_SSH should appear in the web interface ready to be checked, and will come up with an appropriate status, including the load average as read via SSH to the target host. To Nagios Core, the results of the check are just the same as if they'd come via NRPE.

How it works...

Checking services via NRPE and SSH is actually a reasonably similar process; the central idea is that we're using another network service shared by the monitoring server and the target host to instruct the target host to run a plugin, and return the results to the monitoring server.

In the case of check_by_ssh, this is done over an SSH connection. It's quite typical for administrators to run commands on remote hosts using the ssh client, simply by adding the command to be run to the command line:

`$ hostname`

`olympus.naginet`

`$ ssh roma.naginet hostname`

`roma.naginet`

All that the check_by_ssh plugin does is formalizes this process into a Nagios plugin context. The value for the command_line directive for the command we defined can be broken down as follows:

▸ $USER1$/check_by_ssh: This is the path to the plugin, as is typical in command definitions, using the $USER1$ macro to expand to /usr/local/nagios/libexec.

▸ -H $HOSTADDRESS$: This specifies that the plugin should connect to the applicable host for any host or service that uses this command.

- ▶ `-i /usr/local/nagios/keys/id_rsa`: This specifies the location of the private key to be used for identification with the remote host.

- ▶ `-C '$ARG1$'`: This specifies that the command run by `check_by_ssh` on the target host is given in the first argument the service defines in its `check_command`; in this case, our command is:

```
/usr/local/nagios/libexec/check_load -w 15,10,5 -c 30,25,20
```

Note that it's important that $ARG1$ is in quotes, because we want to pass the whole command as one argument to `check_by_ssh`.

There's more...

Using `check_by_ssh` instead of `check_nrpe` allows full authentication via public key, rather than merely by having the right IP address. It also encrypts all traffic implicitly, minimizing the risk of sensitive data, such as usernames or passwords, from being intercepted. Which of the two plugins you should use will depend very much on the nature of your network and your security policy. There is no reason you can't use both of them if you wish.

Be careful not to confuse this plugin with `check_ssh`, which checks that the SSH service itself is running, and is discussed in the *Monitoring SSH for any host* recipe in *Chapter 5, Monitoring Methods*.

See also

- ▶ The *Monitoring local services on a remote machine with NRPE* recipe in this chapter
- ▶ The *Monitoring SSH for any host* recipe in *Chapter 5, Monitoring Methods*

Using the Web Interface

7

In this chapter, we will cover the following recipes:

- ▶ Using the Tactical Overview
- ▶ Viewing and interpreting availability reports
- ▶ Viewing and interpreting trends
- ▶ Viewing and interpreting notification history
- ▶ Adding comments on hosts or services in the web interface
- ▶ Viewing configuration in the web interface
- ▶ Scheduling checks from the web interface
- ▶ Acknowledging a problem via the web interface

Introduction

The Nagios Core web interface is an administrator's first port of call to see the current status of the network being monitored. By way of CGI and PHP scripts, it allows an overview of the general performance of all the hosts and services being monitored. It also provides information about their current states and how checks are performed. This allows considerably more detail than that which is normally contained in e-mailed notifications.

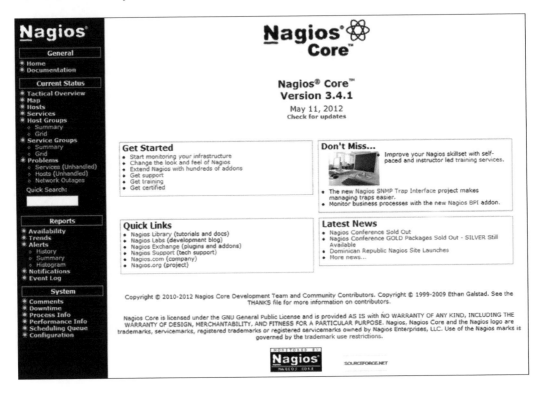

In most respects, the Nagios Core web interface (without any addons) is designed for the display of information rather than controlling or configuring the server, but there are some things that can be done from it to actually change the way Nagios Core is running. These include the following:

▶ Disabling or enabling active and passive checks, event handlers, notifications, and flap detection, whether for all hosts and services or specific ones

▶ Sending custom notifications about a host or service that don't necessarily correspond to an actual state change

▶ Rescheduling checks, commonly done to prioritize a check when there have been problems that the administrator thinks are now resolved and wishes to recheck

▶ Acknowledging problems, to allow administrators to suppress further notifications from problems that they're working on fixing

▶ Scheduling downtime to suppress notifications for a certain time period; this was discussed in the *Scheduling downtime for a host or service* recipe in *Chapter 3, Working with Checks and States*

▶ Leaving comments on hosts and services for the information of any other administrator who inspects them; many of the other actions in this list will do this implicitly

We won't offer a comprehensive survey of the web interface here, as much of its use is explained in other chapters, or otherwise reasonably self-explanatory. Instead, we'll explore a few runtime behavior changes that we can arrange through the web interface listed in the preceding section, and on using and interpreting the reports available under the **Reports** heading of the left navigation menu.

Another important and extremely useful part of the web interface, the **Network Status Map**, is discussed in several recipes in *Chapter 8, Managing Network Layout*. We won't discuss it here, as it's so useful that it merits a chapter in itself.

Using the Tactical Overview

In this recipe, we'll take a look at the **Tactical Overview** screen of the Nagios Core web interface. As its name implies, this screen provides a one-page summary of the current operating status of both the monitored hosts and services and the Nagios Core server itself.

Getting started

You will need access to the Nagios Core web interface. In the QuickStart install, the `nagiosadmin` user will have all of the necessary privileges.

How to do it...

We can take a look at **Tactical Overview** as follows:

1. Log in to the Nagios Core web interface.
2. Click the **Tactical Overview** item in the left menu:

You should see the **Tactical Monitoring Overview** screen appear in the right frame:

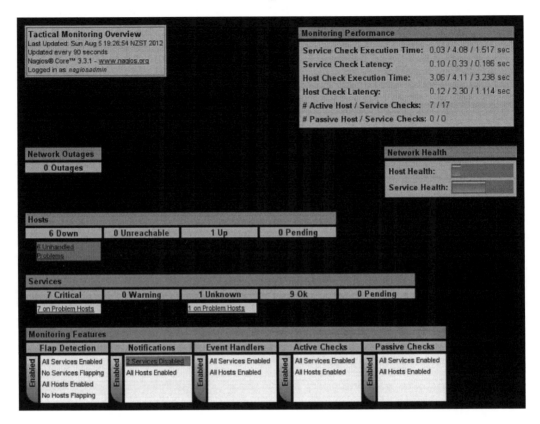

3. Try clicking on some of the items under **Hosts** and **Services**, for example the **Up** count under **Hosts**. Note that you're presented with a listing of all the hosts that comprise that section.

4. Return to **Tactical Overview**, and try clicking on some of the items under the **Monitoring Features** heading, for example the **Enabled** item under **Flap Detection**. Note that clicking on these brings you to a screen where you can quickly turn the relevant feature on or off (provided your user has the appropriate privileges).

How it works...

The Tactical Overview is a good first port of call whenever you become aware of problems with the monitored network, particularly if you've a reason to believe that the problems are on more than one host. It's also a good place to visit to adjust monitoring features. For example, if a very large segment of your network is going to be down and it's not practical to schedule downtime for all of the affected hosts, then you could simply suppress notifications completely for a while in order to fix the problem with no distractions.

Note that the screen includes an overall assessment of the monitoring performance of the server in the top-right corner; this can be a useful first place to look if you suspect that the monitoring server is struggling to keep up with its tasks, or want to get some idea of how many checks it's making.

Beneath that is a simple bar graph showing the general state of the network. It will change its color depending on the severity of the problems; in the preceding screenshot, there are serious problems with some of the hosts and services on this network, and as a result the bar is short and red.

There's more...

If you find the Tactical Overview useful, it may be a good idea to make it the home page for the web interface, rather than the default page which mostly just shows the Nagios Core branding, version, and some links. We can arrange this by changing the value of `$corewindow` in `/usr/local/nagios/share/index.php` from `main.php` to `cgi-bin/tac.cgi`:

```
$corewindow="cgi-bin/tac.cgi";
```

With this done, when we visit the `/nagios/` URL on the monitoring host, the **Tactical Overview** should come up immediately. This can be done with any of the pages in the menu. The **Services** item is another good choice for an alternative homepage.

See also

> ▶ The *Viewing configuration in the web interface* recipe in this chapter

Viewing and interpreting availability reports

In this recipe, we'll learn how to use the **Availability Report** to build a table showing uptime statistics for a host, hostgroup, service, or servicegroup. This is useful as a quick metric of overall availability, perhaps to meet the terms of a service-level agreement.

Getting started

You will need access to the Nagios Core web interface, and permission to run commands from the CGIs. The sample configuration installed by following the Quick Start Guide grants all the necessary privileges to the `nagiosadmin` user when authenticated via HTTP.

If you find that you don't have this privilege, then check the `authorized_for_all_services` and `authorized_for_all_hosts` directives in `/usr/local/nagios/etc/cgi.cfg`, and include your username in both; for example, for the user `tom`, the directives might look similar to the following:

```
authorized_for_all_servicess=nagiosadmin,tom
authorized_for_all_hosts=nagiosadmin,tom
```

Alternatively, you should also be able to see a host or service's information if you are authenticating with the same username as the nominated contact for the host or service you want to check. This is explained in the *Using authenticated contacts* recipe in *Chapter 10, Security and Performance*.

In this example, we'll view a month's history for a `PING` service on `troy.naginet`, a Linux server.

How to do it...

We can arrange an availability report for the last month for our `troy.naginet` server as follows:

1. Log in to the Nagios Core web interface.
2. Click on the **Availability** link in the left menu, beneath **Reports**:

3. Select the type of report, either **Host(s)**, **Hostgroup(s)**, **Service(s)**, or **Servicegroup(s)**:

4. Select a specific host or service on which to report, or optionally choose to run it for all the hosts, hostgroups, services, or servicegroups:

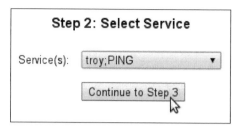

5. Define some options for the report. The defaults are sensible, so we'll use them for now; we'll go over the effect of each of the other fields in the next section. Click on **Create Availability Report!** when done:

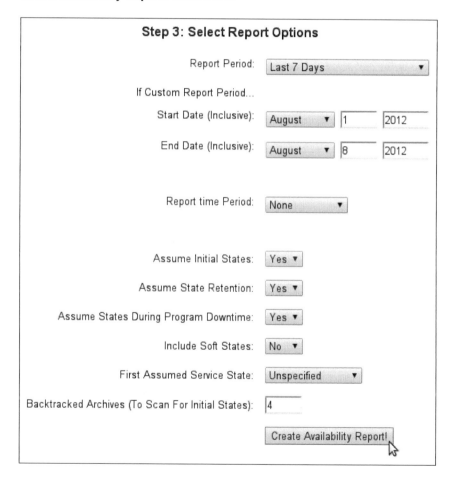

You should be presented with a table showing the percentage of time the host or service has spent in each state. A healthy service might look similar to the following screenshot, with a few blips or none at all:

Service State Breakdowns:

State	Type / Reason	Time	% Total Time	% Known Time
	Unscheduled	6d 22h 49m 56s	99.305%	99.305%
OK	Scheduled	0d 0h 0m 0s	0.000%	0.000%
	Total	**6d 22h 49m 56s**	**99.305%**	**99.305%**
	Unscheduled	0d 0h 10m 0s	0.099%	0.099%
WARNING	Scheduled	0d 0h 0m 0s	0.000%	0.000%
	Total	**0d 0h 10m 0s**	**0.099%**	**0.099%**
	Unscheduled	0d 1h 0m 4s	0.596%	0.596%
UNKNOWN	Scheduled	0d 0h 0m 0s	0.000%	0.000%
	Total	**0d 1h 0m 4s**	**0.596%**	**0.596%**
	Unscheduled	0d 0h 0m 0s	0.000%	0.000%
CRITICAL	Scheduled	0d 0h 0m 0s	0.000%	0.000%
	Total	**0d 0h 0m 0s**	**0.000%**	**0.000%**
	Nagios Not Running	0d 0h 0m 0s	0.000%	
Undetermined	Insufficient Data	0d 0h 0m 0s	0.000%	
	Total	0d 0h 0m 0s	0.000%	
All	Total	7d 0h 0m 0s	100.000%	100.000%

A more problematic service might have large percentages of time in a WARNING or CRITICAL state:

Service State Breakdowns:

State	Type / Reason	Time	% Total Time	% Known Time
	Unscheduled	2d 9h 35m 1s	34.276%	34.276%
OK	Scheduled	0d 0h 0m 0s	0.000%	0.000%
	Total	**2d 9h 35m 1s**	**34.276%**	**34.276%**
	Unscheduled	4d 14h 19m 59s	65.674%	65.674%
WARNING	Scheduled	0d 0h 0m 0s	0.000%	0.000%
	Total	**4d 14h 19m 59s**	**65.674%**	**65.674%**
	Unscheduled	0d 0h 0m 0s	0.000%	0.000%
UNKNOWN	Scheduled	0d 0h 0m 0s	0.000%	0.000%
	Total	**0d 0h 0m 0s**	**0.000%**	**0.000%**
	Unscheduled	0d 0h 5m 0s	0.050%	0.050%
CRITICAL	Scheduled	0d 0h 0m 0s	0.000%	0.000%
	Total	**0d 0h 5m 0s**	**0.050%**	**0.050%**
	Nagios Not Running	0d 0h 0m 0s	0.000%	
Undetermined	Insufficient Data	0d 0h 0m 0s	0.000%	
	Total	0d 0h 0m 0s	0.000%	
All	Total	7d 0h 0m 0s	100.000%	100.000%

Above the table appears a quick visual summary of the time spent in each state, which will link to **Trends Report** with the same criteria if clicked. Additionally, below the table are any log entries for the service or host changing state.

How it works...

Nagios Core assembles state changes from its log files for the specified time period, and constructs the table of state changes by percentage. The availability report, therefore, only works for times covered by your archived log files. The third step of building the report involves a lot of possible options:

- ▸ **Report Period**: This dropdown allows choosing a fixed period for convenience, relative to the current date; alternatively, a custom time period may be used by selecting the final **CUSTOM TIME PERIOD** option and selecting dates in the two fields that follow:
  - ❑ **Start Date (Inclusive)**: This field specifies the date on which the report should start, if the custom time period option has been set.
  - ❑ **End Date (Inclusive)**: This field specifies the date on which the report should end, if the custom time period option has been set.

- ▸ **Report Time Period**: This is the time period for which the availability should be assessed. The default is **None**, meaning that the service or host's state at any time will be used in the calculations. You could, for example, set this to `workhours` to see the percentage of uptime during a time that the server is expected to be busy.

- ▸ **Assume State Retention**: If Nagios Core was restarted one or more times during the reporting period, checking this option would make the report assume that the state before any restart was retained by Nagios Core until it started again; this is enabled with the `retain_state_information` directive in `nagios.cfg`.

- ▸ **Assume Initial States**: If Nagios Core can't figure out the initial state of the service at the time the report begins until the first check, it will assume it based on the value of the **First Assumed Host State** or **First Assumed Service State** fields.

- ▸ **Assume States During Program Downtime**: If Nagios Core finds that it was down for a period in its log files, it will assume the final state it read from the host or service before it went down.

- ▸ **Include Soft States**: Nagios Core will graph `SOFT` states, meaning that it will include state changes that occur, but that return to their previous state, before `max_check_attempts` is exhausted. Otherwise, it will only graph states that have endured right through the retry checks, or `HARD` states.

- ▸ **First Assumed Host State** or **First Assumed Service State**: This is the value Nagios Core should assume for the host or service state, if it can't determine it from the log files.

- ▸ **Backtracked Archives**: This specifies the number of archived log files back the Nagios Core process should check to try and find initial states for the host or service.

There's more...

You can choose to run the report for a hostgroup or servicegroup as well, which will yield an indexed table showing both the per-host or per-service percentage state time, and also the average uptime for all the hosts or services in the group.

See also

▸ The *Viewing and interpreting trends* and *Viewing and interpreting notification history* recipes in this chapter

▸ The *Using authenticated contacts* recipe in *Chapter 10, Security and Performance*

Viewing and interpreting trends

In this recipe, we'll learn how to use the **Host** and **Service State Trends** reporting tool on a host or service to show a graph of states over some fixed period of time. This can be useful to determine not only overall availability, perhaps to meet the terms of a service-level agreement, but also to ascertain whether there are certain intervals or consistent times that the host enters a non-OK state. It's a good way to look for patterns in the downtime of your hosts.

Getting started

You will need access to the Nagios Core web interface, and permission to run commands from the CGIs. The sample configuration installed by following the Quick Start Guide grants the nagiosadmin user all the necessary privileges when authenticated via HTTP.

If you find that you don't have this privilege, then check the authorized_for_all_ services and authorized_for_all_hosts directives in /usr/local/nagios /etc/cgi.cfg, and include your username in both; for the user tom, the directives might look similar to the following:

```
authorized_for_all_services=nagiosadmin,tom
authorized_for_all_hosts=nagiosadmin,tom
```

Alternatively, you should also be able to see a host or service's information if you are authenticating with the same username as a nominated contact for the host or service you want to check.

In this example, we'll view a month's history for the HTTP service on athens.naginet, a web server for which we've been running checks.

How to do it...

We can arrange a **Service State Trends** report for the last month for our `athens.naginet` server as follows:

1. Log in to the Nagios Core web interface.

2. Click on the **Trends** link in the left menu, beneath **Reports**:

3. Select the type of report, either **Host** or **Service**:

4. Select a specific host or service on which you would like to report:

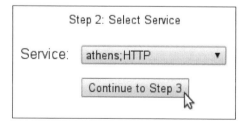

5. Define some options for the report. The defaults are sensible, so we'll use them for now; we'll go over the effect of each of the other fields in the next section. Click on **Create Report** when done:

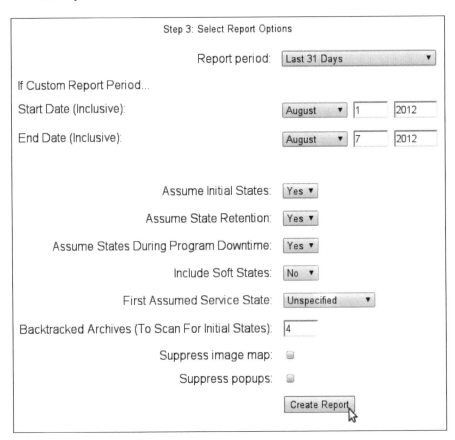

You should be presented with a graph showing the state of the host or service over time, along with markings of time for when the state changed, and a percentage breakdown of the relative states on the right.

A healthy service might look similar to the following screenshot, with a few blips or none at all:

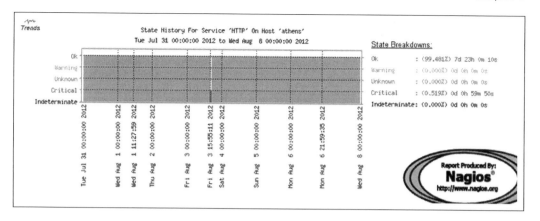

A more problematic service might have long periods of time in a WARNING or CRITICAL state:

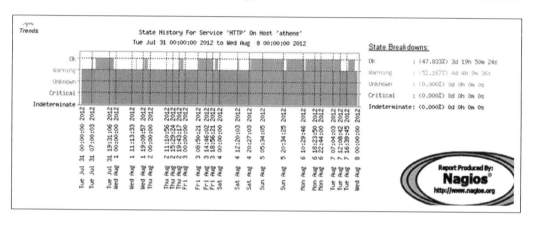

You can click on sections of the graph to "zoom in" on it, provided that you did not select the **Suppress image map** option on the **Select Report Options** page.

How it works...

Nagios Core assembles state changes from its log files for the specified time period and constructs the graph of state changes by color, delineating the dates on the horizontal axis and at regular intervals. The trends graph, therefore, only works for times covered by your archived log files. The third step of building the report involves a lot of possible options:

- **Report period**: This dropdown allows choosing a fixed period for convenience, relative to the current date; alternatively, a custom time period may be used by selecting the final **CUSTOM TIME PERIOD** option and selecting dates in the two fields that follow:
  - **Start Date (Inclusive)**: This field specifies the date on which the report should start, if the custom time period option has been set.
  - **End Date (Inclusive)**: This field specifies the date on which the report should end, if the custom time period option has been set.

- **Assume State Retention**: If Nagios Core was restarted one or more times during the reporting period, checking this option will make the report assume that the state before any restart was retained by Nagios Core until it started again; this is enabled with the `retain_state_information` directive in `nagios.cfg`.

- **Assume Initial States**: If Nagios Core can't figure out the initial state of the service at the time the report begins until the first check, it will assume it based on the value of the **First Assumed Host State** or **First Assumed Service State** fields.

- **Assume States During Program Downtime**: If Nagios Core finds that it was down for a period in its log files, it will assume the final state it read from the host or service while it was down.

- **Include Soft States**: Nagios Core will graph `SOFT` states, meaning that it will include state changes that occur, but that return to their previous states, before `max_check_attempts` is exhausted. Otherwise, it will only graph states that have endured right through the retry checks, or `HARD` states.

- **First Assumed Host State** or **First Assumed Service State**: This is the value Nagios Core should assume for the host or service state, if it can't determine it from the log files.

- **Backtracked Archives**: This specifies the number of archived log files back the Nagios Core process should check to try and find initial states for the host or service.

- **Suppress image map**: This prevents the graph from being clickable to zoom in on a particular region of it, perhaps for reasons of browser compatibility.

- **Suppress popups**: This prevents the graph from showing popups when hovering over sections of it, perhaps for reasons of browser compatibility.

There's more...

Note that it's important to ensure that checks have actually been running for the entire time for which you're running the report, as otherwise the **State Breakdowns** section will have distorted statistics. There is not much point running a yearly report for a host that has only existed for six months! In general, the more frequent and consistent your checks, the more accurate the trends graph will be.

See also

▶ The *Viewing and interpreting availability reports and Viewing and interpreting notification history* recipes in this chapter

Viewing and interpreting notification history

In this recipe, we'll see how to get both complete listings and convenient summaries of the alerts and notifications being generated by Nagios Core in response to hosts and services changing state. These options are all available under the **Reports** section of the sidebar:

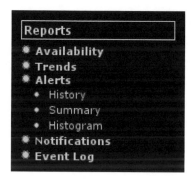

It's important to distinguish between alerts and notifications in this section. An **alert** is generated in response to an event such as a host or service changing state. A **notification**, in turn, may or may not be generated as a response to that alert, and be sent to the appropriate contacts. SOFT state changes constitute alerts; only HARD state changes generally make notifications.

It's likely that a production monitoring server will not be sending notifications for every alert, particularly if you're making good use of the max_check_attempts, scheduled downtime, and problem acknowledgement features. You should make sure you're checking the correct section.

Getting started

You will need access to the Nagios Core web interface and permission to run commands from the CGIs. The sample configuration installed by following the Quick Start Guide grants all the necessary privileges to the `nagiosadmin` user when authenticated via `HTTP`.

How to do it...

We can get an overview of the notifications, alerts, and other events being generated on the Nagios Core server as follows:

1. Start with the **Notifications** report. The resulting screen should show you the day's notifications as read from the current log file.

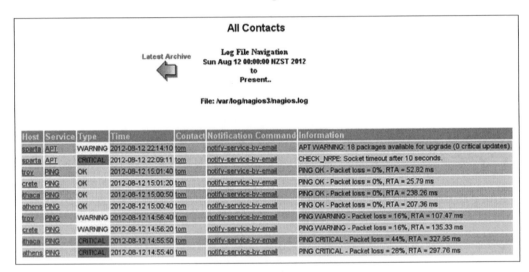

2. Note that if you're using the **log rotation** feature of Nagios Core, configured with the `log_rotation_method` directive, then you can use the arrows above the table to navigate to the previous period's monitoring (generally 24 hours worth). Additionally, note that the information includes the following:

   ❑ Links to the hosts and services that generate them

   ❑ The contacts to which they were sent

   ❑ The notification commands that were run

   ❑ The output of the commands that prompted the alert and notification

Also note that you're able to filter for any particular kind of notification, and change the sorting order, using the form in the top-right corner:

3. Next, move to the **Alerts** or **Alerts | History report**. Rather than a tabular format, this shows you all of the alerts generated by hosts and services as a list, showing red exclamation icons for CRITICAL or DOWN states, green icons for OK states, and others. The list is broken into intervals of one hour:

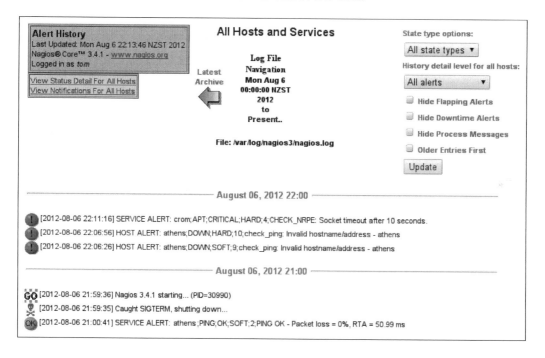

Note that these alerts also include the server being started or shut down. Also note that you're again able to filter for specific alert types with the form in the top-right corner.

4. The other two items in the **Alerts** menu allow generating complex reports with many criteria. The first, **Summary**, presents its results in tabular format according to the criteria entered in a form. For now, try clicking on **Create Summary Report** at the bottom of the first page, with all of the fields on their defaults, to get a feel for the results it generates:

Alert Summary Report
Last Updated: Mon Aug 6 22:37:05 NZST 2012
Nagios® Core™ 3.4.1 - www.nagios.org
Logged in as *tom*

Most Recent Alerts

2012-07-30 22:37:05 to 2012-08-06
22:37:05
Duration: 7d 0h 0m 0s

Report Options Summary:

Alert Types:	*Host & Service Alerts*
State Types:	*Soft & Hard States*
Host States:	*Up, Down, Unreachable*
Service States:	*Ok, Warning, Unknown, Critical*

Generate New Report

Displaying most recent 25 of 1059 total matching alerts

Time	Alert Type	Host	Service	State	State Type	Information
2012-08-06 22:21:06	Service Alert	sparta	APT	WARNING	HARD	APT WARNING: 12 packages available for upgrade (0 critical updates).
2012-08-06 22:15:56	Service Alert	athens	PING	OK	SOFT	PING OK - Packet loss = 0%, RTA = 39.10 ms
2012-08-06 22:15:36	Service Alert	troy	PING	OK	SOFT	PING OK - Packet loss = 0%, RTA = 36.79 ms
2012-08-06 22:14:56	Service Alert	troy	PING	WARNING	SOFT	PING WARNING - Packet loss = 16%, RTA = 62.74 ms
2012-08-06 22:14:36	Service Alert	crete	PING	CRITICAL	SOFT	PING CRITICAL - Packet loss = 37%, RTA = 45.88 ms
2012-08-06 22:11:16	Service Alert	sparta	APT	CRITICAL	HARD	CHECK_NRPE: Socket timeout after 10 seconds.

The **Histogram** report generates something similar, showing a breakdown of the alerts generated for nominated hosts or services over a fixed period of time:

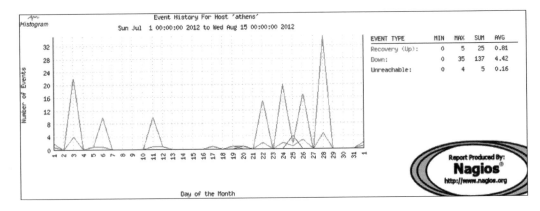

How it works...

Nagios Core saves the data for both alerts and notifications on a long-term basis, allowing for reports like this to be generated dynamically from its archives. Note that the data presented in these reports is for alerts and notifications, not the actual states of the services over time. To get useful statistics such as the percentage of uptime, you'll want to generate an availability report, as discussed in the *Viewing and interpreting availability reports* recipe in this chapter.

The same notifications data can also be translated into a MySQL database format via the NDOUtils extension, so that reading the alerts and notifications data programmatically to generate custom reports is possible. See the *Reading status into a MySQL database with NDOUtils* recipe in *Chapter 11, Automating and Extending Nagios*, for information on how to do this.

There's more...

The remaining item in the menu is the **Event Log**, which presents a more comprehensive summary of Nagios Core's overall activity without filtering only for alerts or notifications. This screen can include information such as the application of external commands. It tends to be quite verbose, but it's a useful way to read the `nagios.log` file from the web interface. Your username will need to be included in the `authorized_for_system_information` directive in `/usr/local/nagios/etc/cgi.cfg` to use this:

```
authorized_for_system_information=nagiosadmin,tom
```

See also

- The *Viewing and interpreting availability reports* and *Viewing and interpreting trends* recipes in this chapter
- The *Reading status into a MySQL database with NDOUtils* recipe in *Chapter 11, Automating and Extending Nagios*

Adding comments on hosts or services in the web interface

In this recipe, we'll learn how to add comments to hosts or services in the Nagios Core web interface, to keep track of information about them for all the web interface users.

Getting started

You will need access to the Nagios Core web interface, and permission to run commands from the CGIs. The sample configuration installed by following the Quick Start Guide grants all the necessary privileges to the `nagiosadmin` user when authenticated via `HTTP`. You will also need at least one host or service.

If you find that you don't have this privilege, then check the `authorized_for_all_service_commands` and `authorized_for_all_host_commands` directives in `/usr/local/nagios/etc/cgi.cfg`, and include your username in both; for example, for the user `tom`, the directives might look similar to the following:

```
authorized_for_all_service_commands=nagiosadmin,tom
authorized_for_all_host_commands=nagiosadmin,tom
```

How to do it...

We can add a comment to a host or service as follows:

1. Log in to the Nagios Core web interface, and click on the hostname or service description on which you wish to leave the comment. You can get to this via the **Hosts** or **Services** menu items. Here, I'm leaving a comment on my **sparta.naginet** host:

    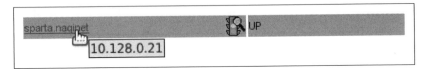

2. Click on the **Add a new comment** link at the bottom of the page:

3. Fill out the resulting form and include the following details:

- ❏ **Host Name**: This is the host name for the host or service on which the comment should be made. This should be filled in automatically.

- ❏ **Persistent**: Check this box if you would like the comment to remain on the host even after Nagios Core is restarted.

- ❏ **Author (Your Name)**: This is the name of the person acknowledging the fault. This should default to your name or username; it may be grayed out and unchangeable, depending on the value of `lock_author_names` in `/usr/local/nagios/etc/cgi.cfg`.

- ❏ **Comment**: This is the text of the comment itself.

Note that explanatory notes also appear to the right of the command description. Click on **Commit** when done:

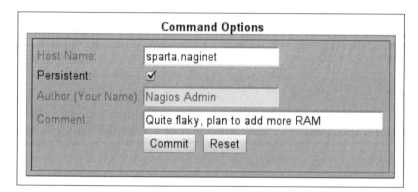

With this done, a comment should be added to the host or service. It may take a little while for the command to be processed. You will find that there is an icon added to the host or service's link in its menu, and that a comment has been added:

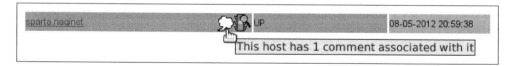

How it works...

Like most changes issued from the Nagios Core web interface, adding a comment to a host or service is a command issued for processing by the server, along with its primary task of executing plugins and recording states. This is why it can sometimes take a few seconds to apply even on an idle server. This is all written to the command file, by default stored at `/usr/local/nagios/var/rw/nagios.cmd`, which the Nagios Core system regularly reads.

When the command is executed, a comment is added to the host or service that can be viewed by anyone with appropriate permissions in the web interface.

There's more...

You can view a list of all comments with the **Comments** link in the sidebar:

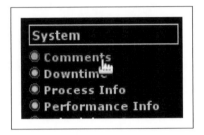

This will bring up a complete list of comments for all hosts and services, including both automated and manual ones:

[Host Comments | Service Comments]

Host Comments

Add a new host comment

Host Name	Entry Time	Author	Comment	Comment ID	Persistent	Type	Expires	Actions
sparta.naginet	08-05-2012 20:59:40	Nagios Admin	Quite flaky, plan to add more RAM	1	Yes	User	N/A	

Service Comments

Add a new service comment

Host Name	Service	Entry Time	Author	Comment	Comment ID	Persistent	Type	Expires	Actions
There are no service comments									

See also

► The *Acknowledging a problem via the web interface* recipe in this chapter

Viewing configuration in the web interface

In this recipe, we'll learn how to view a table of all the objects currently configured for the running Nagios Core instance. This is a very convenient way to view how the system has understood your configuration. If you use a lot of configuration tricks, such as object inheritance and patterns for hostnames, this can really help you make sense of things.

Some administrators aren't aware of this feature, because it's tucked away at the bottom of the Nagios Core web interface's navigation menu. It's very simple to use as there are only really two steps involved.

Getting started

You will need access to the Nagios Core web interface, and permission to run commands from the CGIs. The sample configuration installed by following the Quick Start Guide grants all the necessary privileges to the `nagiosadmin` user when authenticated via `HTTP`.

If you find that you don't have this privilege, then check the `authorized_for_configuration_information` directive in `/usr/local/nagios/etc/cgi.cfg`, and include your username in it; for example, for the user `tom`, the directives might look like the following:

```
authorized_for_configuration_information=nagiosadmin,tom
```

How to do it...

We can view the configuration of different object types in the web interface as follows:

1. Log in to the Nagios Core web interface, and click on the **Configuration** item in the navigation menu:

2. Select the object type you wish to view, and click on **Continue**. In this example, I want to view all the hosts I have defined:

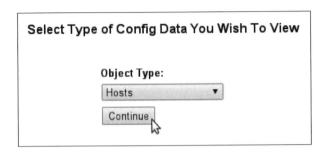

You should be presented with a complete table showing the directive values of all the hosts defined in your system. It will likely be wider than the screen, and will hence require horizontal scrolling.

Host Name	Alias/Description	Address	Parent Hosts	Max. Check Attempts	Check Interval	Retry Interval	Host Check Command	Check Period	Obsess Over	Enable Active Check
athens.naginet	athens	10.128.0.22		10	0h 0m 5s	0h 0m 1s	check-host-alive	24x7	Yes	Yes
imap.naginet	imap	10.128.0.33		10	0h 0m 5s	0h 0m 1s	check-host-alive	24x7	Yes	Yes
localhost	localhost	127.0.0.1		10	0h 0m 5s	0h 0m 1s	check-host-alive	24x7	Yes	Yes
pop3.naginet	pop3	10.128.0.32		10	0h 0m 5s	0h 0m 1s	check-host-alive	24x7	Yes	Yes
roma.naginet	roma	10.128.0.61		10	0h 0m 5s	0h 0m 1s	check-host-alive	24x7	Yes	Yes

How it works...

This is simply a convenient shortcut for viewing the configuration of your hosts as Nagios Core understands them. The following object types can be viewed:

- Hosts
- Host dependencies
- Host escalations
- Host groups
- Services
- Service groups
- Service dependencies
- Service escalations
- Contacts
- Contact groups
- Time periods
- Commands
- Command expansion

This shortcut is particularly convenient for definitions that can sometimes be quite complex, such as hosts and services that inherit from templates, or time period definitions. It's a good way to check that Nagios Core has interpreted your configuration the way you expected.

There's more...

It's important to note that the output doesn't actually tell you anything about the state of hosts or services; it only shows how they're configured. If you need to get both the configuration and state information in an accessible format for processing by a custom script, an excellent way to arrange this is with the NDOUtils addon, which allows you to translate this information into a MySQL database format. See the *Reading status into a MySQL database with NDOUtils* recipe in *Chapter 11, Automating and Extending Nagios Core* for information on how to do this.

See also

- The *Reading status into a MySQL database with NDOUtils* and *Writing customized Nagios Core reports* recipes in *Chapter 11, Automating and Extending Nagios Core*

Scheduling checks from the web interface

In this recipe, we'll learn how to manually schedule checks of hosts and services from the web interface, overriding the automatic scheduling normally done by Nagios Core. This can be convenient to hurry along checks for hosts or services that have just been added, or which have just had problems, or to force a check to be made even when active checks are otherwise disabled on a host for whatever reason.

In this example, we'll schedule a check for a service, but checks for hosts can be established in just the same way.

Getting started

You will need access to the Nagios Core web interface, and permission to run commands from the CGIs. The sample configuration installed by following the Quick Start Guide grants all the necessary privileges to the nagiosadmin user when authenticated via HTTP.

If you find that you don't have this privilege, then check the authorized_for_all_service_commands and authorized_for_all_host_commands directives in /usr/local/nagios/etc/cgi.cfg, and include your username in both; for example, for the user tom, the directives might look like the following:

```
authorized_for_all_service_commands=nagiosadmin,tom
authorized_for_all_host_commands=nagiosadmin,tom
```

How to do it...

We can schedule a check for an existing service as follows:

1. Log in to the Nagios Core web interface, and find the link to the host or service for which you want to schedule a check. In this example, we're forcing a check of the **LOAD** service on the **sparta.naginet** host:

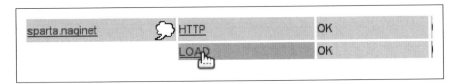

2. Click on the **Re-schedule the next check of this service** or **Re-schedule the next check of this host** link in the menu on the right:

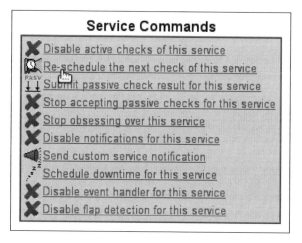

3. Complete the resulting form and include the following details:

- **Host Name**: This is the host name for the host or service having the problem. This should be filled in automatically.

- **Service**: This is the service description for the service having problems, if applicable. This will also be filled in automatically.

- **Check Time**: This is the time at which Nagios Core should reschedule the check.

- **Force Check**: This specifies whether it's required to force a check regardless of active checks being disabled for this host or service.

Note that explanatory notes also appear to the right of the command description. Click on **Commit** when done:

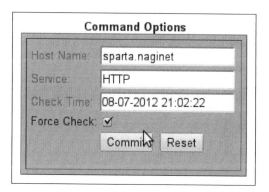

With this done, after Nagios Core processes the new command, viewing the service should show the new time for its next scheduled check, and the check will be run at the nominated time and its return values processed normally.

How it works...

Scheduling checks in this manner is a means of "jumping the queue" for a particular host or service. Check scheduling is otherwise an automated process that Nagios Core figures out based on host and service directives such as `check_interval` and `retry_interval`.

Like all external commands issued from the web interface, a command is written to the commands file, usually at `/usr/local/nagios/var/rw/nagios.cmd`, for processing by the system.

There's more...

We can inspect the enqueued checks by clicking on the **Scheduling Queue** link under the **System** section of the sidebar:

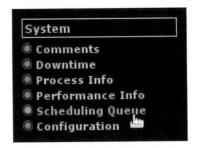

This will bring up a list of the pending checks, and the times at which they'll take place:

Entries sorted by **next check time** (ascending)						
Host ↑	Service ↑	Last Check ↑	Next Check ↑↓	Type	Active Checks	Actions
sparta.naginet	LOAD	08-05-2012 22:07:17	08-05-2012 22:07:27	Normal	ENABLED	✕ 🖧
pop3.naginet	POP3	08-05-2012 22:07:17	08-05-2012 22:07:27	Normal	ENABLED	✕ 🖧
localhost	VULN_KERNEL	08-05-2012 22:07:17	08-05-2012 22:07:27	Normal	ENABLED	✕ 🖧
localhost	Total Processes	08-05-2012 22:07:17	08-05-2012 22:07:27	Normal	ENABLED	✕ 🖧
localhost	Swap Usage	08-05-2012 22:07:17	08-05-2012 22:07:27	Normal	ENABLED	✕ 🖧
localhost	SSH	08-05-2012 22:07:17	08-05-2012 22:07:27	Normal	ENABLED	✕ 🖧

We can also get more detailed information about the queuing process and performance by using the -s flag with the `nagios` command:

```
# /usr/local/nagios/bin/nagios -s /usr/local/nagios/etc/nagios.cfg
```

This will print a lot of information to the terminal, too much to reproduce here! It is probably helpful to pipe it through a paging tool like `less` to read it:

```
# /usr/local/nagios/bin/nagios -s /usr/local/nagios/etc/nagios.cfg | less
```

See also

> ▸ The *Viewing and interpreting notification history* recipe in this chapter
> ▸ The *Checking Nagios Core performance with Nagiostats* recipe in *Chapter 10, Security and Performance*
> ▸ The *Allowing passive checks*, and *Running passive checks from a remote host with NSCA* recipes in *Chapter 11, Automating and Extending Nagios Core*

Acknowledging a problem via the web interface

In this recipe, we'll learn how to acknowledge problems with a host or service, in order to prevent further notifications coming from it and to signal that the problem is being worked on. This is useful if more than one administrator has access to the Nagios Core web interface, to prevent more than one administrator trying to fix a problem, and to prevent unnecessary notifications for a longer-term problem after the operations team has been made aware of it. The exact changes in behavior that the acknowledgement causes are defined at the time it's submitted.

Getting started

To acknowledge a notification, there needs to be at least one host or service suffering problems. Any host or service in a WARNING, CRITICAL, or UNKNOWN state can be acknowledged.

You will need access to the Nagios Core web interface, and permission to run commands from the CGIs. The Quick Start configuration grants all the necessary privileges to the `nagiosadmin` user when authenticated via HTTP.

If you find that you don't have this privilege, check the `authorized_for_all_service_commands` and `authorized_for_all_host_commands` directives in `/usr/local/nagios/etc/cgi.cfg`, and include your username in both; for example, for the user `tom`, the directives might look like the following:

```
authorized_for_all_service_commands=nagiosadmin,tom
authorized_for_all_host_commands=nagiosadmin,tom
```

How to do it...

We can acknowledge a host or service problem as follows:

1. Log in to the Nagios Core web interface, and click on the **Hosts** or **Services** section in the left menu, to visit the host or service having problems. In this example, I'm acknowledging a problem with the **APT** service on my machine **athens**; Nagios Core is reporting upgrades available, but they're not critical and I can't run them right now. Hence I'm going to acknowledge them, so that other administrators know I've got a plan for the problem:

2. Click on the **Acknowledge this service problem** link under the **Service Commands** menu:

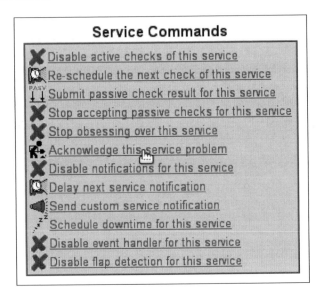

3. Complete the resulting form and include the following details:

- ❑ **Host Name**: This is the host name for the host or service having the problem. This should be filled in automatically.

- ❑ **Service**: This is the service description for the service having problems, if applicable. This will also be filled in automatically.

- ❑ **Sticky Acknowledgement**: If checked, notifications will be suppressed until the problem is resolved; the acknowledgement will not go away if Nagios Core is restarted.

- ❑ **Send Notification**: If checked, an ACKNOWLEDGEMENT notification will be sent to all the contacts and contact groups for the host or service.

- ❑ **Persistent Comment**: Acknowledgements always leave comments on the host or service in question. By default, these are removed when the host or service recovers, but if you wish you can check this to arrange to have them take the form of a permanent comment.

- ❑ **Author (Your Name)**: This is the name of the person acknowledging the fault. This should default to your name or username; it may be grayed out and unchangeable, depending on the value of `lock_author_names` in `/usr/local/nagios/etc/cgi.cfg`.

- ❑ **Comment**: This is an explanation of the acknowledgement; this is generally a good place to put expected times to resolution, and what's being done about the problem.

Note that explanatory notes also appear to the right of the command description. Click on **Commit** when done:

With this done, the effects you chose for the downtime should take effect shortly. It may take a little while for the command to be processed. You will find that there is an acknowledgement icon added to the host or service's link in its menu, and that a comment has been added:

Your contacts may also receive an **ACKNOWLEDGEMENT** notification:

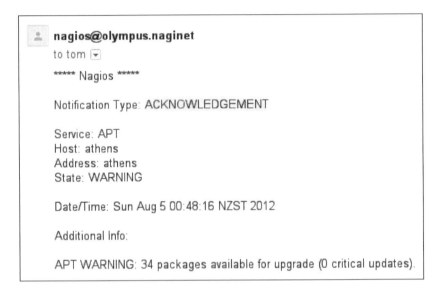

How it works...

Like most changes issued from the Nagios Core web interface, acknowledging a host or service is a command issued for processing by the server, along with its primary task of executing plugins and recording states. This is why it can sometimes take a few seconds to apply even on an idle server. This is all written to the command file, which is by default stored at `/usr/local/nagios/var/rw/nagios.cmd`. The Nagios Core system regularly reads this file, provided external command processing is enabled in `/usr/local/nagios/etc/nagios.cfg`.

When the command is executed and the **Sticky Acknowledgement** option is selected, the effect is that the filters normally applied by Nagios Core will notice that the host or service has had its problems acknowledged before dispatching a notification, and will therefore prevent the notification from being sent.

When the host recovers (a RECOVERY event), a notification to that effect will be sent, and the acknowledgement will be removed as it's no longer needed. Future problems with the host or service, even if they're exactly the same problem, will need to be themselves acknowledged.

There's more...

Acknowledging host and service problems is a really good habit to get into for administrators, particularly if working in a team, as it may prevent a lot of confusion or duplication of work. It's therefore helpful in the same way comments are, in keeping your team informed about what's going on with the network.

The distinction between scheduled downtime and acknowledgements is important. **Downtime** is intended to be for planned outages to a host or service; an **acknowledgement** is intended as a means of notification that an unanticipated problem has occurred, and is being worked on.

If we're getting nagged repeatedly by notifications for problems that we already know about, as well as using acknowledgements, then it may be appropriate to review the notification_interval directive for the applicable hosts or services, to limit the frequency with which notifications are sent. For example, to only send repeat notifications every four hours, we could write the following code snippet:

```
define host {
    ...
    notification_interval   240
}
```

For low-priority hosts, for example, it's perhaps not necessary to send notifications every 10 minutes!

Do not confuse this directive with notification_period, which is used to define the times during which notifications may be sent, another directive that may require review:

```
define host {
    ...
    notification_period   24x7
}
```

See also

- ▶ The *Adding comments on hosts or services in the web interface* recipe in this chapter
- ▶ The *Scheduling downtime for a host or service* recipe in *Chapter 3, Working with Checks and States*

8
Managing Network Layout

In this chapter, we will cover the following recipes:

- ▸ Creating a network host hierarchy
- ▸ Using the network map
- ▸ Choosing icons for hosts
- ▸ Establishing a host dependency
- ▸ Establishing a service dependency
- ▸ Monitoring individual nodes in a cluster
- ▸ Using the network map as an overlay

Introduction

While Nagios Core is still very useful when configured to monitor only a simple list of hosts and services, it includes some optional directives that allow defining some structural and functional properties of the monitored network; specifically, how the hosts and services interrelate. Describing this structure in the configuration allows some additional intelligent behavior in the monitoring and notification that Nagios Core performs.

There are two main approaches to working with network structure in Nagios Core:

▶ Host parent definitions allow an administrator to define a hierarchy of connectivity to monitored hosts from the "point of view" of the Nagios Core server. An example might be a server with the monitored address in another subnet linked to the Nagios Core server by a router. If the router enters a DOWN state, it triggers Nagios Core's host reachability logic to automatically determine which hosts become inaccessible, and flags these as UNREACHABLE rather than DOWN, allowing refined notification behavior.

▶ Host and service dependencies allow the formalization of relationships between hosts or services, usually for the purposes of suppressing unnecessary notifications. An example might be a service that tests a login to a mail service, that itself requires a database service to work properly. If Nagios Core finds that the database service and the login service are both down, a service dependency allows the suppressing of the notification about the login service; the administrator would therefore only be notified about the database service being down, which is more likely to be the actual problem.

There is some overlap of functionality here, but the general pattern is that host parent definitions describe the structure of your network from the vantage point of your monitoring server, and host and service dependencies describe the way it functions, independent of the monitoring server. We will define both parent definitions and dependencies in this chapter, with the primary goal of filtering and improving the notifications that Nagios Core sends in response to failed checks, which can assist greatly in diagnosing problems.

We'll also look at another, more subtle benefit of establishing host parent definitions in making the network map of the Nagios Core web interface useful, and once a basic hierarchy is set up, we'll show how to customize the map's appearance (including defining icons for hosts), to make it generally useful as a network weather map.

Creating a network host hierarchy

In this recipe, we'll learn how to establish a parent-child relationship for two hosts in a very simple network, in order to take advantage of Nagios Core's reachability logic. Changing this configuration is very simple; it involves adding only one directive, and optionally changing some notification options.

Getting ready

You will need to be running a Nagios Core 3.0 or newer server, and have at least two hosts, one of which is only reachable via the other. The host that allows communications with the other is the **parent host**. You should be reasonably confident that a loss of connectivity to the parent host necessarily implies that the child host becomes unreachable from the monitoring server.

Access to the web interface of Nagios Core would also be useful, as making this change will change the appearance of the network map, discussed in the *Using the network map* recipe in this chapter.

Our example will use a Nagios Core monitoring server, `olympus.naginet`, monitoring three hosts:

- `calpe.naginet`, a router
- `janus.naginet`, another router
- `corsica.naginet`, a web server

The hosts are connected as shown in the following diagram:

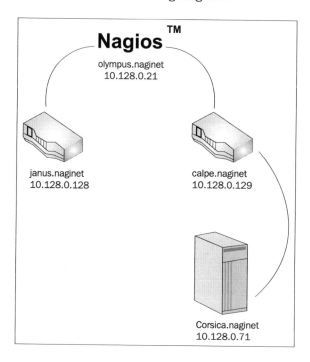

Note that the Nagios Core server `olympus.naginet` is only able to communicate with the `corsica.naginet` web server if the router `calpe.naginet` is working correctly. If **calpe. naginet** were to enter a **DOWN** state, we would see **corsica.naginet** enter a **DOWN** state too:

Host ↑↓	Status ↑↓	Last Check ↑↓
calpe.naginet	DOWN	08-20-2012 20:29:33
corsica.naginet	DOWN	08-20-2012 20:29:34
janus.naginet	UP	08-20-2012 20:29:36

This is a little misleading, as we don't actually know whether `corsica.naginet` is down. It might be, but with the router in between the hosts not working correctly, Nagios Core has no way of knowing. A more informative and accurate status for the host would be UNREACHABLE; this is what the configuration we're about to add will arrange.

How to do it...

We can configure a parent-child relationship for our two hosts as follows:

1. Change to the `objects` configuration directory for Nagios Core. The default path is `/usr/local/nagios/etc/objects`. If you've put the definition for your host in a different file, then move to its directory instead.

    ```
    # cd /usr/local/nagios/etc/objects
    ```

2. Edit the file containing the definition for the child host. In our example, the child host is `corsica.naginet`, the web server. The host definition might look something similar to the following code snippet:

    ```
    define host {
            use             linux-server
            host_name       corsica.naginet
            alias           corsica
            address         10.128.0.71
    }
    ```

3. Add a new `parents` directive to the host's definition, and give it the same value as the `host_name` directive of the host on which it is dependent for connectivity. In our example, that host is `calpe.naginet`.

    ```
    define host {
            use             linux-server
            host_name       corsica.naginet
            alias           corsica
            address         10.128.0.71
            parents         calpe.naginet
    }
    ```

4. Validate the configuration and restart the Nagios Core server:

    ```
    # /usr/local/nagios/bin/nagios -v /usr/local/nagios/etc/nagios.cfg
    # /etc/init.d/nagios restart
    ```

With this done, if the parent host enters a **DOWN** state and the child host can't be contacted, then the child host will enter an **UNREACHABLE** state rather than also being flagged as **DOWN**:

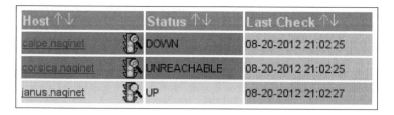

Host ↑↓		Status ↑↓	Last Check ↑↓
calpe.naginet		DOWN	08-20-2012 21:02:25
corsica.naginet		UNREACHABLE	08-20-2012 21:02:25
janus.naginet		UP	08-20-2012 21:02:27

The child host's contacts will also receive UNREACHABLE notifications instead of DOWN notifications for the child host, provided the u flag is included in `notification_options` for the host, and `host_notification_options` for the contacts. See the *Specifying which states to be notified about* recipe in *Chapter 4, Configuring Notifications*, for details on this.

How it works...

This is a simple application of Nagios Core's reachability logic. When the check to `calpe.naginet` fails for the first time, Nagios Core notes that it is a parent host for one child host, `corsica.naginet`. If during checks for the child host it finds it cannot communicate with it, it flags an UNREACHABLE state instead of the DOWN state, firing a different notification event.

The primary advantages to this are twofold:

▶ The DOWN notification is only sent for the nearest problem parent host. All other hosts beyond that host fire UNREACHABLE notifications. This means that Nagios Core's reachability logic automatically determines the point of failure from its perspective, which can be very handy in diagnosing which host is actually experiencing a problem.

▶ If the host is a parent to a large number of other hosts, the configuration can be arranged not to send urgent notifications for UNREACHABLE hosts. There may not be much point sending a hundred pager or e-mail messages to an administrator when a very central router goes down; they know there are problems with the downstream hosts, so all we would be doing is distracting them with useless information.

With a little planning and some knowledge of the network, all we need to do is add a few `parents` directives to host definitions to build a simple network structure, and Nagios Core will behave much more intelligently as a result. This is one of the easiest ways to refine the notification behavior of Nagios Core; it can't be recommended enough!

There's more...

Note that a child host can itself be a parent to other hosts in turn, allowing a nesting network structure. Perhaps in another situation, we might find that the `corsica.naginet` server is two routers away from the monitoring server:

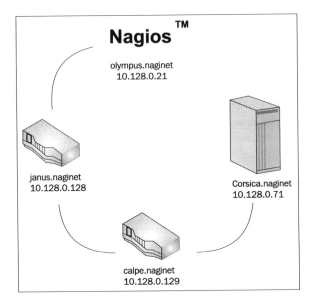

In this case, not only is `corsica.naginet` the child host of `calpe.naginet`, but `calpe.naginet` is itself the child host of `janus.naginet`. We could specify this relationship in exactly the same way:

```
define host {
    use         linux-router
    host_name   calpe.naginet
    alias       calpe
    address     10.128.0.129
    parents     janus.naginet
}
```

It's also possible to set multiple parents for a host, if there are two possible paths to the same machine:

```
define host {
    use         linux-server
    host_name   corsica.naginet
    alias       corsica
    address     10.128.0.71
    parents     calpe.naginet,janus.naginet
}
```

With this configuration, `corsica.naginet` would only be deemed UNREACHABLE if both of its parent hosts were down. This kind of configuration is useful to account for redundant paths in a network; use cases could include spanning tree technologies, or dynamic routing failover.

After you've set up a good basic structure for your network using the `parents` directive, definitely check out the *Using the network map* recipe in this chapter to get some automatic visual feedback about your network's structure as generated from your new configuration.

See also

▶ The *Using the network map* and *Establishing a host dependency* recipes in this chapter

▶ The *Specifying which states to be notified about* and *Configuring notification groups* recipes in *Chapter 4, Configuring Notifications*

Using the network map

In this recipe, we'll examine our network hierarchy in the network map (or status map) in the Nagios Core web interface. The network map takes the form of a generated graphic showing the hierarchy of hosts and their current states. You can learn how to establish such a hierarchy in the recipe *Creating a network host hierarchy* in this chapter. The network map allows filtering to show specific hosts, and clicking on hosts to navigate through larger networks.

Getting ready

You will need to be running a Nagios Core 3.0 or newer server, and have access to its web interface. You will also need permission to view the states of hosts, preferably all hosts. You can arrange this by adding your username in the `authorized_for_all_hosts` directive, normally in `/usr/local/nagios/etc/cgi.cfg`; for example, for the user `tom`, we might configure the directive to read as follows:

```
authorized_for_all_hosts=nagiosadmin,tom
```

By default, the `nagiosadmin` user should have all the necessary permissions to view the complete map.

The network map is not particularly useful without at least a few hosts configured and arranged in a hierarchy, so if you have not set any `parents` directives for your hosts, then you may wish to read the *Creating a network host hierarchy* recipe in this chapter first, and arrange your monitored hosts as it explains.

How to do it...

We can inspect the network map for our newly configured host hierarchy like so:

1. Log in to the Nagios Core web interface.
2. Click on the **Map** item in the menu on the left:

You should be presented with a generated graphic showing all the hosts in your network that your user has permissions to view:

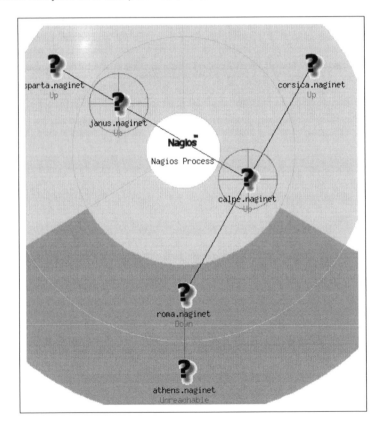

3. Hover over any host with the mouse to see a panel breaking down the host's current state:

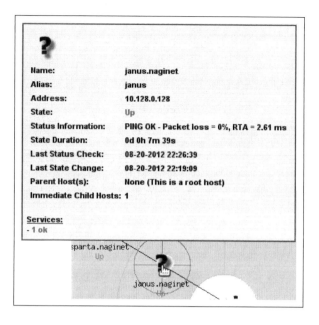

Name:	janus.naginet
Alias:	janus
Address:	10.128.0.128
State:	Up
Status Information:	PING OK - Packet loss = 0%, RTA = 2.61 ms
State Duration:	0d 0h 7m 39s
Last Status Check:	08-20-2012 22:26:39
Last State Change:	08-20-2012 22:19:09
Parent Host(s):	None (This is a root host)
Immediate Child Hosts:	1

Services:
- 1 ok

4. By default, the network map is centered around the Nagios Process icon. Try clicking on one of your hosts to recenter the map; in this example, it's recentered on `calpe.naginet`:

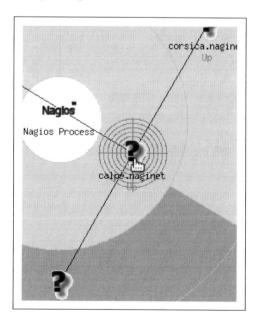

How it works...

The network map is automatically generated from your host configuration. By default, it arranges the hosts in sectors, radiating outward from the central Nagios Process icon, using lines to show dependencies, and adjusting background colors to green for UP states, and red for DOWN or UNREACHABLE states.

This map is generated via the **GD2 library**, written by Thomas Boutell. It takes the form of a linked image map. This means that you can simply right-click the image to save it while the network is in a particular state for later reference, and also that individual nodes can be clicked to recenter the map around the nominated host. This is particularly useful for networks with a large number of hosts and very many levels of parent/child host relationships.

There's more...

Note that the form in the panel in the top-right allows customizing the appearance of the map directly:

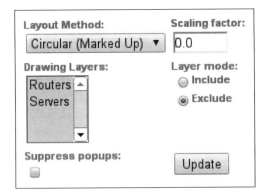

- ▶ **Layout Method**: This allows you to select the algorithm used to arrange and draw the hosts. It's worth trying each of these to see which you prefer for your particular network layout.

- ▶ **Scaling factor**: Change the value here to reduce or increase the size of the map image; values between 0.0 and 1.0 will reduce the image's size, and values above 1.0 will increase it.

- ▶ **Drawing Layers**: If your hosts are organized into hostgroups, you can filter the map to only display hosts belonging to particular groups.

- ▸ **Layer mode**: If you selected any host groups in the **Drawing Layers** option, this allows you to select whether you want to include hosts in those groups in the map, or exclude them from it.

- ▸ **Suppress popups**: If you find the yellow information popups that appear when hovering over hosts annoying, then you can turn them off by selecting this checkbox.

After selecting or changing any one of these options, you will need to click on **Update** to apply them.

The appearance of the status map can be configured well beyond this by changing directives in the Nagios Core configuration file, and adding some directives to your hosts; take a look at the recipes under the *See also* section of this recipe for some examples of how this is done.

See also

- ▸ The *Customizing appearance of the network map, Choosing icons for hosts, Specifying coordinates for a host on the network map*, and *Using the network map as an overlay* recipes in this chapter

Choosing icons for hosts

In this recipe, we'll learn how to select graphics for hosts, to appear in various parts of the Nagios Core web interface. This is done by adding directives to a host to specify the paths to appropriate images to represent it.

Adding these definitions has no effect on Nagios Core's monitoring behavior; they are mostly cosmetic changes, although it's useful to see at a glance whether a particular node is a server or a workstation, particularly on the network map.

Getting ready

You will need to be running a Nagios Core 3.0 or newer server, and have access to its web interface. You must also be able to edit the configuration files for the server.

It's a good idea to check that you actually have the required images installed. The default set of icons is included in `/usr/local/nagios/share/images/logos`. Don't confuse this with its parent directory, `images`, which contains images used as part of the Nagios Core web interface itself.

In the `logos` directory, you should find a number of images in various formats. In this example, we're interested in the `router` and `rack-server` icons:

```
$ ls /usr/local/nagios/share/images/logos/{router,rack-server}.*
/usr/local/nagios/share/images/logos/rack-server.gd2
/usr/local/nagios/share/images/logos/rack-server.gif
/usr/local/nagios/share/images/logos/router.gd2
/usr/local/nagios/share/images/logos/router.gif
```

To get the full benefit of the icons, you'll likely want to be familiar with using the network map, and have access to view it with the appropriate hosts in your own Nagios Core instance. The network map is introduced in the *Using the network map* recipe in this chapter.

How to do it...

We can define images to be used in displaying our host as follows:

1. Change to the `objects` configuration directory for Nagios Core. The default path is `/usr/local/nagios/etc/objects`. If you've put the definition for your host in a different file, then move to its directory instead.

   ```
   # cd /usr/local/nagios/etc/objects
   ```

2. Add three new directives to each of the hosts to which you want to apply the icons. In this example, the `rack-server` icon is assigned to `corsica.naginet`, and the `router` icon to both `calpe.naginet` and `corsica.naginet`:

   ```
   define host {
           use                 linux-server
           host_name           corsica.naginet
           alias               corsica
           address             10.128.0.71
           icon_image          rack-server.gif
           icon_image_alt      Rack Server
           statusmap_image     rack-server.gd2
   }
   define host {
           use                 linux-router
           host_name           janus.naginet
           alias               janus
           address             10.128.0.128
           icon_image          router.gif
           icon_image_alt      Router
           statusmap_image     router.gd2
   }
   ```

```
define host {
      use                linux-router
      host_name          calpe.naginet
      alias              calpe
      address            10.128.0.129
      icon_image         router.gif
      icon_image_alt     Router
      statusmap_image    router.gd2
}
```

3. Validate the configuration and restart the Nagios Core server:

    ```
    # /usr/local/nagios/bin/nagios -v /usr/local/nagios/etc/nagios.cfg
    # /etc/init.d/nagios restart
    ```

With this done, a visit to the status map should display the appropriate hosts with icons rather than question marks:

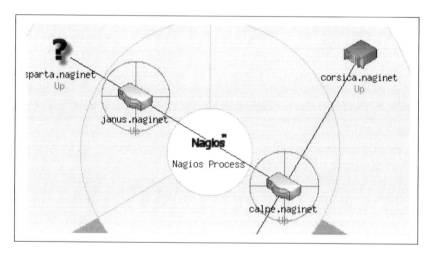

The **Hosts** list should also include a scaled-down version of the image:

Host ↑↓		Status ↑↓	Last Check ↑↓
athens.naginet		UNREACHABLE	08-21-2012 18:52:20
calpe.naginet		UP	08-21-2012 18:52:20
corsica.naginet		UP	08-21-2012 18:52:20
janus.naginet		UP	08-21-2012 18:52:20
roma.naginet		DOWN	08-21-2012 18:52:20
sparta.naginet		UP	08-21-2012 18:52:20

How it works...

When a host list, service list, or network status map is generated, it checks for the presence of `icon_image` or `statusmap_image` values for each host object, reads the appropriate image if defined, and includes that as part of its processing. The network status map defaults to displaying only a question mark in the absence of a value for the `statusmap_image` directive.

Note that for the `statusmap_image` directive, we chose the `.gd2` version of the icon rather than the `.gif` version. This is for performance reasons; the status map is generated with the GD2 library, which deals more efficiently with its native `.gd2` format.

The `icon_image_alt` directive defines the value for the `alt` attribute when the image is displaying in an `<img>` HTML tag. Most web browsers will show the contents of this tag after briefly hovering over the icon.

Nagios Core 3.0 allows you to put these directives in a separate `hostextinfo` object, but this object type is officially deprecated as of Nagios Core 4.0, so it's recommended to avoid it.

There's more

If you have a number of hosts that need to share the same image, it's a good practice to inherit from a common host template with the appropriate directives set. For our example, we might define a template as follows:

```
define host {
    name              router-icon
    icon_image        router.gif
    icon_image_alt    Router
    statusmap_image   router.gd2
    register          0
}
```

We could then apply the image settings directly to both our routers simply by inheriting from that template, by adding it to the `use` directive:

```
define host {
    use         linux-router,router-icon
    host_name   janus.naginet
    alias       janus
    address     10.128.0.128
}
define host {
    use         linux-router,router-icon
    host_name   calpe.naginet
```

```
alias       calpe
address     10.128.0.129
}
```

If you don't like the included icon set, there are many icon sets available online on the Nagios Exchange site at `http://exchange.nagios.org/`. If you want, you could even make your own, out of pictures of your physical hardware, saved in standard PNG or GD2 format.

See also

> ▸ The *Using the network map* and *Specifying coordinates for a host on the network map* recipes in this chapter

Establishing a host dependency

In this recipe, we'll learn how to establish a host dependency between two hosts. This feature can be used to control how Nagios Core checks hosts and notifies us about problems in situations where if one host is DOWN, it implies that at least one other host is necessarily DOWN.

Getting ready

First of all, it's very important to note that this is not quite the same thing as a host being UNREACHABLE, which is what the parents directive is for, as discussed in the *Creating a network host hierarchy* recipe in this chapter. Most of the time, a host actually being DOWN does not mean that other hosts actually go DOWN by definition. It's more typical for a child host to simply be UNREACHABLE; it might be working fine, but Nagios Core can't check it because of the DOWN host in its path.

However, there's one particularly broad category where host dependencies are definitely useful: the host/guest relationship of virtual machines. If you are monitoring both a host physical machine and one or more guest virtual machines, then the virtual machines are definitely dependent on the host; if the host machine is actually in a DOWN state and has no redundant failover, then it would imply that the guests were DOWN as well, and not simply UNREACHABLE.

We'll use **virtualization** as an example, with two virtual machines zeus.naginet and athena.naginet running on a host machine, ephesus.naginet. All three are already monitored, but we'll establish a host dependency so that Nagios Core doesn't notify anyone about the guests' state if it determines that the host is DOWN.

You will need a Nagios Core 3.0 or newer server, and have shell access to change its backend configuration.

How to do it...

We can establish our host dependencies as follows:

1. Change to the `objects` configuration directory for Nagios Core. The default path is `/usr/local/nagios/etc/objects`. If you've put the definition for your host in a different file, then move to its directory instead.

   ```
   # cd /usr/local/nagios/etc/objects
   ```

2. Create or edit an appropriate file that will be included by the configuration in `/usr/local/nagios/etc/nagios.cfg`. A sensible choice could be `/usr/local/nagios/etc/objects/dependencies.cfg`:

   ```
   # vi dependencies.cfg
   ```

3. Add a `hostdependency` definition. In our case, the definition looks similar to the following code snippet. Note that you can include multiple dependent hosts by separating their names with commas:

   ```
   define hostdependency {
        host_name                      ephesus.naginet
        dependent_host_name            zeus.naginet,athena.naginet
        execution_failure_criteria     n
        notification_failure_criteria  d,u
   }
   ```

4. Validate the configuration and restart the Nagios Core server:

   ```
   # /usr/local/nagios/bin/nagios -v /usr/local/nagios/etc/nagios.cfg
   # /etc/init.d/nagios restart
   ```

With this done, if the `ephesus.naginet` host goes down and takes both the `zeus.naginet` and `athena.naginet` hosts down with it, then checks to all three hosts will continue but notifications will be suppressed for the two guest hosts.

How it works...

The host dependency object's four directives are as follows:

- `host_name`: This is the name of the host on which at least one other host is dependent. We'll refer to this as the dependency host. This can also be a comma-separated list of host names.

- `dependent_host_name`: This is the name of the dependent host. Again, this can be a comma-separated list.

- execution_failure_criteria: This defines a list of states for the dependency host. If that host is in any of these states, then Nagios Core will skip checks for the dependent hosts. This can be a comma-separated list of any of the following flags:

    - o: Dependency host is UP

    - d: Dependency host is DOWN

    - u: Dependency host is UNREACHABLE

    - p: Dependency host is PENDING (not checked yet)

    Alternatively, the single flag n can be used (as it is in this example), to specify that the checks should take place regardless of the dependency host's state.

- notification_failure_criteria: This defines a list of states for the dependency host. If that host is in any of these states, then notifications for the dependent host will not be sent. The flags are the same as for execution_failure_criteria; in this example, we've chosen to suppress the notifications if the dependency host is DOWN or UNREACHABLE.

When Nagios Core notices that the zeus.naginet or athena.naginet hosts have apparently gone DOWN as a result of a failed host check, it refers to its configuration to check if there are any dependencies for the host, and finds that they depend on ephesus.naginet.

It then checks the status of ephesus.naginet and finds it to be DOWN. Referring to the execution_failure_criteria directive and finding n, it continues to run checks for both of the dependent hosts as normal. However, referring to the notification_failure_criteria directive and finding d, u, it determines that notifications should be suppressed until the host returns to an UP state.

There's more...

We can specify groups rather than host names for dependencies using the hostgroup_name and dependent_hostgroup_name directives:

```
define hostdependency {
        hostgroup_name                   vm-hosts
        dependent_hostgroup_name         vm-guests
        execution_failure_criteria       n
        notification_failure_criteria    d,u
}
```

We can also provide comma-separated lists of dependency hosts:

```
define hostdependency {
    host_name                   ephesus.naginet,alexandria.naginet
    dependent_host_name  zeus.naginet,athena.naginet
    execution_failure_criteria      n
    notification_failure_criteria  d,u
}
```

If a host depends on more than one host, the check or notification rules apply if any of its dependencies are not met, rather than all of them. For the previous example, this means that if ephesus.naginet was DOWN, but alexandria.naginet was UP, then the dependency would still suppress checks or notifications for all dependent hosts.

This means that host dependencies are not really suitable in redundant scenarios where the loss of one of the depended-upon hosts does not necessarily imply the loss of all its dependent hosts. You are likely to find that monitoring nodes as a cluster is a better fit for this situation; this is discussed in the *Monitoring individual nodes as a cluster* recipe, also in this chapter.

See also

▶ The *Establishing a service dependency, Creating a network host hierarchy,* and *Monitoring individual nodes as a cluster* recipes in this chapter

Establishing a service dependency

In this recipe, we'll learn how to establish a service dependency between two services. This feature can be used to control how Nagios Core checks services and notifies us about problems in situations where if one service is in a PROBLEM state, it implies that at least one other service is necessarily also in a PROBLEM state.

Getting ready

You will need a Nagios Core 3.0 or newer server, and have shell access to change its backend configuration. You will also need to have at least two services defined, one of which is by definition dependent on the other; this means that if the dependency service were to enter CRITICAL state, then it would imply that the dependent service would also be CRITICAL.

We'll use a simple example: suppose we are testing authentication to a mail server marathon.naginet with a service MAIL_LOGIN, and also checking a database service MAIL_DB on the same host, which stores the login usernames and password hashes.

In this situation, it might well be the case that if `MAIL_DB` is not working, then `MAIL_LOGIN` will almost certainly not be working either. If so, then we can configure Nagios Core to be aware that the `MAIL_LOGIN` service is dependent on the `MAIL_DB` service.

How to do it...

We can establish our service dependency as follows:

1. Change to the `objects` configuration directory for Nagios Core. The default path is `/usr/local/nagios/etc/objects`. If you've put the definition for your host in a different file, then move to its directory instead.

   ```
   # cd /usr/local/nagios/etc/objects
   ```

2. Create or edit an appropriate file that will be included by the configuration in `/usr/local/nagios/etc/nagios.cfg`. A sensible choice could be `/usr/local/nagios/etc/objects/dependencies.cfg`:

   ```
   # vi dependencies.cfg
   ```

3. Add a `servicedependency` definition. In our case, the definition looks similar to the following code snippet:

   ```
   define servicedependency {
           host_name                       marathon.naginet
           service_description             MAIL_DB
           dependent_host_name             marathon.naginet
           dependent_service_description   MAIL_LOGIN
           execution_failure_criteria      c
           notification_failure_criteria   c
   }
   ```

4. Validate the configuration and restart the Nagios Core server:

   ```
   # /usr/local/nagios/bin/nagios -v /usr/local/nagios/etc/nagios.cfg
   # /etc/init.d/nagios restart
   ```

With this done, if the `MAIL_DB` service fails for whatever reason and enters a `CRITICAL` state, the `MAIL_LOGIN` service will skip its checks of that service, and also skip any notifications that it would normally send about its own problems, if any. Note that the web interface may still show Nagios Core is scheduling checks, but it won't actually run them.

How it works...

The service dependency object's five directives are as follows:

- `host_name`: This is the name of the host with which these services are associated. We'll refer to this as the dependency host.

- `service_description`: This is the description of the service being depended upon. It can be a comma-separated list. We'll refer to this as the dependency service.

- `dependent_service_description`: This is the description of the dependent service. It can also be a comma-separated list.

- `execution_failure_criteria`: This defines a list of states for the dependency service. If that service is in any of these states, then Nagios Core will skip the checks for the dependent services. It can be a comma-separated list of any of the following flags:

- o: Dependency service is OK

    - w: Dependency service is WARNING

    - c: Dependency service is CRITICAL (as in this example)

    - u: Dependency service is UNKNOWN

    - p: Dependency service is PENDING (not checked yet)

    Alternatively, the single flag n can be used to specify that the checks should take place regardless of the dependency service's state. In this example, we've chosen the value c to suppress service checks only if the dependency service is CRITICAL.

- `notification_failure_criteria`: This defines a list of states for the dependency service. If that service is in any of these states, then notifications for the dependent service will not be sent. The flags are the same as for `execution_failure_criteria`; in this example, we've again chosen the value c to suppress the notifications only if the dependency service is CRITICAL.

When Nagios Core notices the MAIL_DB service has gone CRITICAL as a result of a failed service check, it refers to its configuration to check if there are any dependencies for the service, and finds that they depend on MAIL_LOGIN.

It then checks the status of MAIL_DB and finds it to be CRITICAL. Referring to the `execution_failure_criteria` directive and finding c, it prevents checks for both of the dependent services. Referring to the `notification_failure_criteria` directive and also finding c, it also decides that notifications should be suppressed until the service returns to any other state.

There's more...

Note that services do not have to be on the same host to depend upon one another. We can add
dependent_host_name or dependent_hostgroup_name directives to specify other hosts:

```
define servicedependency {
        host_name                       marathon.naginet
        service_description             MAIL_DB
        dependent_host_name             sparta.naginet
        dependent_service_description   WEBMAIL_LOGIN
        execution_failure_criteria      c
        notification_failure_criteria   c
}
```

In this example, the WEBMAIL_LOGIN service on sparta.naginet is defined as dependent
on the MAIL_DB service on marathon.naginet. Note that the values for host_name and
dependent_host_name are different.

In versions of Nagios Core before 3.3.1, the dependent_host_name directive is required,
even if it is the same as the host_name.

See also

> ▸   The *Establishing a host dependency* and *Monitoring individual nodes as a cluster*
>   recipes in this chapter

Monitoring individual nodes in a cluster

In this recipe, we'll learn how to monitor a collection of hosts in a cluster, using the
check_cluster plugin included in the standard Nagios Plugins. Being able to monitor
more than one host collectively is useful in situations with redundancy; one of a set of hosts
being DOWN, perhaps for power conservation or maintenance reasons, is not necessarily a
cause for notification. However, if a larger number or all of the hosts were down, we would
definitely want to be notified. Using check_cluster allows us to arrange this.

Getting ready

You will need a Nagios Core 3.0 or newer server, and have shell access to change its backend
configuration. You will also need to have at least two monitored hosts in a redundant setup for
some function, such as database replication, DNS servers, or load-balanced web servers.

You should also be familiar with the way hosts and services are defined, and in particular defining commands; these concepts are discussed in *Chapter 1, Understanding Hosts, Services, and Contacts*.

For this example, we'll work with three blade servers with hostnames `achilles.naginet`, `odysseus.naginet`, and `agamemnon.naginet`, running in a redundant cluster to support a virtual hosting environment. All three hosts are already being monitored to send an e-mail message if one of them goes down. We will arrange a `check_cluster` service on a "dummy host" in such a way that:

▶ If none of the blades is down, the service is `OK`

▶ If one of the blades is down, the service enters `WARNING` state, again notifying us as appropriate

▶ If two or all three of the blades are down, the service enters `CRITICAL` state, again notifying us as appropriate

How to do it...

We can arrange a cluster check for our hosts as follows:

1. Change to the `objects` configuration directory for Nagios Core. The default path is `/usr/local/nagios/etc/objects`. If you've put the definition for your host in a different file, then move to its directory instead.

   ```
   # cd /usr/local/nagios/etc/objects
   ```

2. Create or edit an appropriate file for defining a new command. A sensible choice might be `/usr/local/nagios/etc/objects/commands.cfg`.

3. Define two new commands in this file, `check_dummy` and `check_host_cluster`:

   ```
   define command {
       command_name    check_dummy
       command_line    $USER1$/check_dummy $ARG1$ $ARG2$
   }
   define command {
       command_name    check_host_cluster
       command_line    $USER1$/check_cluster -h -d $ARG1$ -w $ARG2$ -c
   $ARG3$
   }
   ```

4. Create or edit an appropriate file that will be included by the configuration in `/usr/local/nagios/etc/nagios.cfg`. A sensible choice might be `/usr/local/nagios/etc/objects/clusters.cfg`.

5. Define a dummy host for the cluster with the following values:

```
define host {
    use                   generic-host
    host_name             naginet-blade-cluster
    alias                 Naginet Blade Cluster
    address               127.0.0.1
    max_check_attempts    1
    contact_groups        admins
    check_command         check_dummy!0!"Dummy host only"
}
```

Note that the `address` directive has the value `127.0.0.1`; this is deliberate, as the dummy host itself does not really need to be actively checked or send any notifications.

6. Add a service for the dummy host:

```
define service {
    use                   generic-service
    host_name             naginet-blade-cluster
    service_description   CLUSTER
    check_command         check_host_
cluster!$HOSTSTATEID:achilles.naginet$,$HOSTSTATEID:odysseus.
naginet$,$HOSTSTATEID:agamemnon.naginet$!@1:!@2:
    notification_options  c,w,r
}
```

The suggestion of inheriting from `generic-service` is only an example; you will likely want to use your own template or values. Note that the value for `check_command` is all on one line, with no spaces. You should substitute the hostnames of your own machines.

7. Validate the configuration and restart the Nagios Core server:

```
# /usr/local/nagios/bin/nagios -v /usr/local/nagios/etc/nagios.cfg
# /etc/init.d/nagios restart
```

With this done, the `CLUSTER` service on the `naginet-blade-cluster` dummy host should be available for viewing. It will change state and send notifications the same way as any other service if the hosts in the cluster come up or go down:

naginet-blade-cluster	CLUSTER	OK	08-22-2012 21:27:44	0d 0h 8m 2s	1/3	CLUSTER OK: Host cluster: 3 up, 0 down, 0 unreachable
naginet-blade-cluster	CLUSTER	WARNING	08-22-2012 21:32:25	0d 0h 0m 10s	1/3	CLUSTER WARNING: Host cluster: 2 up, 1 down, 0 unreachable
naginet-blade-cluster	CLUSTER	CRITICAL	08-22-2012 21:33:42	0d 0h 0m 9s	3/3	CLUSTER CRITICAL: Host cluster: 1 up, 2 down, 0 unreachable

How it works...

The host added in this recipe is just a "hook" for the `CLUSTER` service, which performs the actual check. This is why we used a command using the `check_dummy` plugin to always return an `OK` state:

```
# /usr/local/nagios/libexec/check_dummy 0 "Dummy host only"
OK: Dummy host only
```

The `check_cluster` command is actually quite simple. It performs no actual checks of its own. Instead, it determines states based on the current state of other hosts or services.

This is why the `$HOSTSTATEID:hostname$` macros are used in the `check_command` directive for the service; they evaluate to a number indicating the state of the host, with the hostname specified after the colon.

For example, if `achilles.naginet` and `odysseus.naginet` were UP, but `agamemnon.naginet` was DOWN, then the command run by Nagios Core for the check would look similar to the following code snippet after the macros were expanded:

```
/usr/local/nagios/libexec/check_cluster -h -d 0,0,1 -w @1: -c @2:
```

We can run this ourselves as the `nagios` user to check the output:

```
# sudo -s -u nagios
$ /usr/local/nagios/libexec/check_cluster -h -d 0,0,1 -w @1: -c @2:
CLUSTER WARNING: Service cluster: 2 ok, 1 warning, 0 unknown, 0 critical
```

The comma-separated states given in the `-d` option to the plugin correspond to two hosts being UP (state ID of 0), and one host being DOWN (state ID of 1). The `-w` option's value of `@1:` means that a `WARNING` state will be entered if one or more of the hosts is down. Similarly, the `-c` option's value of `@2:` means that a `CRITICAL` state will be entered if two or more of the hosts go down.

This allows you to customize notifications to be sent based on the number of hosts in the DOWN state, rather than merely monitoring the hosts individually. Once you're confident this is working correctly, you may even choose to prevent the individual hosts from sending notifications to your pager, and have the CLUSTER service notify you instead.

There's more...

If you have a cluster of services rather than hosts to monitor, this can be done by using the -s option to check_cluster, rather than the -h option. In this case, instead of the $HOSTSTATEID:<host_name>$ macro, you would use the $SERVICESTATEID:<host_name>:<service_description>$ macro. An example configuration might look similar to the following code snippet for a cluster of two web servers, sparta.naginet and athens.naginet, given a dummy host named naginet-http-cluster:

```
define command {
    command_name    check_service_cluster
    command_line    $USER1$/check_cluster -s -d $ARG1$ -w $ARG2$ -c
$ARG3$
}
define service {
    use                     generic-service
    host_name               naginet-http-cluster
    service_description     CLUSTER_HTTP
    check_command           check_service_cluster!$SERVICESTATEID:sparta.
naginet:HTTP$,$SERVICESTATEID:athens.naginet:HTTP$!@1:!@2:
}
```

See also

▶   The *Establishing a host dependency* recipe in this chapter

Using the network map as an overlay

In this recipe, we'll learn how to use a background for the network map and deliberate placement of hosts in specific points on it, to make a kind of network status weather map to see host statuses at a glance in a geographical context.

Getting ready

You will need a Nagios Core 3.0 or newer server, and have shell access to change its backend configuration. You should also have at least a couple of hosts configured to place on the map, and understand the basics of using the Nagios network map and icons for hosts. These are discussed in the *Using the network map* and *Choosing icons for hosts* recipes, in this chapter.

You should also select a background image on which you can meaningfully place hosts. If you are monitoring an office network, this could be a floor plan of the building or server room. If you're monitoring a nationwide Internet service provider, then you could use a map of your state or country. Some administrators even like to use pictures of physical equipment, and place the Nagios Core hosts over their physical analogues. In this example, we'll use a map of Australia, 640 by 509 pixels in size, a public domain image retrieved from the Natural Earth website at `http://www.naturalearthdata.com/`:

The background image can be anything you like, and several graphics formats including PNG can be used. However, for the sake of quick map rendering, it's recommended to use an image in the GD2 file format, with extension .gd2. If you have your image in a PNG format, you can generate a GD2 image from it using the free tool pngtogd2:

```
$ pngtogd2 australia.png australia.gd2 0 1
```

This tool is available on Debian-derived systems in the `libgd-tools` package. Its source code is also available online at `http://www.libgd.org/`.

How to do it...

We can set up a background for our network map as follows:

1. Copy your GD2 format image into the `images` subdirectory of the `physical_html_path` directory. In the default installation, this is `/usr/local/nagios/share/images`; if it is different, you can find the definition of `physical_html_path` in `/usr/local/nagios/etc/cgi.cfg`.

   ```
   # cp /home/tom/australia.gd2 /usr/local/nagios/share/images
   ```

2. Change to the configuration directory for Nagios Core. In the default installation, this is `/usr/local/nagios/etc`. Edit the file `cgi.cfg`.

   ```
   # cd /usr/local/nagios/etc
   # vi cgi.cfg
   ```

3. Look for the directive `statusmap_background_image` in this file. Uncomment it and make its value the name of your image:

   ```
   statusmap_background_image=australia.gd2
   ```

4. Look for the directive `default_statusmap_layout` in the same file. Change it to 0, which corresponds to the **User-defined coordinates** layout.

   ```
   default_statusmap_layout=0
   ```

5. Change to the `objects` configuration directory for Nagios Core. In the default installation, this is `/usr/local/nagios/etc/objects`. Add `2d_coords` directives to each of the hosts you want to display on the map. You might like to include definitions for `statusmap_image` here too, which is done as follows:

   ```
   # vi australia.cfg
   define host {
           use              linux-server
           host_name        adelaide.naginet
           address          10.128.0.140
           2d_coords        390,360
           statusmap_image  rack-server.gd2
   }
   define host {
           use              linux-server
           host_name        cairns.naginet
           address          10.128.0.141
           2d_coords        495,100
           statusmap_image  rack-server.gd2
   }
   ... etc ...
   ```

6. For the directive `2d_coords`, supply two comma-separated values describing the coordinates for the placement of the host. For example, `adelaide.naginet` is 390 pixels from the left, and 360 pixels from the top. A convenient way to get the coordinates is by using GIMP, the open source imaging tool, or even a simple tool such as MS Paint; load the image and hover over the point you wish to use to find its pixel coordinates.

7. Validate the configuration and restart the Nagios Core server:

```
# /usr/local/nagios/bin/nagios -v /usr/local/nagios/etc/nagios.cfg
# /etc/init.d/nagios restart
```

With this done, on visiting the network map in the Nagios Core web interface by clicking on **Map** on the left-hand side menu, your hosts will be placed in their corresponding positions on the map, including the normal lines and colors to specify child-parent relationships and reachability:

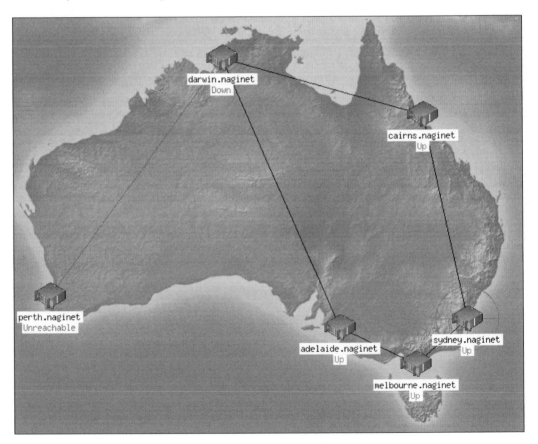

How it works...

The `default_statusmap_layout` directive fixes the network map into the **User-supplied coords** mode by default. In this mode, only hosts with values for `2d_coords` are shown, and they are displayed at fixed points on the map, rather than being dynamically placed.

It's possible to use this display mode without a background if we wish, but we can give a lot of useful context to the picture of the network generated by taking the extra step of using an actual background image.

Note that if you don't have any hosts with coordinates defined, you'll receive an error that looks similar to the following screenshot:

```
You have not supplied any host drawing coordinates, so you cannot use this layout method.
Read the FAQs for more information on specifying drawing coordinates or select a different layout method.
```

There's more...

Using the network map with an image background can be particularly helpful for seeing not only the statuses of individual hosts at a glance, but in the case of outages from multiple hosts, looking for possible geographical causes. If all of the nodes in one part of the city or country went down at once, we would be able to see that at a glance. This makes the network map an excellent choice for a network monitoring display, or as one of the first ports of call in diagnosing large-scale problems.

The network map is very useful in this way, and graphically it is probably the most impressive part of the Nagios Core web interface. If you would like even more options and an impressive range of visualizations for host statuses, you may like to consider looking at the excellent **NagVis** extension, which could fill a whole book in itself. There is a brief introduction to its usage in the *Getting extra visualizations with NagVis* recipe, in *Chapter 11, Automating and Extending Nagios*.

See also

▶ The *Creating a network host hierarchy*, *Using the network map*, and *Choosing icons for hosts* recipes in this chapter

▶ The *Getting extra visualizations with NagVis* recipe in *Chapter 11, Automating and Extending Nagios*

9
Managing Configuration

In this chapter, we will cover the following recipes:

- ▶ Grouping configuration files in directories
- ▶ Keeping configuration under version control
- ▶ Configuring host roles using groups
- ▶ Building groups using regular expressions
- ▶ Using inheritance to simplify configuration
- ▶ Defining macros in a resource file
- ▶ Dynamically building host definitions

Introduction

A major downside of Nagios Core's configuration being so flexible is that without proper management, a configuration can easily balloon out into hundreds of files with thousands of objects, all having unclear dependencies. This can be frustrating when attempting to make significant changes to a configuration, or even for something as simple as removing a host, sifting through dependencies to find what's causing errors in the configuration and prevents you from restarting Nagios Core.

It's therefore important to build your configuration carefully using as much abstraction as possible, to allow adding, changing, and removing hosts and service definitions from the configuration painlessly, and to avoid duplication of configuration. Nagios Core provides a few ways of dealing with this, most notably in the judicious use of groups and templates for the fundamental objects. Duplication of network-specific and volatile data, such as passwords, is also to be avoided; it's best done with the use of custom macros defined in a resource file.

This chapter's recipes will run through some examples of good practice for the configuration of a large network. The most important recipes are the first two, *Grouping configuration files in directories* and *Configuring host roles using groups*. If you're looking to untangle and revamp a messy configuration, then these two recipes would be the best place to start.

At the end of the chapter, the final recipe, *Dynamically building host definitions,* will show one of the primary advantages of a tidy configuration in being able to easily generate configuration according to a list of hosts and services kept in some other external information source, such as a **Configuration Management Database** (**CMDB**).

Grouping configuration files in directories

In this recipe, we'll learn to group configuration files in directories to greatly ease the management of configuration. We'll do this by configuring Nagios Core to load every file it can find ending with a `.cfg` extension in a given directory, including recursing through subdirectories. The end result will be that to have Nagios Core load a file, we only need to include it somewhere in that directory with an appropriate extension; we don't need to define exactly which files are being loaded in `nagios.cfg`.

Getting ready

You will need to have a server running Nagios Core 3.0 or later, and have access to the command line to change its configuration. You should be familiar with the loading of individual configuration files using the `cfg_file` directive in `/usr/local/nagios/etc/nagios.cfg`.

In particular, you should have a directory prepared that contains all of the configuration files you would like to be loaded by Nagios Core. In this example, we'll prepare a new directory called `/usr/local/nagios/etc/naginet`, which will contain three configuration files, each defining information for one host:

```
# ls -1 /usr/local/nagios/etc/naginet
athens.cfg
ithaca.cfg
sparta.cfg
```

You will need to ensure that the directory, files, and subdirectories within it are all readable (though not necessarily owned) by the `nagios` user.

How to do it...

We can arrange for Nagios Core to include all the files in a directory as follows:

1. Change to the directory containing the `nagios.cfg` file. In the default installation, it is located at `/usr/local/nagios/etc/nagios.cfg`.

   ```
   # vi nagios.cfg
   ```

2. Edit the file, and below any other `cfg_file` or `cfg_dir` directives, add the following line referring to the absolute path of the directory containing your `.cfg` files:

   ```
   cfg_dir=/usr/local/nagios/etc/naginet
   ```

   Note that this directive is `cfg_dir`, rather than `cfg_file`.

3. Remove any `cfg_file` definitions pointing to `.cfg` files in the new directory. This is to prevent loading the same objects twice. In our example, we would need to comment out our previous rules loading these files individually:

   ```
   #cfg_file=/usr/local/nagios/etc/naginet/sparta.cfg
   #cfg_file=/usr/local/nagios/etc/naginet/athens.cfg
   #cfg_file=/usr/local/nagios/etc/naginet/ithaca.cfg
   ```

4. Validate the configuration and restart the Nagios Core server:

   ```
   # /usr/local/nagios/bin/nagios -v /usr/local/nagios/etc/nagios.cfg
   # /etc/init.d/nagios restart
   ```

With this done, Nagios Core should have loaded all of the files with the extension `.cfg` found in the `naginet` directory or any of its subdirectories, saving us the burden of specifying them individually.

How it works...

At load time, Nagios Core interprets the `cfg_dir` directive to mean that it should identify all of the `.cfg` files in a particular directory, including recursing through its subdirectories. It ignores the files that do not have that extension, allowing us to include metadata or other file types (such as version control information directories) without causing problems.

As a result, defining a new host or service becomes as simple as adding the file in an appropriate included directory, without needing to edit `nagios.cfg`.

There's more...

It's important to note that this directive will include all the .cfg files in subdirectories as well. This might allow us to meaningfully group the configuration files:

```
$ find /usr/local/nagios/etc/naginet
/usr/local/nagios/etc/naginet
/usr/local/nagios/etc/naginet/hosts
/usr/local/nagios/etc/naginet/hosts/athens.cfg
/usr/local/nagios/etc/naginet/hosts/sparta.cfg
/usr/local/nagios/etc/naginet/hosts/ithaca.cfg
/usr/local/nagios/etc/naginet/commands
/usr/local/nagios/etc/naginet/commands/webserver-checks.cfg
/usr/local/nagios/etc/naginet/services
/usr/local/nagios/etc/naginet/services/webservers.cfg
```

For large networks, it's worth deciding on some suitable organizing principle for directories. One common approach is having a separate directory for hosts, services, and command definitions, relevant to a particular **Domain Name System** (**DNS**) zone or larger subnet.

If you want to prevent a file from being included at any point, all you need to do is either move it out of the directory, or rename it so that it no longer has a .cfg extension. One possibility is adding the suffix .exclude:

```
# mv unwanted-file.cfg unwanted-file.cfg.exclude
```

This will prevent Nagios Core from picking it up as part of its cfg_dir searching algorithm.

See also

▶ The *Using inheritance to simplify configuration* and *Keeping configuration under version control* recipes in this chapter

Keeping configuration under version control

In this recipe, we'll place a Nagios Core configuration directory under version control, in an attempt to keep track of changes made to it, and to enable us to reverse changes if there are problems.

Getting ready

You should choose an appropriate version control system. The recipe will vary considerably depending on which system you use; there are too many options to demonstrate here, so we'll use the popular open source content tracker **Git**, the basics of which are very easy to use for this kind of version control and do not require an external server. However, there's no reason you can't use **Subversion** or **Mercurial**, if you'd prefer. You should have the client for your chosen system (git, hg, svn, and so on) installed on your server.

This will all work with any version of Nagios Core. It does not involve directly changing any part of the Nagios Core configuration, only keeping track of the files in it.

How to do it...

We can place our configuration directory under version control as follows:

1. Change to the root of the configuration directory. In the default installation, this is /usr/local/nagios/etc:

   ```
   # cd /usr/local/nagios/etc
   ```

2. Run git init to start a repository in the current directory:

   ```
   # git init
   Initialized empty Git repository in /usr/local/nagios/etc/.git/.
   ```

3. Add all the files in the configuration directory with git add:

   ```
   # git add .
   ```

4. Commit the files with git commit:

   ```
   # git commit -m "First commit of configuration"
   [master (root-commit) 6a2c605] First commit of configuration.
    39 files changed, 3339 insertions(+), 0 deletions(-)
    create mode 100644 naginet/athens.naginet.cfg
    create mode 100644 naginet/ithaca.naginet.cfg
    create mode 100644 naginet/sparta.naginet.cfg
    ...
   ```

With this done, we should now have a .git repository in /usr/local/nagios/etc, tracking all the changes made to the configuration files.

How it works...

Changes to the configuration files in this directory can now be reviewed for commit with `git status`. For example, if we changed the IP addresses of one of our hosts, we might check the changes by typing the following:

```
# git status -s
M naginet/hosts/sparta.cfg
```

We could then commit this change with an explanatory message:

```
# git commit -am "Changed IP address of host"
[master d5116a6] Changed IP address of host
1 files changed, 1 insertions(+), 1 deletions(-)
```

We can review the change with `git log`:

```
# git log --oneline
d5116a6 Changed IP address of host
6a2c605 First commit of configuration
```

If we want to inspect exactly what was changed later on, we can use `git diff` followed by the short commit ID given in the first column of the preceding output:

```
# git diff 6a2c605
diff --git a/naginet/hosts/sparta.cfg b/naginet/hosts/sparta.cfg
index 0bb3b0b..fb7c2a9 100644
--- a/naginet/hosts/sparta.cfg
+++ b/naginet/hosts/sparta.cfg
@@ -2,7 +2,7 @@ define host {
        use                     linux-server
        host_name               sparta.naginet
        alias                   sparta
-       address                 10.128.0.101
+       address                 10.128.0.102
}
```

The full functionality of Git for managing these changes, including reverting to older revisions, is out of scope here. You can read more about how to use Git in general in Scott Chacon's excellent book entitled *Pro Git*, free to read online at `http://git-scm.com/book`.

There's more...

Version control is particularly useful in this way when more than one person is editing a configuration, because it allows us to determine who made a change and when. It also allows us to see the exact changeset to review why it was changed, and to undo or edit it if it is causing problems.

If you're going to use this method, it's a good idea to keep your configuration reasonably granular, using at least several files rather than just one or two. It will still work if you have two big files such as `hosts.cfg` and `services.cfg` for your network, but the differences between each commit will not be as clear. This is therefore a very good recipe to combine with the *Grouping configuration files in directories* recipe, also in this chapter.

Rather than merely the configuration directory, you may prefer to keep the entire Nagios Core directory under version control, including the plugins and other scripts and binaries. This could be particularly handy if you upgrade your installation with new releases and want to see what's changed in your files, in case it breaks anything. In this case, be careful to use your chosen version control system's "ignore" functionality to prevent tracking temporary files or log files. For Git, take a look at the output of `git help ignore`.

See also

▸ The *Grouping configuration files in directories* recipe in this chapter

Configuring host roles using groups

In this recipe, we'll learn how to use the abstraction of host and service groups to our advantage in order to build a configuration where hosts and services can be added or removed more easily. We'll do this by defining roles for hosts by using a hostgroup structure, and then assigning relevant services to the hostgroup, rather than to the hosts individually.

Getting ready

You will need to have a server running Nagios Core 3.0 or later, have access to the command line to change its directories, and understand the basics of how host and service groups work. These are covered in the *Creating a new hostgroup* and *Creating a new servicegroup* recipes in *Chapter 1*.

In this example, we'll create two simple hostgroups; one called `servers`, for which a `PING` check should be made for its member hosts, and another called `webservers`, which should include `HTTP` checks for its member hosts. Once this is set up, we'll then add an example host `sparta.naginet` to both groups, thereby easily assigning all the appropriate services to the host in one definition, which we can cleanly remove simply by deleting the host.

How to do it...

We can create our group-based roles for hosts as follows:

1. Change to the `objects` configuration directory. In the default installation, this is `/usr/local/nagios/etc/objects`. If you have already followed the *Grouping configuration files in directories* recipe in this chapter, then your own directory may differ.

   ```
   # cd /usr/local/nagios/etc/objects
   ```

2. In an appropriate file, perhaps `hostgroups.cfg`, define new hostgroups with names corresponding to the roles for the hosts. Do not assign them any members just yet.

   ```
   define hostgroup {
       hostgroup_name   servers
       alias            Servers
   }
   define hostgroup {
       hostgroup_name   web-servers
       alias            Web Servers
   }
   ```

3. In a second appropriate file, perhaps `services.cfg`, define new services and assign them `hostgroup_name` values, corresponding to the hostgroups added in the previous step:

   ```
   define service {
       use                   generic-service
       hostgroup_name        servers
       service_description   PING
       check_command         check_ping!100,10%!200,20%
   }
   define service {
       use                   generic-service
       hostgroup_name        web-servers
       service_description   HTTP
       check_command         check_http
   }
   ```

   Note that the use of the `generic-service` template is an example only; you will probably want to inherit from your own particular service template.

4. Add or edit your existing hosts to make them a part of the appropriate hostgroups, using the `hostgroups` directive:

   ```
   define host {
       use             linux-server
   ```

```
        host_name     sparta.naginet
        alias         sparta
        address       10.128.0.21
        hostgroups    servers,web-servers
}
define host {
        use           linux-server
        host_name     athens.naginet
        alias         athens
        address       10.128.0.22
        hostgroups    servers,web-servers
}
```

5. If you already had services with the same value for their `service_description` directives as the ones you're adding in this recipe, you will need to remove them, as this may cause a conflict with the services added in the previous step.

6. Validate the configuration and restart the Nagios Core server:

```
# /usr/local/nagios/bin/nagios -v /usr/local/nagios/etc/nagios.cfg
# /etc/init.d/nagios restart
```

With this done, you should now find that all of the services you defined for the hostgroups you created have been attached to the appropriate hosts:

Host ↑↓	Service ↑↓	Status ↑↓
athens.naginet	HTTP	PENDING
	PING	OK
sparta.naginet	HTTP	PENDING
	PING	OK

How it works...

The configuration added in the preceding section avoids assigning services directly to hosts, instead assigning them to hostgroups, thereby creating roles for services that hosts can adopt or discard simply by becoming part of or leaving the group.

Apart from making the configuration shorter, another advantage to this approach is that if services are added this way, adding or deleting a host from the Nagios Core configuration requires nothing but the adding or removing of the host definition. Similarly, if a host takes on another role (for example, a web server adding some database functionality), then we can modify the services being checked on it simply by modifying its hostgroups. This ends up being much easier than adding dependencies in other files.

Another advantage is that having hostgroups organized by host function is helpful for applying batch operations such as scheduled downtime in one easy action, or for checking all the services for one particular type of host. Once a hostgroup is defined, we can run operations on all the hosts within it by clicking on its name in the brackets, in any of the hostgroup views:

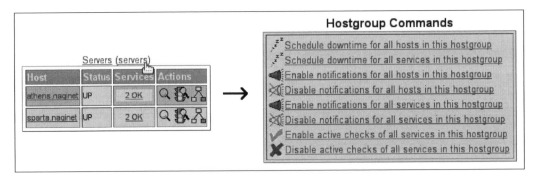

If we had twenty web servers that we knew were going to be down, for example, this would be much easier than scheduling downtime for each of them individually!

There's more...

It's worth noting that hostgroups can have subgroups, meaning that all of the hosts added to any of their subgroups are implicitly added to the parent group.

For example, we could define the hostgroup web servers as a subgroup of the `servers` hostgroup, using the `hostgroup_members` directive:

```
define hostgroup {
    hostgroup_name      servers
    alias               Servers
    hostgroup_members   web-servers
}
```

This would allow us to implicitly add hosts to both groups, without needing to refer to the parent group, and with all the services assigned to both groups assigned to the host:

```
define host {
    use         linux-server
    host_name   athens.naginet
    alias       athens
    address     10.128.0.22
    hostgroups  web-servers
}
```

This can be very useful for sorting "subcategories" of services. Other examples might include a `dns-servers` group with subgroups `dns-authoritative-servers` and `dns-recursive-servers`, or a `database-servers` group with subgroups `oracle-servers` and `mysql-servers`.

See also

▶ The *Building groups using regular expressions* and *Using inheritance to simplify configuration* recipes in this chapter

▶ The *Creating a new hostgroup, Creating a new servicegroup*, and *Running a service on all hosts in a hostgroup* recipes in *Chapter 1, Understanding Hosts, Services, and Contacts*

Building groups using regular expressions

In this recipe, we'll learn a shortcut for building groups of hosts using regular expressions tested against their hostnames.

This recipe is likely only of use to you if you use a naming convention for your hosts that allows them to be reasonably grouped by location, function, or some other useful metric by a common string in their hostnames.

Getting ready

You will need to have a server running Nagios Core 3.0 or later, have access to the command line to change its configuration, and understand the basics of how hostgroups and servicegroups work. These are covered in the *Creating a new hostgroup* and *Creating a new servicegroup* recipes in *Chapter 1*.

In this example, we'll group three existing hosts named `web-server-01`, `web-server-02`, and `web-server-03` into a new hostgroup, `web-servers`, based only on their hostnames.

It would help to have some familiarity with regular expressions, but the recipe includes a simple example, which should meet many use cases for this trick. An excellent site about regular expressions including tutorials can be found at `http://www.regular-expressions.info/`.

How to do it...

We can build a hostgroup by matching regular expressions to hostnames as follows:

1. Change to the Nagios configuration directory. In the default installation, this is `/usr/local/nagios/etc`. Edit the `nagios.cfg` file in this directory.

   ```
   # cd /usr/local/nagios/etc
   # vi nagios.cfg
   ```

2. Search for the `use_regexp_matching` directive. Uncomment it if necessary and set it to `1`.

   ```
   use_regexp_matching=1
   ```

3. Search for the `use_true_regexp_matching` directive. Uncomment it if necessary, and ensure it's set to `0`, which it should be by default.

   ```
   use_true_regexp_matching=0
   ```

4. Change to the `objects` configuration directory. In the default installation, this is `/usr/local/nagios/etc/objects`. If you have already followed the *Grouping configuration files in directories* recipe in this chapter, then your own directory may differ.

   ```
   # cd /usr/local/nagios/etc/objects
   ```

5. In an appropriate file, perhaps `hostgroups.cfg`, add a definition similar to the following. In this case, `.+` means "any string at least one character in length"; you will probably want a pattern of your own, devising appropriate to your own host names.

   ```
   define hostgroup {
        hostgroup_name    web-servers
        members           web-server-.+
        alias             Web Servers
   }
   ```

6. Validate the configuration and restart the Nagios Core server:

   ```
   # /usr/local/nagios/bin/nagios -v /usr/local/nagios/etc/nagios.cfg
   # /etc/init.d/nagios restart
   ```

With this done, if your regular expression was correctly formed to match all the appropriate hostnames, then you should find that the hosts become part of the group:

Web Servers (web-servers)			
Host	**Status**	**Services**	**Actions**
web-server-01	UP	2 PENDING	🔍 ⓕ ⓐ
web-server-02	UP	2 PENDING	🔍 ⓕ ⓐ
web-server-03	UP	2 PENDING	🔍 ⓕ ⓐ

How it works...

With the `use_regexp_matching` directive set to 1, Nagios Core will attempt to use hostname strings containing the strings *, ?, +, or \. as regular expressions to match against hostnames. Because `web-server-01`, `web-server-02`, and `web-server-03` all match the regular expression `web-server-.+` given in the `members` directive for the `web-servers` hostgroup, all three hosts are added to the group.

We keep `use_true_regexp_matching` off. If it were on, it would use every hostname pattern as a regular expression, whether or not it had any special regular expression characters. This is probably not what you want for most configurations.

There's more...

This matching works in other places aside from hostgroup definitions; for example, you can also use it in the `host_name` definitions for services:

```
define service {
    use                  generic-service
    host_name            web-server-.+
    service_description  HTTP
    check_command        check_http
}
```

This is one of a number of very good suggestions for simplifying object definitions suggested in the Nagios Core manual: `http://nagios.sourceforge.net/docs/3_0/objecttricks.html`.

See also

▸ The *Building groups using regular expressions* and *Using inheritance to simplify configuration* recipes in this chapter

▸ The *Creating a new hostgroup* and *Creating a new servicegroup* recipes in Chapter 1, *Understanding Hosts, Services, and Contacts*

Using inheritance to simplify configuration

In this recipe, we'll learn how to use inheritance to handle the situation where hosts and services share a lot of values in common, amounting to a large amount of undesirable redundancy in configuration.

Some Nagios Core objects, particularly hosts and services, have a rather long list of possible directives, and the default values for these are not always suitable. It's therefore worthwhile to be able to declare the values you want for these directives once, and then spend only a few lines on the actual host definition by copying those values from a template, making the configuration shorter and easier to read.

Previous examples in this book have already demonstrated the use of this in suggesting you inherit from the `linux-server` host template or the `generic-service` service template, for the sake of brevity; in this example, we'll define our own templates, and show how these can be used to streamline a configuration.

Getting ready

You will need to have a server running Nagios Core 3.0 or later, have access to the command line to change its configuration, and be familiar with how to define hosts and services. These are covered in the *Creating a new host* and *Creating a new service* recipes in *Chapter 1*.

In this example, we'll define a template, `critical-host`, which we'll use as the basis for any host that needs to be checked and notified around the clock, with a very stringent value for its `check_command` directive, and with all notification types enabled. We'll also define two hosts named `phobos.naginet` and `deimos.naginet` that inherit from this template.

How to do it...

We can define a host template and then define hosts to inherit from it as follows:

1. Change to the `objects` configuration directory. In the default installation, this is `/usr/local/nagios/etc/objects`. If you have already followed the *Grouping configuration files in directories* recipe in this chapter, then your own directory may differ.

   ```
   # cd /usr/local/nagios/etc/objects
   ```

2. In an appropriate file, perhaps `templates.cfg`, add the following definition. Note the use of the special directives `name` and `register`:

   ```
   define host {
           name                    critical-host
           register                0
   ```

```
    check_command          check_ping!25,10%!50,20%
    max_check_attempts     3
    check_interval         1
    notification_interval  1
    notification_period    24x7
    notification_options   d,u,r,f,s
    check_period           24x7
    contact_groups         admins
}
```

3. In another file, or separate files if you prefer to keep your hosts to one per file, define hosts to inherit from this template. Add in the remaining required directives for hosts, and include a `use` directive referring to the established template:

```
define host {
    use         critical-host
    host_name   phobos.naginet
    alias       phobos
    address     10.128.0.151
}
define host {
    use         critical-host
    host_name   deimos.naginet
    alias       deimos
    address     10.128.0.152
}
```

4. Validate the configuration and restart the Nagios Core server:

```
# /usr/local/nagios/bin/nagios -v /usr/local/nagios/etc/nagios.cfg
# /etc/init.d/nagios restart
```

You might receive warnings about no services being defined for the hosts, but you can ignore those for now.

With this done, two new hosts should be registered in your configuration, **phobos.naginet** and **deimos.naginet**:

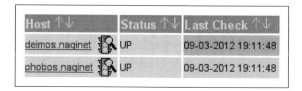

No other new hosts should be added, as the template itself was explicitly not registered as an object with the `register` directive.

How it works...

The configuration added in the preceding section defines a new template with the `name` directive of `critical-host`. Because the value for the host's register directive is `0`, where it normally defaults to `1`, the host is not registered as an object with Nagios Core. Instead, it becomes a snippet of configuration that can be referenced by real objects of the same type, by referring to its name.

Note that in the template, the normally required values of `host_name`, `alias`, and `address` are missing; this means that the host is not complete and wouldn't work if we tried to register it as an actual host anyway.

Instead, we use its values as the basis for other hosts, `phobos.naginet` and `deimos.naginet`. Both of these hosts inherit from `critical-host`, and fill in the rest of the missing values in their own definitions. This frees us from having to repeat the same directives in two different hosts.

If an object inherits a value for a directive from its parent, it's possible to override that directive by redefining it in the inheriting object definition. For example, if we wanted `phobos.naginet` to have a different value for `max_check_attempts`, we can add that to its definition:

```
define host {
    use                 critical-host
    host_name           deimos.naginet
    alias               deimos
    address             10.128.0.152
    max_check_attempts  5
}
```

There's more...

The most important thing to note about templates is that they work for a variety of Nagios Core objects, most importantly including hosts, services, and contacts. You can therefore set up and inherit from a service template in the same way:

```
define service {
    name      critical-service
    register  0
    ...etc...
}
define service {
    use       critical-service
    ...etc...
}
```

Or a contact template:

```
define contact {
    name        critical-contact
    register  0
    ...etc...
}
define contact {
    use         critical-contact
    ...etc...
}
```

Note that inheritance can stack. For example, `critical-host` could itself inherit from a template, perhaps `generic-host`, by adding its own `use` directive:

```
define host {
    use         generic-host
    name        critical-host
    register  0
    ...etc...
}
```

This allows the setting up of an inheritance structure of arbitrary complexity, but you should avoid too much depth to prevent confusing yourself or anyone else trying to read your configuration. Two levels is probably a sensible limit.

The rules around how inheritance is handled are discussed in more depth in the Nagios Core manual, including a treatment of multiple inheritance. It's useful to know about this, but in the interests of keeping configuration clear, it's best used sparingly: `http://nagios.sourceforge.net/docs/3_0/objectinheritance.html`.

See also

- ▸ The *Configuring host roles using groups* recipe in this chapter
- ▸ The *Creating a new host, Creating a new service,* and *Creating a new contact* recipes in *Chapter 1, Understanding Hosts, Services, and Contacts*

Defining macros in a resource file

In this recipe, we'll learn how to define custom user macros in resource files. This is good practice for strings used in `check_command` definitions or other directives that are shared by more than one host or service. For example, in lieu of writing the full path in a `command_name` directive as follows:

```
command_name=/usr/local/nagios/libexec/check_ssh $HOSTADDRESS$
```

We could instead write:

```
command_name=$USER1$/check_ssh $HOSTADDRESS$
```

As a result, if the location of the `check_ssh` script changes, we only need to change the value of $USER1$ in the appropriate resource file to update all of its uses throughout the configuration.

Most of the macros in Nagios Core are defined automatically by the monitoring server, but up to 32 user-defined macros can be used as well, in the form $USERn$.

Getting ready

You will need to have a server running Nagios Core 3.0 or later, and have access to the command line to change its configuration, in particular the `resource.cfg` file.

In this example, we'll add a new macro, $USER2$, to contain the SNMP community name `snagmp`, as used for various `check_snmp` requests.

How to do it...

We can define our user macro as follows:

1. Change to the Nagios configuration directory. In the default installation, this is `/usr/local/nagios/etc`. Edit the `resource.cfg` file in this directory.

   ```
   # cd /usr/local/nagios/etc
   # vi resource.cfg
   ```

2. Ensure that the $USER2$ macro is not already defined in the file. If it is, we could define $USER3$ instead, and so on.

3. Add the following definition to the end of the file:

   ```
   $USER2$=snagmp
   ```

4. Change to the `objects` configuration directory for Nagios Core. In the default installation, this is `/usr/local/nagios/etc/objects`.

   ```
   # cd /usr/local/nagios/etc/objects
   ```

5. Edit any of the `object` configuration files in which you wish to use the value of the macro, and replace the inline values with $USER2$. In our example, we might find various uses of the literal `checksnmp` community string:

   ```
   define command {
       . . .
       command_line  $USER1$/check_snmp -H $HOSTADDRESS$ -C snagmp -o
   .1.3.6.1.2.1.1.5.0 -r $ARG1$
   }
   define service {
       . . .
       check_command  check_snmp!snagmp
   }
   ```

   We could swap these out to use the macro instead:

   ```
   define command {
       . . .
       command_line  $USER1$/check_snmp -H $HOSTADDRESS$ -C $USER2$
   -o .1.3.6.1.2.1.1.5.0 -r $ARG1$
   }
   define service {
       . . .
       check_command  check_snmp!$USER2$
   }
   ```

6. Validate the configuration and restart the Nagios Core server:

   ```
   # /usr/local/nagios/bin/nagios -v /usr/local/nagios/etc/nagios.cfg
   # /etc/init.d/nagios restart
   ```

With this done, all the monitoring should be working the same as it was before, but we're now using macro expansion to centralize configuration.

How it works...

Before Nagios Core processes directives such as `command_line` and `check_command`, it will first expand all the macros referenced, including the user-defined macros we added in the `resource.cfg` resource file.

One common use for the $USERn$ macros is for defining the full path of directories where Nagios Core resources such as plugins or event handler scripts are located— in fact, the sample configuration included in Nagios Core defines $USER1$ in `resource.cfg` as `/usr/local/nagios/libexec`, the default location for plugin scripts and binaries.

It's worth noting that you can load more than one resource file by adding more `resource_file` directives in `/usr/local/nagios/etc/nagios.cfg`. For example, to load another file called `resource-extra.cfg`, we could add a second line as follows:

```
resource_file=/usr/local/nagios/etc/resource.cfg
resource_file=/usr/local/nagios/etc/resource-extra.cfg
```

There's more...

There's also a security benefit to using resource files—for sensitive information, we can prevent users other than `nagios` from reading them by making them readable only to the `nagios` user:

```
# cd /usr/local/nagios/etc
# chown nagios.nagios resource.cfg
# chmod 0600 resource.cfg
```

This makes it a decent way to store credentials, such as usernames and passwords, for example to be used in `check_command` for MySQL:

```
define command {
    command_name   check_mysql_secure
    command_line   check_mysql -H $HOSTADDRESS$ -u naguser -d nagdb -p
$USER3$
}
```

You can also define per-host macros, by using custom directives preceded with an underscore in the host definition:

```
define host {
    use             critical-host
    host_name       sparta.naginet
    alias           sparta
    address         10.128.0.21
    _mac_address    08:00:27:7e:7c:d2
}
```

In the preceding example, we're able to include the host's MAC address in a custom directive; this can be referenced in services as `$_HOSTMAC_ADDRESS$`:

```
define service {
    use                  generic-service
    host_name            sparta.naginet
    service_description  ARP
    check_command        check_arp!$_HOSTMAC_ADDRESS$
}
```

The same trick can also apply for contacts and services. This special use of custom macros is discussed in the *Custom Object Variables* chapter of the Nagios documentation at `http://nagios.sourceforge.net/docs/3_0/customobjectvars.html`.

See also

▸ The *Monitoring the output of an SNMP query* recipe in *Chapter 5, Monitoring Methods*

▸ The *Monitoring individual nodes in a cluster* recipe in *Chapter 8, Understanding the Network Layout*

Dynamically building host definitions

In this recipe, we'll learn one possible method of building Nagios configuration dynamically, to avoid having to compose or copy-paste a lot of directives for new hosts or services. In other words, this recipe is about generating configuration using templates.

To demonstrate how this is useful, we'll use the m4 macro language utility, which should be available on virtually any UNIX-like system, including GNU/Linux and BSD. As a tool designed for macro expansion, m4 is particularly well-suited to creating verbose plain text configuration files such as the ones used by Nagios Core.

The principles here should apply just as easily to your favored programming or templating language, perhaps Python or Perl, or shell scripts.

Getting ready

You will need to have the m4 macro language tool available to you, preferably but not necessarily on the same system as the one running Nagios Core. It is a very standard tool and should be already installed, or available as part of a package. The version used in this example is **GNU m4**, documented at `http://www.gnu.org/software/m4/manual/m4.html`. This recipe does not assume any familiarity with m4, and will show you the basics.

You may like to work in a new subdirectory in your home directory:

```
$ mkdir $HOME/nagios-dynamic-hosts
$ cd $HOME/nagios-dynamic-hosts
```

How to do it...

We can create and apply an example Nagios Core configuration template as follows:

1. Create a new file `host-service-template.m4` with the following contents:

```
define(`NAGHOST', `
    define host {
        host_name               $1
        alias                   $2
        address                 $3
        contact_groups          ifelse(`$#', `4', `$4', `admins')
        check_command           check-host-alive
        check_interval          5
        check_period            24x7
        max_check_attempts      3
        notification_interval   30
        notification_options    d,r
        notification_period     24x7
    }
    define service {
        host_name               $1
        contact_groups          ifelse(`$#', `4', `$4', `admins')
        check_command           check_ping!100,10%!200,20%
        check_interval          5
        check_period            24x7
        max_check_attempts      3
        notification_interval   30
        notification_period     24x7
        retry_interval          1
        service_description     PING
    }
')
```

2. Create a second file in the same directory called `sparta.host.m4` with the following contents:

```
include(`host-service-template.m4')
NAGHOST(`sparta', `Sparta Webserver', `10.0.128.21')
```

3. Create a third file in the same directory called `athens.host.m4` with the following contents:

```
include(`host-service-template.m4')
NAGHOST(`athens', `Athens Webserver', `10.0.128.22', `ops')
```

4. Run the following commands and note the output:

```
$ m4 sparta.host.m4
define host {
        host_name              sparta
        alias                  Sparta Webserver
        address                10.0.128.21
        contact_groups         admins
        check_command          check-host-alive
        check_interval         5
        check_period           24x7
        max_check_attempts     3
        notification_interval  30
        notification_options   d,r
        notification_period    24x7
}
define service {
        host_name              sparta
        contact_groups         admins
        check_command          check_ping!100,10%!200,20%
        check_interval         5
        check_period           24x7
        max_check_attempts     3
        notification_interval  30
        notification_period    24x7
        retry_interval         1
        service_description    PING
}
$ m4 athens.host.m4
define host {
        host_name              athens
        alias                  Athens Webserver
        address                10.0.128.22
        contact_groups         ops
        check_command          check-host-alive
```

```
        check_interval          5
        check_period            24x7
        max_check_attempts      3
        notification_interval   30
        notification_options    d,r
        notification_period     24x7
}
define service {
        host_name               athens
        contact_groups          ops
        check_command           check_ping!100,10%!200,20%
        check_interval          5
        check_period            24x7
        max_check_attempts      3
        notification_interval   30
        notification_period     24x7
        retry_interval          1
        service_description     PING
}
```

As seen in the preceding output, we can now generate a basic host and service configuration with a two-line m4 script referring to a template, simply by writing the output to a .cfg file:

```
$ m4 sparta.host.m4 > sparta.cfg
```

How it works...

The files `sparta.host.m4` and `athens.host.m4` both called an m4 macro with arguments, after including the template for the host and service in the `host-service-template.m4` file. This was expanded into the full definition, and the arguments given were substituted as follows:

▶ $1 was replaced with the first argument, host_name

▶ $2 was replaced with the second argument, alias

▶ $3 was replaced with the third argument, address

▶ $4 was replaced with the fourth argument, contact_group

Note that two of these values, $1 and $4, were used in both the host and the PING service definitions.

Also note that the argument $4 is optional; the `if-else` construct tests the number of arguments, and if it finds there are four, it uses the value of the fourth argument; for `athens.naginet`, this is the contact group `ops`. If there is no fourth argument, it defaults instead to the value `admins`. This allows us to set default values for arguments if we so choose.

The rest of the directives are all written directly into the template. The configuration made by this process is valid for Nagios Core, assuming that the `check_command` and `contact_groups` used are defined.

There's more...

To automate things even further, we could use `make` to automatically generate `.cfg` files from anything with the extension `.host.m4` with the following `Makefile`:

```
%.cfg : %.host.m4
    m4 $< > $*.cfg
```

Note that correct `Makefile` syntax usually requires a literal *Tab* character to indent the second line, not four spaces.

With this in the same directory as all the preceding files, in order to build the configuration for the `sparta.naginet` host, we would only need to use a `make` call to generate the file:

```
$ make sparta.cfg
m4 sparta.host.m4 > sparta.cfg
$ make athens.cfg
m4 athens.host.m4 > athens.cfg
```

Note that it's better practice to avoid repeating directives, and instead to use hostgroups and host and service templates to define "roles" for new hosts. This makes adding and removing the hosts much easier, and both processes are explained in this chapter, in the *Configuring host roles using groups* and *Using inheritance to simplify configuration* recipes.

David Douthitt goes into considerably more depth about the possibilities of using m4 for Nagios configuration at `http://administratosphere.wordpress.com/2009/02/19/configuring-nagios-with-m4/`.

See also

- ▸ The *Configuring host roles using groups* and *Using inheritance to simplify configuration* recipes in this chapter

10
Security and Performance

In this chapter, we will cover the following recipes:

- ▶ Requiring authentication for the web interface
- ▶ Using authenticated contacts
- ▶ Writing debugging information to the Nagios log file
- ▶ Monitoring Nagios performance with Nagiostats
- ▶ Improving startup times with pre-cached object files
- ▶ Setting up a redundant monitoring host

Introduction

Most administrators of even mid-size networks will choose to dedicate an entire server to monitoring software, and sometimes a whole server just for Nagios Core. This is because of two main factors common to most comprehensive Nagios Core setups:

- ▶ They have a lot of privileges, because in order to inspect the running state of so many different hosts and services, they need to be conferred appropriate network access. This often means that their IP addresses are whitelisted all over the network. A user who is able to assume that privilege could potentially do a lot of damage.

> ▸ They have a lot of work to do, and hence ideally have dedicated software and hardware resources to run what can be thousands of host and service checks smoothly and to promptly notice problems and recoveries. If a Nagios Core server is not able to keep up with its check schedule, it could cause delays in notifications about very important services.

It's therefore very important to take into account the security and performance of your Nagios Core server when building your configuration.

General best network security practices apply to Nagios Core management and will not be discussed in depth here. The following general guidelines are just as relevant to securing a Nagios Core server as they are any other kind of server:

> ▸ **Don't run the server as root**: This is probably not a concern unless you've changed it yourself, as if you've installed using the Quick Start Guides the server should be set up to run as the unprivileged `nagios` user. Nagios Core should not need `root` privileges under most circumstances.

> ▸ **Use a firewall**: The protections offered by Nagios Core, NSCA, and NRPE's host checking are very basic and are not a replacement for a software or hardware firewall policy. Even a simple `iptables` or `pf` software firewall would be a very good idea to protect a monitoring server.

> ▸ **Use the principle of least privilege**: Don't confer Nagios Core or any of its plugins or processes more privileges than they need, and lock down writable files, such as `logs`, and state information only to appropriate users. Similarly, only allow Nagios Core access through firewalls for what it needs to check, and nothing else.

> ▸ **Encrypt sensitive information**: Don't put credentials in plain text in any of the configuration files if you can avoid it, and if you can't avoid it, define them in resource files that are only readable by the `nagios` user.

You should therefore not consider this chapter a complete guide to securing and optimizing your Nagios Core server. For a more comprehensive treatment of security and optimization procedures, be sure to take a look at these pages in the Nagios Core documentation:

> ▸ **Security Considerations**: `http://nagios.sourceforge.net/docs/3_0/security.html`

> ▸ **Enhanced CGI Security and Authentication**: `http://nagios.sourceforge.net/docs/3_0/cgisecurity.html`

> ▸ **Tuning Nagios for Maximum Performance**: `http://nagios.sourceforge.net/docs/3_0/tuning.html`

In particular, this chapter will focus on securing the CGIs, as the web interface is readily exposing Nagios Core's information to the world, and is particularly vulnerable to abuse if misconfigured. It will also include methods to assess how Nagios Core is performing.

Requiring authentication for the web interface

In this recipe, we'll explore the use of basic authentication for the Nagios Core web interface, probably the single most important configuration step in preventing abuse of the software by malicious users.

By default, the Nagios Core installation process takes the sensible step of locking down the authentication by default in its recommended Apache configuration file, with standard HTTP authentication for a default user named nagiosadmin, with full privileges.

Unfortunately, some administrators take the step of removing this authentication or never installing it, in spite of the recommendations in the installation guide. It's a good idea to install it and keep it in place even on private networks, and especially if the server running Nagios Core is open to the Internet in any way (generally not advised).

This is not just because of the security benefits, but also because it allows you to set up basic access control, allowing certain users the permission to read state or run commands on certain resources, but not on others. It also has other more subtle benefits, such as recording the names of users that carry out actions for logging purposes.

Getting ready

You'll need access to the backend of a Nagios Core server with version 3.0 or greater, to change its configuration and restart it. You'll also need a functioning web interface. Much of this recipe will assume the web interface is running on the recommended **Apache HTTPD server**; you may also need to be able to edit this configuration. Some familiarity with Apache HTTPD is assumed here; the documentation available online is excellent if you need to consult it:

```
https://httpd.apache.org/docs/
```

This recipe will be in two parts: we'll first ensure that all the recommended settings are in place to properly require authentication, and we'll then demonstrate adding a user named helpdesk with read-only permissions for the server's web interface. This user will be able to read the states of all the hosts and services, but will not be able to (for example) issue commands, or submit passive check results.

How to do it...

We can ensure proper authentication is in place for the Nagios Core web interface as follows:

1. Clear your browser of all cookies and saved authentication data, and try to visit the web interface. If your browser does not challenge you for a username or password as follows, then it's likely that your authentication is disabled or not working correctly:

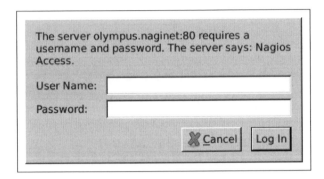

2. On the server, move to the Nagios Core configuration directory and open the `cgi.cfg` file. In the default installation, this is saved in `/usr/local/nagios/etc/cgi.cfg`.

    ```
    # cd /usr/local/nagios/etc
    # vi cgi.cfg
    ```

3. Ensure that the value for `use_authentication` is uncommented and set to 1:

    ```
    use_authentication=1
    ```

4. Ensure that the `default_user_name` directive is commented out:

    ```
    #default_user_name=guest
    ```

5. In the `nagios.conf` file in your Apache configuration, check that the following lines are included to refer to the `htpasswd.users` file:

    ```
    AuthName "Nagios Access"
    AuthType Basic
    AuthUserFile /usr/local/nagios/etc/htpasswd.users
    Require valid-user
    ```

    This file should be somewhere in the configuration directory for Apache, for example `/etc/apache/conf.d/nagios.conf`. If you need to make changes to Apache's configuration to fix this, you will need to restart Apache to have the changes take effect.

We can add a read-only user named `helpdesk` as follows:

1. Add the user to the `htpasswd.users` file using `htpasswd`, the Apache HTTPD password manager. Its location will vary depending on your system; common locations are `/usr/bin` and `/usr/local/apache/bin`.

   ```
   # htpasswd /usr/local/nagios/etc/htpasswd.users helpdesk
   New password:
   Re-type new password:
   Adding password for user helpdesk
   ```

   You may like to make the `htpasswd.users` file only readable by the web server user if you are concerned about the hashes being stolen by users on the system.

2. In `cgi.cfg`, uncomment the `authorized_for_read_only` directive and add the new `helpdesk` user to its value:

   ```
   authorized_for_read_only=helpdesk
   ```

3. Add the user to the values for the `authorized_for_all_services` and `authorized_for_all_hosts` directives:

   ```
   authorized_for_all_services=nagiosadmin,helpdesk
   authorized_for_all_hosts=nagiosadmin,helpdesk
   ```

   Be careful not to confuse these with the `authorized_for_all_service_commands` and `authorized_for_all_host_commands` directives.

You should not need to restart the Nagios Core server for these changes to take effect as you normally would with other `.cfg` files.

With this done, you should only be able to access the Nagios Core web interface with a valid username and password. The default `nagiosadmin` user created on installation should have full privileges, and the `helpdesk` user added in this recipe should be able to view host and service states, but will be unable to issue any commands such as rescheduling checks or submitting passive check results.

How it works...

It's important to note that it isn't actually Nagios Core itself prompting for the username and password and running the authentication check; this is a function performed by the web server, as specified in the `nagios.conf` file recommended for installation with Apache HTTPD.

After login, however, Nagios Core uses the permissions defined in the `cgi.cfg` file each time one of the CGI scripts in the web interface is accessed, to ensure that the user as authenticated with the web server has permissions to view the requested page, or execute the requested action.

We disable the `default_user_name` directive by commenting it out, because this specifies a user that Nagios Core will "assume" for users who access the CGIs without authenticating. This is a potentially dangerous setting and is best avoided in most circumstances, particularly with a server with publicly accessible addresses.

The following directives in `cgi.cfg` allow refining permissions for using the CGIs, to form a simple kind of access control list:

- ▶ `authorized_for_configuration_information`: The specified users are allowed to view configuration information for hosts in the web interface
- ▶ `authorized_for_system_information`: The specified users are allowed to view Nagios Core process and performance information
- ▶ `authorized_for_system_commands`: The specified users are allowed to run commands affecting the Nagios Core process, such as shutdowns and restarts
- ▶ `authorized_for_all_services`: The specified users are allowed to view status information and history for all services
- ▶ `authorized_for_all_hosts`: The specified users are allowed to view status information and history for all hosts
- ▶ `authorized_for_all_service_commands`: The specified users are allowed to run commands on all services, such as rescheduling checks or submitting passive check results
- ▶ `authorized_for_all_host_commands`: The specified users are allowed to run commands on all hosts, such as rescheduling checks or submitting passive check results

Further refining access per-service and per-host is done with authenticated contacts, demonstrated in the *Using authenticated contacts* recipe in this chapter. This is highly recommended for teams with mixed responsibilities that all require access to the same Nagios Core web interface.

There's more...

Besides authentication via Apache HTTPD, it's also often sensible to limit the IP addresses allowed access to the Nagios Core instance, using `Order` and `Allow` Apache directives. We could extend the `nagios.conf` file loaded by Apache as follows:

```
<Directory "/usr/local/nagios/sbin">
    Options ExecCGI
    AllowOverride None
    AuthName "Nagios Access"
    AuthType Basic
    AuthUserFile /usr/local/nagios/etc/htpasswd.users
```

```
    Require valid-user
    Order Allow,Deny
    Deny from all
    Allow from 127.0.0.0/16
    Allow from 10.128.0.1
</Directory>
```

This would only allow local addresses and `10.128.0.1` to access the CGIs, denying access with `403 Forbidden` to anyone else. Similarly, we could arrange to only allow connections over HTTPS, perhaps with an `SSLRequireSSL` directive; in general, we can configure Apache to carefully control even accessing the CGIs, let alone abusing them.

Note that none of this should take the place of an appropriate firewall solution and policy. A monitoring server should be protected as carefully as any other mission-critical server.

See also

- ▶ The *Using authenticated contacts* recipe in this chapter
- ▶ The *Viewing configuration in the web interface* and *Scheduling checks from the web interface* recipes in *Chapter 7, Working With the Web Interface*

Using authenticated contacts

In this recipe, we'll learn how to use authenticated contacts to refine our control of access to information in the Nagios Core web interface. This recipe is useful in situations where a particular user requires information on the status of certain hosts and services but should not be allowed to view others, a setup which can't be managed with the directives in `cgi.cfg`.

As a simple example, on a given monitoring server, we might have two hosts configured thus:

```
define host {
        use             linux-server
        host_name       sparta.naginet
        alias           sparta
        address         10.128.0.21
        contacts        nagiosadmin
}
define host {
        use             linux-server
        host_name       athens.naginet
        alias           athens
        address         10.128.0.22
        contacts        nagiosadmin
}
```

We might like to add a new user `athensadmin` with permissions to view the status of and run commands on the `athens.naginet` host and its services, but not the `sparta.naginet` host or its services.

Getting ready

You'll need access to the backend of a Nagios Core server with version 3.0 or greater, to change its configuration and restart it. You'll also need a functioning web interface with authentication running, and be familiar with how it works; the *Requiring authentication for the web interface* recipe in this chapter explains how to do this.

How to do it...

We can add an authenticated contact as follows:

1. Create a new user in the `htpasswd.users` file named `athensadmin`, using the `htpasswd` tool:

   ```
   # htpasswd /usr/local/nagios/etc/htpasswd.users athensadmin
   New password:
   Re-type new password:
   Adding password for user athensadmin
   ```

2. Log in to the Nagios Core web interface with the credentials you just added, and click on **Hosts** in the left menu to verify that you are not able to view any information yet:

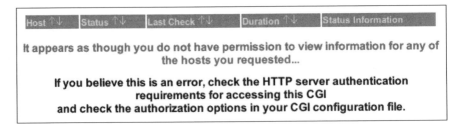

3. Back on the command line, change to the Nagios Core objects configuration directory. In the quick start guide installation, this is `/usr/local/nagios/etc/objects`.

   ```
   # cd /usr/local/nagios/etc/objects
   ```

4. Edit the `contacts.cfg` file to include a definition for a new contact object, `athensadmin`. Here, we've used the `generic-contact` template. You can use your own template or values if you prefer; the value for `contact_name` is the important part:

```
define contact {
        use             generic-contact
        contact_name    athensadmin
        alias           Athens Administrator
        email           athens@example.com
}
```

5. Edit the hosts or services to which you want to allow the `athensadmin` user
    access, and add `athensadmin` to its list of contacts. For our example, this means
    the definition for `athens.naginet` looks similar to the following code snippet:

```
define host {
        use             linux-server
        host_name       athens.naginet
        alias           athens
        address         10.128.0.22
        contacts        nagiosadmin,athensadmin
}
```

6. Validate the configuration and restart the Nagios Core server:

```
# /usr/local/nagios/bin/nagios -v /usr/local/nagios/etc/nagios.cfg
# /etc/init.d/nagios restart
```

With this done, logging in as the `athensadmin` user should allow you to view the details of
the `athens.naginet` host, but nothing else:

Host ↑↓	Status ↑↓	Last Check ↑↓	Duration ↑↓	Status Information
athens.naginet	UP	09-12-2012 22:13:10	0d 0h 1m 1s	PING OK - Packet loss = 0%, RTA = 0.37 ms

1 Matching Host Entries Displayed

You should also be able to issue commands related to that host, such as rescheduling checks
and acknowledging issues.

How it works...

When logging in as an authenticated user with Apache HTTPD, Nagios Core checks the
username to see if it matches the `contact_name` directive of any configured contacts.
If it does, then privileges to inspect the state of that contact's associated hosts and
services are granted, along with the ability to run commands on only those hosts and
services. The web interface otherwise works in just the same way. To the authenticated
contact, it appears as if no other hosts or services are being monitored.

If your network includes co-located equipment or teams with mixed monitoring responsibilities, this will allow you to restrict the Nagios Core interface to certain hosts for certain users. This can be very useful for confidentiality, transparency, and delegation purposes.

There's more...

If you want to allow an authenticated user read-only access to the details for their associated hosts or services, you can arrange that by adding their username to the values of the `authorized_for_read_only` directive in `cgi.cfg`:

```
authorized_for_read_only=athensadmin
```

The `athensadmin` user will then still be able to view the same host and service information, but will not be able to issue any commands:

> **Host Commands**
> Your account does not have permissions to execute commands.

See also

▸ The *Requiring authentication for the web interface* recipe in this chapter

▸ The *Creating a new contact* recipe in *Chapter 1, Understanding Hosts, Services, and Contacts*

Writing debugging information to a Nagios log file

In this recipe, we'll learn how to use the debugging log file in Nagios Core to get various kinds of process information from the running program, considerably more than available in the file specified by the standard `log_file` directive. This is useful not just for debugging purposes when Nagios Core is doing something unexpected at runtime, but also to get a better idea of how the server is working in general and with your particular configuration.

Getting ready

You will need a Nagios Core server with version 3.0 or greater. More debugging options are available in versions after 3.0, but these will be noted in the recipe. You will need access to change the `nagios.cfg` file and to restart the server.

In this example, we'll simply log everything we possibly can, and then explain how to refine the logging behavior if necessary in the *How it works...* section.

How to do it...

We can enable very verbose debugging for our monitoring server as follows:

1. Change to the configuration directory for Nagios Core. In the default installation, this is /usr/local/nagios/etc. Edit the file nagios.cfg:

    ```
    # cd /usr/local/nagios/etc
    # vi nagios.cfg
    ```

2. Look for the debug_level, debug_verbosity, and debug_file directives. Ensure they are uncommented or add them to the end of the file if they don't exist, and define them as follows:

    ```
    debug_level=-1
    debug_verbosity=2
    debug_file=/usr/local/nagios/var/nagios.debug
    ```

3. Validate the configuration and restart the Nagios Core server:

    ```
    # /usr/local/nagios/bin/nagios -v /usr/local/nagios/etc/nagios.cfg
    # /etc/init.d/nagios restart
    ```

With this done, the /usr/local/nagios/var/nagios.debug file should start filling with information about the running process quite quickly. You may find it instructive to watch it for a while with tail -f, which will show you the contents of the file as it updates:

```
# tail -f /usr/local/nagios/var/nagios.debug

[1347529967.839794] [008.2] [pid=14621] No events to execute at
the moment. Idling for a bit...

[1347529967.839799] [001.0] [pid=14621] check_for_external_
commands()

[1347529967.839805] [064.1] [pid=14621] Making callbacks (type
8)...

[1347529968.089971] [008.1] [pid=14621] ** Event Check Loop

[1347529968.090027] [008.1] [pid=14621] Next High Priority Event
Time: Thu Sep 13 21:52:52 2012

[1347529968.090038] [008.1] [pid=14621] Next Low Priority Event
Time:  Thu Sep 13 21:53:00 2012

...
```

How it works...

The `debug_level` directive specifies how much information (and of what kind) should be written to the debugging log. Here we've used the value `-1`, which is a shortcut for specifying that all debugging information should be written to the debugging log file.

In practice, however, we often only want to get information about particular kinds of Nagios Core tasks. In this case, we can use OR values for `debug_level` to specify which ones.

The different kinds of debugging information can be specified with the following numbers:

- ▶ `1`: Function enter and exit debugging
- ▶ `2`: Configuration debugging
- ▶ `4`: Process debugging
- ▶ `8`: Scheduled event debugging
- ▶ `16`: Host and service check debugging
- ▶ `32`: Notification debugging
- ▶ `64`: Event broker debugging

In version 3.3 and later of Nagios Core, the following can also be specified. There may be even more added in subsequent versions:

- ▶ `128`: External commands debugging
- ▶ `256`: Commands debugging
- ▶ `512`: Scheduled downtime debugging
- ▶ `1024`: Comments debugging
- ▶ `2048`: Macros debugging

Rather than comma-separating these values to specify more than one, they are added together. For example, if we wanted to save process and scheduled event debugging information and nothing else, we would use `4 + 8 = 12`:

```
debug_level=12
```

We can turn the debugging off completely by changing `debug_level` back to `0`, its default value.

There's more...

Nagios Core generates a great deal of information at the highest level of debugging, with over 30 lines per second even on minimal configurations, so be careful not to leave this running permanently if you don't always need it, as it can slowly fill a disk. You can avoid this situation by using the `max_debug_file_size` directive to specify a maximum size in bytes for the file. For example, to restrict the file to one megabyte, we could define the following:

```
max_debug_file_size=1000000
```

Nagios Core will "roll" an existing debugging log by adding the extension `.old` when it exceeds this size, and will start a new one. It will also automatically delete any previous logs with the `.old` extension when it does this.

See also

> ▸ The *Monitoring Nagios performance with Nagiostats* recipe in this chapter
> ▸ The *Viewing and interpreting notification history* recipe in *Chapter 7, Working With the Web Interface*

Monitoring Nagios performance with Nagiostats

In this recipe, we'll learn how to use the `nagiostats` utility to get some statistics about the performance of a Nagios Core process, and the states of the hosts and services that it monitors.

Optionally, we'll also show how to use the `mrtg.cfg` file built in the Nagios Core source distribution at `./configure` time to set up graphs built by `mrtg` (**Multi-Router Traffic Grapher**), and link to the graphs in the menu of the web interface. The Nagios Core source distribution includes some files to assist with this, which we'll use here.

Getting ready

You will need a Nagios Core 3.0 or newer server installed and running to invoke `nagiostats`. Older versions do include the utility, but there is not quite as much information returned.

If you would like to run the `mrtg` graphing as well, which is highly recommended, you should have `mrtg` and its helper program, `indexmaker`, installed on your system. If you are already graphing other things with `mrtg`, don't worry, this recipe should not interfere with that.

The recipe does not assume any familiarity with `mrtg`, but if you have any problems with it, you may like to consult its documentation online at `http://oss.oetiker.ch/mrtg/doc/index.en.html`.

You should also have access to the sources from which your installation of Nagios Core was compiled. If you need to retrieve the sources again, you can download them from the Nagios Core website (`http://www.nagios.org/`).

In this case, you will need to run `./configure` again to generate the file required, `sample-config/mrtg.cfg`.

How to do it...

We can invoke `nagiostats` itself in one step whenever we want to get some statistics about the server's performance:

1. Run the following command:

   ```
   # /usr/local/nagios/bin/nagiostats -c /usr/local/nagios/etc/
   nagios.cfg
   ```

   This should give you output beginning with the following:

   ```
   Nagios Stats 3.4.1

   Copyright (c) 2003-2008 Ethan Galstad (www.nagios.org)

   Last Modified: 05-11-2012

   License: GPL

   CURRENT STATUS DATA

   ------------------------------------------------------------
   Status File:                          /usr/local/nagios/var/
   status.dat
   Status File Age:                      0d 0h 0m 2s
   Status File Version:                  3.4.1
   Program Running Time:                 2d 2h 25m 23s
   Nagios PID:                           2487
   Used/High/Total Command Buffers:      0 / 0 / 4096
   Total Services:                       60
   Services Checked:                     60

   ...
   ```

2. Run the following command:

```
# /usr/local/nagios/bin/nagiostats -c /usr/local/nagios/etc/
nagios.cfg --help
```

This should give you a complete list of the names and meanings of all the fields returned by the output of `nagiostats`.

If you would like to include `mrtg` graphs of this data, a good starting point is using the sample configuration included in the Nagios Core source distribution, in `sample-config/mrtg.cfg`.

1. Copy `sample-config/mrtg.cfg` into `/usr/local/nagios/etc`:

```
# cp nagios-3.4.1/sample-config/mrtg.cfg /usr/local/nagios/etc
```

2. Create a directory to store the `mrtg` pages and graphs, so that they can be viewed in the Nagios Core web interface:

```
# mkdir /usr/local/nagios/share/stats
```

3. Edit `/usr/local/nagios/etc/mrtg.cfg` to include a `WorkDir` declaration at the top of the file:

```
WorkDir: /usr/local/nagios/share/stats
```

4. Run `mrtg` to create the graphs:

```
# mrtg /usr/local/nagios/etc/mrtg.cfg
```

For this first run, we can safely ignore any errors about missing prior data, or backup log files:

```
2012-09-16 17:01:04, Rateup WARNING: /usr/bin/rateup could not
read the primary log file for nagios-n

2012-09-16 17:01:04, Rateup WARNING: /usr/bin/rateup The backup
log file for nagios-n was invalid as well

2012-09-16 17:01:04, Rateup WARNING: /usr/bin/rateup Can't remove
nagios-n.old updating log file

2012-09-16 17:01:04, Rateup WARNING: /usr/bin/rateup Can't rename
nagios-n.log to nagios-n.old updating log file
```

If you are using a UTF-8 locale in your shell, `mrtg` may fail to run. You can run it in a standard C locale with an `env` prefix:

```
# env LANG=C mrtg /usr/local/nagios/etc/mrtg.cfg
```

5. Run the `indexmaker` helper installed with `mrtg` to create an index to the graphs:

```
# indexmaker /usr/local/nagios/etc/mrtg.cfg --output=/usr/local/
nagios/share/stats/index.html
```

You should only need to do this once, unless you add or remove graph definitions from `mrtg.cfg` later on.

6. Visit `http://olympus.naginet/nagios/stats`, substituting your own Nagios Core server's hostname for `olympus.naginet`. After authenticating (if necessary), we should be able to see some empty `mrtg` graphs:

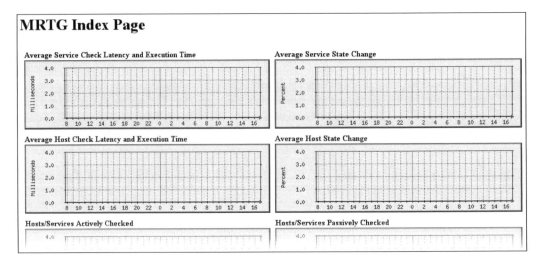

Don't worry that they're empty; we expect that, as we only have one data point for each graph at the moment.

7. If everything has worked up to this point, we can probably add a `cron` task to run every five minutes to add new data points to the graph. Here, we are assuming the `mrtg` program is saved in `/usr/bin`:

```
*/5 * * * *   root   /usr/bin/mrtg /usr/local/nagios/etc/mrtg.cfg
```

The best way to do this will vary between systems. You could put this in `/etc/crontab`, or in its own file in `/etc/cron.d/nagiostats` if you want to be a little tidier.

It is probably safe to leave it running as `root`, but if you are concerned about this, you should also be able to run it as the `nagios` user by including a `--lock-file` option:

```
*/5 * * * *   nagios   /usr/bin/mrtg --lock-file=/usr/local/nagios/
var/mrtg.cfg.lock /usr/local/nagios/etc/mrtg.cfg
```

That might require correcting permissions on the graphs already generated:

```
# chown -R nagios.nagios /usr/local/nagios/share/stats
```

With this done, if the `cron` task is installed correctly, we should start seeing data being plotted over the next few hours:

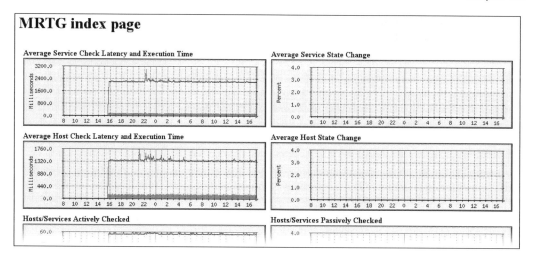

How it works...

The statistics provided by `nagiostats` provide both performance data about Nagios Core itself, how long it's taking to complete its round of checks of all objects and the average time it's taking per check, as well as data such as the number of hosts in various states. By default, running it will return the data in a terse but human-readable format; you can get a good idea of the meaning of each of the fields by running it with `--help` as suggested in the recipe.

The `mrtg.cfg` file included in the Nagios source distribution, which is tailored to your particular system at `./configure` time, contains example definitions of `mrtg` graphs that parse the data retrieved from `nagiostats`. These are not the only possible graphs using the information provided by `nagiostats`, but they are useful examples.

The data used is the same as the data you read if you invoked `nagiostats` from the shell, but the format is slightly different. If you want to see the data being passed to `mrtg` by `nagiostats`, you can run it with the `--mrtg` option and nominate fields to be included in the output with `--data`; for example:

```
# /usr/local/nagios/bin/nagiostats -c /usr/local/nagios/etc/nagios.cfg
--mrtg --data=AVGACTSVCPSC,AVGPSVSVCPSC,PROGRUNTIME,NAGIOSVERPID
0

0

1d 2h 43m 43s

Nagios 3.4.1 (pid=1080)
```

The recipe's call to `indexmaker` is a separate program that builds an `index.html` file with links to all the graphs, just for convenience. Like the `mrtg` call, it refers to the configuration file `/usr/local/nagios/etc/mrtg.cfg` to figure out what it needs to do.

There's more...

Once you're happy with the way your graph's web pages are being displayed, you might like to consider including them in your Nagios Core sidebar. This can be done by editing `/usr/local/nagios/share/side.php`, and adding a new link to the **System** section, perhaps named **Performance Reports**, below the **Performance Info** link. The new line might look similar to the following code snippet:

```
<li><a href="/nagios/stats/" target="<?php echo $link_
target;?>">Performance Reports</a></li>
```

This would make a link to the graphs show up in the web interface as follows:

Note that customizations to the menu like this will be overwritten if you reinstall Nagios Core.

If you like what `mrtg` does with this data, you might like to look at **Cacti**, a very helpful frontend to `rrdtool`, which is similar to `mrtg`. It will allow you a lot of flexibility in defining graphs, although it takes a while to learn (`http://www.cacti.net/`).

If you're interested in more graphing for Nagios Core performance and state data you may like the Nagiosgraph extension, which is discussed in the *Tracking host and service states with NagiosGraph* recipe in *Chapter 11, Automating and Extending Nagios*.

Finally, note that Nagios Core includes some built-in graphing of hosts and states in its reports, so be sure to check those out as well before you try to build a graph for a report that already exists! These are all also discussed in *Chapter 7, Working With the Web Interface*. Check out the references in the *See also* section for this recipe.

See also

▶ The *Using the tactical overview, Viewing and interpreting availability reports, Viewing and interpreting trends*, and *Viewing and interpreting notification history* recipes in *Chapter 7, Working With the Web Interface*

▶ The *Tracking host and service states with Nagiosgraph* recipe in *Chapter 11, Automating and Extending Nagios*

Improving startup times with pre-cached object files

In this recipe, we'll learn how to shorten startup times for large and/or complex Nagios Core configurations. This is done by pre-caching the Nagios Core objects from the configuration, applying all appropriate template and group expansions into a single file that Nagios Core can read much more quickly than a more modular and human-readable configuration.

This will likely only be of interest to you if you are monitoring more than a hundred hosts or services with a reasonably complex template and grouping layout, as suggested by some of the recipes in *Chapter 1* and *Chapter 9*. It will still work on smaller installations, but the gains in startup speed are likely to be minimal.

If you are only running a small setup, then this recipe might be of interest if you want to better understand how Nagios Core expands a configuration that uses a lot of templates and other configuration tricks.

Getting ready

You should be running a Nagios Core 3.0 or newer server, and have access to the server to change its configuration.

You should check that the `precached_object_file` directive in `/usr/local/nagios/etc/nagios.cfg` is uncommented and defined to an accessible file. The setting in the Quick Start configuration is sensible:

```
precached_object_file=/usr/local/nagios/var/objects.precache
```

Having this directive uncommented doesn't actually generate or use the pre-cached objects file; that needs to be done explicitly, as will be explained in the recipe.

Don't confuse this with the `object_cache_file` directive in the same file, which should be left untouched at its current setting.

For this example, we'll use a fairly large configuration with some 20,000 objects defined on a rather slow machine.

How to do it...

We can get some idea of possible performance improvement from using pre-cached object files as follows:

1. Run `nagios` with the `-s` option, and inspect the output. This will print a profile of the processes normally involved in building complete object definitions from the configuration files.

    ```
    # /usr/local/nagios/bin/nagios -s /usr/local/nagios/etc/nagios.cfg
    ```

    In this case, we're particularly interested in the sections of output marked with asterisks, in the section titled OBJECT CONFIG PROCESSING TIMES, which denote times that could be improved by pre-cached object files, including an estimate of the saved time at the end of the TOTAL field:

    ```
    OBJECT CONFIG PROCESSING TIMES        (* = Potential for precache
    savings with -u option)

    ------------------------------------

    Read:                  8.285613 sec

    Resolve:               0.001696 sec   *

    Recomb Contactgroups:  0.000124 sec   *

    Recomb Hostgroups:     1.972412 sec   *

    Dup Services:          0.309333 sec   *

    Recomb Servicegroups:  0.000029 sec   *

    Duplicate:             0.000168 sec   *

    Inherit:               0.102685 sec   *

    Recomb Contacts:       0.000001 sec   *

    Sort:                  0.000000 sec   *

    Register:              0.826046 sec

    Free:                  0.102805 sec

                           ============

    TOTAL:                 11.600912 sec   * = 2.386448 sec (20.57%)
    estimated savings
    ```

    We might decide that 2.3 seconds is a worthwhile saving from our restart time. Perhaps we really don't want to miss any important checks!

2. Run `nagios` with the `-p` and `-v` options, to verify the configuration and also write a pre-cached object file:

    ```
    # /usr/local/nagios/bin/nagios -pv /usr/local/nagios/etc/nagios.
    cfg
    ```

3. Run `nagios` with the `-u` and `-s` options to see how long the startup and scheduling test takes when instructed to use the pre-cached object file:

    ```
    # /usr/local/nagios/bin/nagios -us /usr/local/nagios/etc/nagios.
    cfg
    ```

4. We may note that the TOTAL time taken is now significantly less (even more of an improvement than estimated), and that many of the times are now zero seconds, as Nagios Core did not have to do that step at all:

```
OBJECT CONFIG PROCESSING TIMES        (* = Potential for precache
savings with -u option)
-----------------------------------
Read:                   4.975257 sec
Resolve:                0.000000 sec  *
Recomb Contactgroups:   0.000000 sec  *
Recomb Hostgroups:      0.000000 sec  *
Dup Services:           0.000000 sec  *
Recomb Servicegroups:   0.000000 sec  *
Duplicate:              0.000000 sec  *
Inherit:                0.000000 sec  *
Recomb Contacts:        0.000000 sec  *
Sort:                   0.000000 sec  *
Register:               0.828953 sec
Free:                   0.000758 sec
                        ============
TOTAL:                  5.804968 sec
```

With this done, we should find that restarting Nagios Core with both the `-d` and the `-u` flags should be faster than before. This can be incorporated into any startup scripts (for example, `/etc/init.d/nagios`). It also means that if we make changes to the configuration, we must remember to run `nagios -pv` again to validate and regenerate the pre-cached object file.

How it works...

When run with the `-p` option, Nagios Core parses the configuration as normal into objects with which it can work, expanding out the `hostgroups`, `templates`, and other configuration shortcuts. It writes this information into a single file as specified by the `precached_object_file` directive.

The configuration file is human-readable; if you view it in a text editor, you'll see the expanded definitions that have been built from your configuration, with all of the object inheritance, regular expression hostgroups, and multi-host service definitions expanded.

When next restarted, Nagios Core can be instructed to use this file instead of re-parsing the configuration all over again by including the `-u` option. You may need to incorporate this in any `init.d` scripts you are using.

There's more...

If you don't really have speed problems on Nagios Core restarting, it's best to avoid making this permanent, as it adds another layer of complexity to building configuration; if you forget to rebuild the pre-cached object file after making configuration changes and before restarting Nagios Core, it will continue using the previous configuration, not realizing the difference. Use this with caution!

See also

▶ The *Running a service on all hosts in a group* recipe in *Chapter 1, Understanding Hosts, Services, and Contacts*

▶ The *Configuring host roles using groups* and the *Using inheritance to simplify configuration* recipes in *Chapter 9, Configuration Management*

Setting up a redundant monitoring host

In this recipe, we'll learn how to implement a simple kind of redundancy for Nagios Core, by running a second Nagios Core instance with a near-identical configuration on another machine.

This may seem like it would not need a recipe to implement. It should be reasonably straightforward to simply copy over the configuration for a Nagios Core system and run it concurrently. There are two main problems with this:

▶ Every problem detected on the network will fire notifications events twice. The administrator charged with looking after the pager might well find this unbearable!

▶ Everything will be checked twice. On smaller networks with simple checks, this may not be too much of a concern, but it could be an issue on larger, busier networks.

This recipe will solve the first problem by configuring the slave monitoring server to suppress notifications until it detects an issue with the master server. In the *There's more...* section, we'll discuss extending this solution to solve the second problem as well, by preventing the slave server from making checks as well as sending notifications while the master server is active.

Getting ready

This is the most complex recipe in this book, and one of the longest, tying in concepts from many other recipes and chapters. To follow it, you will likely need to have a good working knowledge of the following:

- ▶ The building blocks of Nagios Core hosts, services, contacts, commands, plugins, and notifications explained in all recipes in Chapters 1 through 4.
- ▶ Remote execution via `check_nrpe` explained in all recipes in *Chapter 6, Enabling Remote Execution*. The recipe will at one point tell you to install NRPE on the master server to run a specific plugin, so you should learn how to do this first.
- ▶ Event handlers and writing to the command file with them, explained in the *Setting up an event handler script* recipe in *Chapter 11*.

The event handler scripts, the most complex part of this setup, are fortunately already written for us; we'll show how to implement them by copying them out of the Nagios Core source package. You'll therefore need to have the sources available for your particular version of Nagios Core. If you need to retrieve the sources again, you can download them again from Nagios Core's website at `http://www.nagios.org/`.

The recipe will start by assuming we have two monitoring servers: `olympus.naginet` (`10.128.0.11`), which will be the master monitoring server, and `everest.naginet` (`10.128.0.12`), which will be the slave. The two servers are configured to monitor the same three hosts, with PING service checks:

- ▶ `sparta.naginet`
- ▶ `athens.naginet`
- ▶ `ithaca.naginet`

The Nagios Core configuration of the two servers is completely identical to start with, and both are sending notifications to an appropriate contact group. However, note that the servers are not yet monitoring one another; this will be an important part of the recipe.

How to do it...

We can arrange a simple redundancy setup for our two Nagios Core servers as follows:

1. Confirm that the `check_nagios` plugin is available on the `master` server, and try running it:

   ```
   # cd /usr/local/nagios/libexec

   # ./check_nagios -e 5 -F /usr/local/nagios/var/status.dat -C
   /usr/local/nagios/bin/nagios

   NAGIOS OK: 1 process, status log updated 3 seconds ago
   ```

2. Install the NRPE daemon on the master server, and define a command `check_nagios` in `nrpe.cfg` (see *Chapter 6*).

```
command[check_nagios]=/usr/local/nagios/libexec/check_nagios -e
5 -F /usr/local/nagios/var/status.dat -C /usr/local/nagios/bin/
nagios
```

3. Include the slave server's address in the `allowed_hosts` directive for `nrpe`, in the file `/usr/local/nagios/etc/nrpe.cfg`:

```
allowed_hosts=127.0.0.1,10.128.0.12
```

Don't forget to restart NRPE to include this change to the configuration.

4. On the slave server, verify that a call to `check_nrpe` can retrieve the results of `check_nagios` on the master server:

```
# cd /usr/local/nagios/libexec
# ./check_nrpe -H olympus.naginet
NRPE v2.13
# ./check_nrpe -H olympus.naginet -c check_nagios
NAGIOS OK: 1 process, status log updated 2 seconds ago
```

You will have to install the `check_nrpe` plugin on the slave server to do this. This is explained in the *Monitoring local services on a remote machine with NRPE* recipe in *Chapter 6*.

5. On the slave server, copy four files (two event handlers and two helper scripts) from the source distribution into the `/usr/local/nagios/libexec/eventhandlers` directory (which you may need to create first):

```
# EHD=/usr/local/nagios/libexec/eventhandlers
# mkdir -p $EHD
# cd /usr/local/src/nagios
# cp contrib/eventhandlers/enable_notifications $EHD
# cp contrib/eventhandlers/disable_notifications $EHD
# cp contrib/eventhandlers/redundancy-scenario1/handle-master-
host-event $EHD
# cp contrib/eventhandlers/redundancy-scenario1/handle-master-
proc-event $EHD
```

The preceding command assumes you are keeping the sources for your Nagios Core distribution in `/usr/local/src`. We define and use the shell variable `$EHD` to refer to the event handlers directory for convenience.

6. In the installed `handle-master-proc-event` script, find and replace `active_service_checks` with `notifications`. The command line tool `sed` works well for this:

```
# sed -i 's/active_service_checks/notifications/g' $EHD/handle-master-proc-event
```

This is because the script as provided issues a command to toggle active checks, rather than notifications. At the time of writing, in Nagios 3.3.1 there is also a bug in `handle-master-proc-event` that may need to be corrected, on line 49:

```
`eventhandlerdir/disable_active_service_checks`
```

It should have a dollar sign added after the first backtick:

```
`$eventhandlerdir/disable_active_service_checks`
```

7. Ensure the event handlers are owned and executable by the `nagios` user:

```
# chown nagios.nagios $EHD/*
```

```
# chmod 0755 $EHD/*
```

8. In `/usr/local/nagios/etc/objects/commands.cfg`, define two new event handler commands:

```
define command {
    command_name    handle-master-host-event
    command_line    $USER1$/eventhandlers/handle-master-host-event
$HOSTSTATE$ $HOSTSTATETYPE$ $HOSTATTEMPT$
}
define command {
    command_name    handle-master-proc-event
    command_line    $USER1$/eventhandlers/handle-master-proc-event
$SERVICESTATE$ $SERVICESTATETYPE$ $SERVICEATTEMPT$
}
```

9. Make a host and service definition on the slave server to monitor the master server. It might look something similar to the following code snippet; change your `host_name`, `alias`, and `address` values as appropriate. The templates used are only examples; you will probably want to choose templates that are defined to run checks often, and during a 24x7 interval.

```
define host {
    use             critical-host-template
    host_name       olympus.naginet
    alias           olympus
    address         10.128.0.11
    event_handler   handle-master-host-event
}
```

```
define service {
    use                  critical-service-template
    host_name            olympus.naginet
    service_description  NAGIOS
    check_command        check_nrpe!check_nagios
    event_handler        handle-master-proc-event
}
```

You can make the master server monitor the slave server as well if you wish.

10. Note that you will need to have the check_nrpe command defined, which the *Monitoring local services on a remote machine with NRPE* recipe in *Chapter 6* explains. If you have followed that recipe then you have probably already done this. If not, the following definition works:

```
define command {
    command_name  check_nrpe
    command_line  $USER1$/check_nrpe -H $HOSTADDRESS$ -c $ARG1$
}
```

11. Finally, in nagios.cfg on the slave server, change enable_notifications to 0:

```
enable_notifications=0
```

12. Validate the configuration and restart the Nagios Core server:

```
# /usr/local/nagios/bin/nagios -v /usr/local/nagios/etc/nagios.cfg
# /etc/init.d/nagios restart
```

With this done, the two Nagios Core servers should both be running, but importantly, notifications on the slave server start out as disabled, as visible in the **Tactical Overview**:

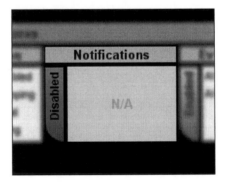

However, all the systems are still being monitored, as visible in the **Services** screen, including the **NAGIOS** service on the host machine:

Host ↑↓	Service ↑↓	Status ↑↓
athens.naginet	PING	OK
ithaca.naginet	PING	OK
olympus.naginet	NAGIOS	OK
sparta.naginet	PING	OK

This means that notifications will only be sent by the master server, since it still has its notifications enabled. However, if the master server goes down or its Nagios process stops working, the event handlers should be called, and notifications on the slave server will be automatically enabled. When the master server or its NAGIOS service comes back up, the notifications will be disabled again, with checks and state changes having continued uninterrupted throughout. We have therefore established a simple kind of redundancy. If you use this setup, you should test it thoroughly to make sure that the slave Nagios Core server will enable and disable its notifications for each contingency (host goes down, service goes down, service comes back, and so on.)

How it works...

The event handlers included in the Nagios Core distribution, which we copied into the eventhandlers directory, are designed to handle toggling notifications and active checks based on the status of a given service or host. They are included for the purposes of demonstrating event handlers and redundancy situations like this one.

We start by setting up the slave server to monitor not just the host on which the master Nagios Core server is running, but also the Nagios Core service itself, using the check_nagios plugin. This plugin checks the age of the log file and the system's process tables to ensure that a Nagios Core service is actually running on the system. Because it's a local plugin that doesn't work for remote checks, we check it from the slave server via NRPE.

The slave server checks the status of the master server and its NAGIOS service as part of its normal routine of active checks. When the master server's host or its NAGIOS service change state, both call their respective event handlers, the two shell scripts handle-master-host-event and handle-master-proc-event, defined in the commands of the same name.

Each time the event handlers are called, they are passed three arguments, in macro form. For `handle-master-host-event`, these are:

- ▸ `$HOSTSTATE$`: This is the new state of the master server
- ▸ `$HOSTSTATETYPE$`: This specifies whether the state is SOFT or HARD
- ▸ `$HOSTATTEMPT$`: This is the number of host checks attempted, up to the value of `max_check_attempts` for the host

`handle-master-proc-event` is passed three analogous arguments, the only difference being they refer to service states rather than host states:

- ▸ `$SERVICESTATE$`: This is the new state of the NAGIOS service on the master server
- ▸ `$SERVICESTATETYPE$`: This specifies whether the service state is SOFT or HARD
- ▸ `$SERVICEATTEMPT$`: This is the number of host checks attempted, up to the value of `max_check_attempts` for the host

The event handlers are written in such a way that they only do anything if the new state is HARD; that is, if the number of `max_check_attempts` has been reached. It ignores SOFT state changes until enough consecutive checks have failed that it can be reasonably confident in concluding that the monitored host or service is suffering a problem.

If the host or service enters a HARD CRITICAL state, the event handlers call the helper script `enable-notifications` to write a command to the `commands` file at `/usr/local/nagios/var/rw/nagios.cmd` for the server to process. This command takes the following form, including the UNIX timestamp for when the command was written:

`[1348129155] ENABLE_NOTIFICATIONS;1348129155`

When Nagios Core processes this command, the effect is that the previously disabled notifications are enabled, and all subsequent notifications generated as a result of checks will be sent.

Similarly, when the host or service recovers from the HARD CRITICAL state, entering a HARD UP or HARD OK state, the `disable-notifications` helper script is called, writing a command in the same manner:

`[1348129231] DISABLE_NOTIFICATIONS;1348129231`

The effect is that when the master server is noted to be down, the slave server notices and assumes its notification behavior, and when it recovers, it stops its own notifications again, allowing the master server to resume its role.

There's more...

If network bandwidth is a concern, we can arrange to leave the slave server more or less idle when not in use, by keeping not only notifications but also service checks off by default. Helper scripts for this are also included in the Nagios Core distribution, in the `disable_active_service_checks` and `enable_active_service_checks` scripts.

The primary issue with this change is the loss of state information as the slave server makes its initial round of checks; this can also be worked around, as explained in the Nagios Core documentation on redundancy at `http://nagios.sourceforge.net/docs/3_0/redundancy.html`.

Once these steps are implemented, the main annoyance with this setup is having to keep the two configuration directories in sync. It's undesirable and error-prone to have to make changes on two servers each time the configuration needs to change, so you may like to consider using a snapshot tool such as `rsync` to keep the two directories the same. More information about `rsync` can be found at `http://en.wikipedia.org/wiki/Rsync`.

A configuration managed with version control is also help here, as recommended in the *Keeping configuration under version control* recipe in *Chapter 9*. That way you can use `git clone` or `svn checkout` to quickly copy and update configuration files on multiple machines.

See also

- ▶ The *Writing debugging information to Nagios log file* recipe in this chapter
- ▶ The *Monitoring local services on a remote machine with NRPE* recipe in *Chapter 6, Enabling Remote Execution*
- ▶ The *Keeping configuration under version control* recipe in *Chapter 9, Configuration Management*
- ▶ The *Setting up an event handler script* recipe in *Chapter 11, Automating and Extending Nagios*

11
Automating and Extending Nagios Core

In this chapter, we will cover the following recipes:

- ▶ Allowing and submitting passive checks
- ▶ Submitting passive checks from a remote host with NSCA
- ▶ Submitting passive checks in response to SNMP traps
- ▶ Setting up an event handler script
- ▶ Tracking host and service states with Nagiosgraph
- ▶ Reading status into a MySQL database with NDOUtils
- ▶ Writing customized Nagios Core reports
- ▶ Getting extra visualizations with NagVis

Introduction

In addition to being useful as a standalone monitoring framework, Nagios Core has a modular design that allows both interaction with and extension by other programs and tools, predominantly using its external command file for controlling the behavior of the server.

One of the most useful ways of interacting with the Nagios Core server in this way is through the use of passive checks: submitting check results to the server directly, rather than as the result of the server's own active checks.

The simplest application of the idea of passive checks is for monitoring some process that might take an indeterminate amount of time to run, and hence resists active checking; instead of the service making active checks of its own, it accepts a check result submitted by another application, perhaps something like a backup script after it has completed its run. These can be sent and accepted via an addon called the **Nagios Service Check Acceptor** (**NSCA**). Similarly, just as plugins and notifications are actually scripted calls to external commands, such as `check_http`, and `mail`, event handlers can be configured to run a specified command every time a host or service changes state. This can be used for the supplementary recording of change state data, or automated attempts at actively resolving the problem, such as restarting a remote server. We also saw event handlers used in the *Setting up a redundant monitoring host* recipe in *Chapter 10, Security and Performance*.

Finally, this chapter also includes installation procedures and discussion of a few of the more popular extensions to Nagios Core:

- ▶ **Nagiosgraph**: This is an advanced web-based graphing solution for Nagios Core, graphing both server performance and host and service status metrics.
- ▶ **NagVis**: This is an advanced web-based visualization extension for Nagios Core data, especially well-suited for administrators who need something more comprehensive than Nagios Core's built-in networking mapping.
- ▶ **NDOUtils**: This applies the translations of Nagios Core data into a standard database system such as MySQL; very useful for performing advanced queries of the Nagios Core data for custom systems such as monitoring displays, or logging with change control systems.

We'll discuss NDOUtils, perhaps the most versatile Nagios Core extension of all, in two separate recipes; first by showing how to install it, and then some ideas on how to apply it to make custom Nagios Core reporting applications of our own, in the form of a **CLI report** written in **Perl**, and an **RSS feed** written in **PHP**.

Allowing and submitting passive checks

In this recipe, we'll learn how to configure Nagios Core to accept passive checks for a service. This allows both users and external applications to directly submit the results of checks to Nagios Core, rather than having the application seek them out itself through polling with active checks, performed via plugins such as `check_http` or `check_ping`.

We'll show one simple example of a passive check, flagging a service called BACKUP for an existing host. We'll show how to do this via the web interface, which is very easy, and via the external commands file, which is slightly more complex but much more flexible and open to automation.

The idea is that when a user or process receives confirmation that the backup process on a host has completed correctly, they are able to supply a check result of OK directly to the service, without Nagios Core needing to poll anything itself.

Getting ready

You should be running a Nagios Core 3.0 or newer server. You should also already have a host configured for which you want to define a service that will accept passive checks. In this example, we'll use the host `ithaca.naginet`, which might be defined as follows:

```
define host {
    use          linux-server
    host_name    ithaca.naginet
    alias        ithaca
    address      10.128.0.21
}
```

You will also need a working Nagios Core web interface to check that passive checks are enabled, and to try out the recipe's method of submitting passive checks.

The recipe will be in two parts: enabling and configuring the service for passive checks only, and actually submitting a passive check via the web interface. In the *There's more...* section, we'll show how to submit a check result via the external commands file, which is a little more complicated, but allows advanced automation behavior.

How to do it...

We can define a new BACKUP service that accepts passive checks only, as follows:

1. Log in to the web interface and ensure that passive checks are enabled. The **Tactical Overview** section shows a panel for it near the bottom. Check that it's green:

If it's not green, you should be able to enable the checks again by clicking on the **Disabled** bar. In this case, you should also check the /usr/local/nagios/etc/ nagios.cfg file to make sure that the accept_passive_service_checks option is set to 1 as well, so that Nagios Core allows passive checks on startup.

2. Change to the Nagios Core objects configuration directory. If you're using the sample configuration, this will likely be /usr/local/nagios/etc/objects.

    ```
    # cd /usr/local/nagios/etc/objects
    ```

3. Edit the `commands.cfg` file, and add a definition for the `check_dummy` command:

```
define command {
        command_name    check_dummy
        command_line    $USER1$/check_dummy $ARG1$ $ARG2$
}
```

If you already followed the *Monitoring individual nodes in a cluster* recipe in *Chapter 8, Understanding the Network Layout*, then you may already have defined this command, in which case you can skip this step, as the definition is the same.

4. Edit the file containing the definition for the existing host. In this example, the host is defined in a file called `ithaca.naginet.cfg`.

```
# vi ithaca.naginet.cfg
```

5. Add the following service definition to the end of the file, substituting the appropriate value for `host_name`.

```
define service {
        use                      generic-service
        host_name                ithaca.naginet
        service_description      BACKUP
        active_checks_enabled    0
        passive_checks_enabled   1
        check_command            check_dummy!1!"Unwanted active check!"
}
```

This example uses the `generic-service` template. You can use any service template you like; the important directives are `active_checks_enabled`, `passive_checks_enabled`, and `check_command`.

6. Validate the configuration and restart the Nagios Core server:

```
# /usr/local/nagios/bin/nagios -v /usr/local/nagios/etc/nagios.cfg
# /etc/init.d/nagios restart
```

With this done, the Nagios Core web interface should show the service as accepting passive checks only in the **Services** listing:

Host ↑	Service ↑	Status ↑	Last Check ↑	Duration ↑	Attempt ↑
ithaca.naginet	BACKUP	PENDING	N/A	0d 0h 1m 36s+	1/3
	HTTP	Active checks of the service have been disabled - only passive checks are being accepted			
	PING	OK	09-28-2012 16:07:34	0d 0h 43m 44s	1/3

It will remain in the `PENDING` state until a passive check result is submitted for it.

We can submit a passive check result via the web interface as follows:

1. Click on the service's name in the **Services** listing, and click on **Submit passive check result for this service** menu item:

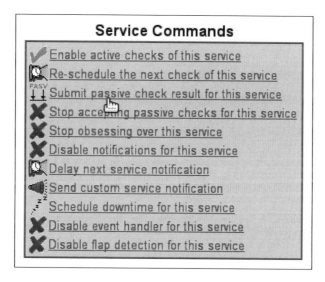

2. Complete the resulting form, with the following values:

    ❑   **Host Name**: This is the host name for which the passive check result should be submitted. This should already be filled out for us.

    ❑   **Service**: This is the service description for which the passive check result should be submitted. This should also already be filled out with `BACKUP`.

    ❑   **Check Result**: This is the particular result you would like to submit for the check. In this case, we choose `OK` to signal that the backup completed successfully. We could just as easily submit a `CRITICAL` result if we wished.

    ❑   **Check Output**: This is a message to attach to the status. In this case, we choose the simple message **Nightly backups were successful**.

    ❑   **Performance Data**: This is the optional extra detail about how the service being checked is performing. We can leave this blank.

3. Click on **Commit** to submit the passive check result:

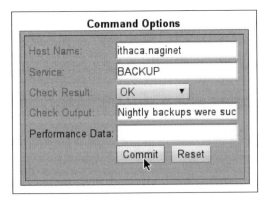

After a short delay, the detail for the service should show it as reflecting the result of the passive check, along with explicitly showing that active checks are disabled:

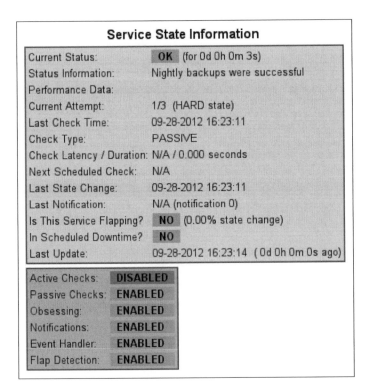

How it works...

The configuration added in the preceding section adds a new service called BACKUP to the existing `ithaca.naginet` host, and is designed to manage and report the status of backups for this host. In our example, this isn't something Nagios Core can check manually; no network service on `ithaca.naginet` can be checked to see if the backups have succeeded.

However, suppose as administrators we do receive a backup report in our inbox every morning, so we know whether the backups have succeeded or failed and would like to register that status in Nagios Core, perhaps for record-keeping purposes or to alert other administrators to problems.

To that end, we disable active checks for the service, and put in place a dummy check command, `check_dummy`, which we never expect to run. If for whatever reason an active check is run, it will always flag a WARNING state, with the message **Unwanted active check!**. The `check_dummy` command never actually checks anything; it is configured to always return the state and output defined in its two arguments.

Instead, we enable passive checks for the service and submit the results manually. If the backups failed, we could just as easily record that with a passive check result of WARNING or CRITICAL.

There's more...

It's also possible (and often desirable) to submit active checks via the external commands file, which is useful for automation purposes. We write details for the check in a single line into the commands file in the following format:

```
[<timestamp>] PROCESS_SERVICE_CHECK_RESULT;<host_name>;<service_
description>;<service_status>;<plugin_output>
```

For our example, the line would be similar to the following code snippet:

```
[1348806599] PROCESS_SERVICE_CHECK_RESULT;ithaca.
naginet;BACKUP;0;Nightly backups were successful
```

We can write this directly to the external commands file as follows:

```
# CHECK="[`date +%s`] PROCESS_SERVICE_CHECK_RESULT;ithaca.
naginet;BACKUP;0;Nightly backups were successful"
# echo $CHECK >>/usr/local/nagios/var/rw/nagios.cmd
```

In this context, the `<service_status>` field needs to be an integer corresponding to the appropriate state. If you use the text value OK or WARNING, the command will not work as expected.

- ▶ 0 for OK
- ▶ 1 for WARNING
- ▶ 2 for CRITICAL
- ▶ 3 for UNKNOWN

If the syntax is correct, then the passive check will be registered just the same way as if it were submitted via the web interface. Writing to the command file thus allows us to submit passive check results with scripts and automated systems, with a little knowledge of an appropriate shell scripting language such as Bash or Perl.

We go into a little more detail about using external commands for passive check results, including a common application with the NSCA add-on, in the *Submitting passive checks from a remote host with NSCA* recipe in this chapter. If you don't want to input your passive checks manually, then you will most likely find this recipe of interest, along with its accompanying explanation of freshness checks.

See also

- ▶ The *Submitting passive checks from a remote host with NSCA*, *Submitting passive checks in response to SNMP traps*, and *Setting up an event handler script* recipes in this chapter

Submitting passive checks from a remote host with NSCA

In this recipe, we'll show how to automate the submission of passive checks by a remote host, using the example of a monitored host, `ithaca.naginet`, submitting a passive check to a Nagios Core server with information about how its BACKUP service is performing.

For example, if the backup process completed successfully, we configure the monitored host to submit a passive check result specifying that the BACKUP service should have the status OK. However, if there were a problem with the backup, the monitored host could send a passive check result with a WARNING or CRITICAL status.

In both cases, Nagios Core does no checking of its own; it trusts the results submitted by its target host.

To do this, we'll use the NSCA add-on. We'll install the NSCA server on the Nagios Core server, and the NSCA client program `send_nsca` on the monitored host.

Getting ready

You should already have followed the *Allowing and submitting passive checks* recipe in this chapter. In this recipe, we will be building on the configuration established in that recipe; specifically, we will assume that you already have a host with a service configured only to accept passive checks.

You will need to be able to install the software on both the monitoring server (the NSCA server) and on the server that will submit passive checks (the NSCA client), and ideally be generally familiar with the `./configure`, `make`, and `make install` process for installing software from source on UNIX-like systems.

You should also be able to define any necessary firewall configuration to allow the NSCA client to send information to TCP port `5667` on the NSCA server. A firewall is absolutely necessary to protect the `nsca` daemon from abuse.

How to do it...

We can set up the NSCA server on the monitoring server (in this example, `olympus.naginet`) as follows:

1. Download the latest version of NSCA using `wget` or a similar tool. You can find download links on the Nagios Exchange page for NSCA at `http://exchange.nagios.org/directory/Addons/Passive-Checks/NSCA--2D-Nagios-Service-Check-Acceptor/details`.

    In this example, we're downloading and compiling it in our home directory on the monitoring server.

    ```
    $ cd
    $ wget http://downloads.sourceforge.net/project/nagios/nsca-2.x/
    nsca-2.7.2/nsca-2.7.2.tar.gz
    ```

2. Inflate the `.tar.gz` file:

    ```
    $ tar -xzf nsca-2.7.2.tar.gz
    ```

3. Move into the new `nsca-2.7.2` directory, and configure and compile the `nsca` daemon. Note that this process may prompt you to install the `libmcrypt` library and its headers, perhaps in `libmcrypt` and `libmcrypt-dev` packages in your system's package manager:

    ```
    $ cd nsca-2.7.2
    $ ./configure
    $ make
    ```

4. Install the NSCA server files manually; you will likely need `root` privileges for this:

```
# cp src/nsca /usr/local/nagios/bin
# cp sample-config/nsca.cfg /usr/local/nagios/etc
```

5. Edit the new file `/usr/local/nagios/etc/nsca.cfg`:

```
# vi /usr/local/nagios/etc/nsca.cfg
```

6. Uncomment the `password` directive, and define it. A random password generated by a tool such as `pwgen` or `makepasswd` will work fine. Don't use the one below; it's just an example!

```
password=yV3aa6S2o
```

7. Check that the NSCA daemon runs with no errors:

```
# /usr/local/nagios/bin/nsca -c /usr/local/nagios/etc/nsca.cfg
--single
```

If it does, you should add this command to an appropriate startup script, perhaps in `/etc/rc.local`, so that the daemon starts when the monitoring server boots. You should consult your system's documentation to find out the best place to add this.

We can set up the NSCA client on the monitored server (in this example, `ithaca.naginet`) as follows:

1. Again, download and expand the latest version of NSCA, and configure and compile it:

```
$ cd
$ wget http://downloads.sourceforge.net/project/nagios/nsca-2.x/
nsca-2.7.2/nsca-2.7.2.tar.gz
$ tar -xzf nsca-2.7.2.tar.gz
$ cd nsca-2.7.2
$ ./configure
$ make
```

2. Install the NSCA client files manually; you will likely need `root` privileges for this, and may need to create the `/usr/local/bin` and `/usr/local/etc` directories beforehand:

```
# mkdir -p /usr/local/bin /usr/local/etc
# cp src/send_nsca /usr/local/bin
# cp sample-config/send_nsca.cfg /usr/local/etc
```

3. Edit the new file `/usr/local/etc/send_nsca.cfg`:

```
# vi /usr/local/etc/send_nsca.cfg
```

4. Uncomment the `password` directive, and define it to be the same as the password given in `nsca.cfg` on the monitoring server:

   `password=yV3aa6S2o`

5. Run the `send_nsca` program to try and submit a passive check result:

   `# CHECK="ithaca.naginet\tBACKUP\t0\tBackup was successful, this check submitted by NSCA\n"`

   `# echo -en $CHECK | send_nsca -c /usr/local/etc/send_nsca.cfg -H olympus.naginet`

   `1 data packet(s) sent to host successfully.`

   Substitute the appropriate host names for the monitoring server (`olympus.naginet`), the monitored server (`ithaca.naginet`), and the service description `BACKUP`.

   Note that the fields are separated by `\t` characters, which expand to literal *Tab* characters with `echo -en`.

If this worked correctly, you should see that the passive check result in the web interface was successfully read by the monitoring server and applied appropriately:

Service State Information

Current Status:	**OK** (for 0d 0h 4m 27s)
Status Information:	Backup was successful, this check submitted by NSCA
Performance Data:	
Current Attempt:	1/3 (HARD state)
Last Check Time:	09-28-2012 18:11:05
Check Type:	PASSIVE
Check Latency / Duration:	N/A / 0.000 seconds
Next Scheduled Check:	N/A
Last State Change:	09-28-2012 18:06:47
Last Notification:	N/A (notification 0)
Is This Service Flapping?	**NO** (0.00% state change)
In Scheduled Downtime?	**NO**
Last Update:	09-28-2012 18:11:14 (0d 0h 0m 0s ago)

How it works...

The `nsca` daemon installed on the monitoring server is designed to listen for submitted service checks from the `send_nsca` client, provided that the password is correct and the data is in the appropriate format:

`<host_name>\t<service_description>\t<check_result>\t<check_output>\n`

Our example passive check took this form:

```
ithaca.naginet\tBACKUP\t0\tBackup was successful, this check
submitted by NSCA\n
```

Here, as with locally submitted passive checks, `check_result` corresponds to a numeric value, to one of the following:

- 0 for `OK`
- 1 for `WARNING`
- 2 for `CRITICAL`
- 3 for `UNKNOWN`

Once received by the `nsca` daemon on the monitoring server, this is translated into a passive check result command, written to the Nagios Core external commands file at `/usr/local/nagios/var/rw/nagios.cmd`, and processed in the same way as a locally submitted passive check would be.

This allows us to include calls to `send_nsca` at the end of scripts such as those managing backups, to immediately and automatically send a passive check result corresponding to whether the backup script succeeded.

Because of the NSCA daemon's very simple design and very basic security checks, it's important to apply a firewall policy to ensure that only the appropriate hosts can write to the NSCA port on the host monitoring system. A password as implemented here is a good first step, but is not sufficient to keep things secure. Make sure you read the `SECURITY` file included in the NSCA sources to ensure your configuration for the daemon is secure. Similar security guidelines apply to the installation of NRPE as discussed in *Chapter 6*.

There's more...

To supplement this setup, it's often a good idea to also have Nagios Core check the freshness of its services. If we have a process that needs to run regularly, such as backups, we will likely want to be notified if we haven't received any passive checks from the host in a given period of time.

This can be managed by configuring the service to run an active check after a certain period of time has elapsed with no passive checks. The configuration might look similar to the following code snippet, adding values for `check_freshness` and `freshness_threshold`:

```
define service {
    use                     generic-service
    host_name               ithaca.naginet
    service_description     BACKUP
```

```
    active_checks_enabled    0
    passive_checks_enabled   1
    check_freshness          1
    freshness_threshold      86400
    check_command            check_dummy!1!"No backups have run for 24
hours"
}
```

In this case, `freshness_threshold` is 86400 seconds, or 24 hours; if there have been no passive checks submitted for 24 hours, `check_command` will be run, even though active checks are disabled. `check_command` is defined to flag a WARNING state for the service with an appropriate explanatory message using the `check_dummy` command and plugin, whenever it is actually run.

Check freshness is discussed in more detail in the Nagios Core documentation, in the section entitled *Service and Host Freshness Checks* at `http://nagios.sourceforge.net/docs/3_0/freshness.html`.

Note that there's no reason that the status of a service has to come from the same host. You can send a passive check from one host to submit information about another. In fact, this is the basis of a distributed monitoring setup; one host can submit check results for any number of other hosts.

This can be particularly useful for working around network connectivity or routing problems; if Nagios Core has no connectivity at all to a host it needs to monitor, but does have connectivity to an intermediate host, that host can be configured to submit checks on behalf of the unreachable host, a slightly complex but often necessary setup.

See also

- The *Allowing and submitting passive checks, Submitting passive checks in response to SNMP traps*, and *Setting up an event handler script* recipes in this chapter
- The *Using an alternative check command* recipe in *Chapter 2, Working with Commands and Plugins*

Submitting passive checks in response to SNMP traps

In this recipe, we'll learn how to configure Nagios Core to process **Simple Network Management Protocol** (**SNMP**) traps, information sent by monitored network devices to a central monitoring server.

Because SNMP traps often contain useful or urgent information about how a host is working, processing them in at least some way can be very helpful, particularly for firmware network devices that can't use `send_nsca` to submit a passive check result in a standard form, as explained in the *Submitting passive checks from a remote host with NSCA* recipe.

As an example, most SNMP-capable hosts can be configured to send SNMP traps when one of their network interfaces changes state, perhaps due to a pulled network cable. These are known as `linkUp` and `linkDown` traps. Monitoring this particular kind of trap is especially useful for devices with a large number of interfaces, such as switches or routers.

Keeping track of these events in Nagios Core is valuable for keeping a unified monitoring interface, rather than having to monitor SNMP traps with a separate application.

Getting ready

There are quite a few prerequisites for getting this recipe to work. It is among the most powerful but also most complex methods of Nagios Core monitoring.

First of all, the recipe assumes some knowledge of SNMP. Unfortunately, SNMP is not very simple, despite its name! You should be familiar with the concepts of **SNMP checks** and **SNMP traps**. The documentation for **Net-SNMP** (the implementation of SNMP used for this example) may help (`http://www.net-snmp.org/docs/readmefiles.html`).

On the same host as your Nagios Core server with version 3.0 or greater, you should have `snmptrapd` installed to collect `trap` information, and `snmptt`, the **SNMP Trap Translator**, to filter useful information from the traps and submit the information to Nagios Core in a workable format. Documentation for SNMPTT is available at `http://snmptt.sourceforge.net/docs/snmptt.shtml`.

Both systems are free software and relatively popular, so check to see if there are packages available for your particular system to save the hassle of compiling them from source. On Debian-derived systems such as Ubuntu, for example, they are available in the `snmpd` and `snmptt` packages.

We will use an event handler called `submit_check_result`, available in the Nagios Core distribution. You will therefore need to have access to the original sources handy. If you have misplaced them, you can download them again from Nagios' website: `http://www.nagios.org/download`.

It's also necessary to use values of `host_name` for your hosts that actually correspond to host names resolvable by DNS from the monitoring server. This is because when the SNMP trap is received by SNMPTT, the only way it can translate it to a host name is with DNS. `host_name` for your host might be `crete.naginet`, but the trap will arrive from an IP address such as `10.128.0.27`. The system will therefore need to be able to resolve this with reverse DNS lookup. An easy way to test this is working is to use `host` or `dig`:

```
$ host 10.128.0.27
27.0.128.10.in-addr.arpa domain name pointer crete.naginet.
$ dig -x 10.128.0.27 +short
crete.naginet.
```

Finally, you should, of course, actually have a device configured to send SNMP traps to your monitoring server, which in turn is configured to listen for SNMP traps with the `snmpd` daemon. I don't really want to encourage you to unplug one of your core switches to test this, so we'll generate a trap manually with `snmptrap` on the monitored server to demonstrate the principle.

How to do it...

We can configure a new service to receive SNMP traps for an existing host as follows:

1. Copy the event handler script `contrib/eventhandlers/submit_check_result` from the Nagios Core source files into `/usr/local/nagios/libexec/eventhandlers`. You may need to create the target directory first. Your source files need not be in `/usr/local/src/nagios`; this is just an example.

   ```
   # mkdir -p /usr/local/nagios/libexec/eventhandlers
   # cp /usr/local/src/nagios/contrib/eventhandlers/submit_check_result /usr/local/nagios/libexec/eventhandlers
   ```

   This script should be made executable as whatever user the `snmptrapd` user runs as.

2. Change to the Nagios Core `objects` configuration directory on the monitoring server. For the default configuration, this is `/usr/local/nagios/etc/objects`.

   ```
   # cd /usr/local/nagios/etc/objects
   ```

3. Edit the file containing the definition for the SNMP-enabled monitored host. In this example, the definition for `crete.naginet` is in its own file, `crete.naginet.cfg`:

   ```
   # vi crete.naginet.cfg
   ```

The host definition might look similar to the following code snippet:

```
define host {
    use         linux-server
    host_name   crete.naginet
    alias       crete
    address     10.128.0.21
}
```

4. Add a service definition for your existing host that accepts only passive checks, and is flagged as `volatile`. Here we have used the `generic-service` template included in the sample configuration. You may prefer to use a different template, but all of the values defined here are important.

```
define service {
    use                     generic-service
    host_name               crete.naginet
    service_description     TRAP
    is_volatile             1
    check_command           check-host-alive
    active_checks_enabled   0
    passive_checks_enabled  1
    max_check_attempts      1
    contact_groups          admins
}
```

5. Validate the configuration and restart the Nagios Core server:

```
# /usr/local/nagios/bin/nagios -v /usr/local/nagios/etc/nagios.cfg
# /etc/init.d/nagios restart
```

In the web interface, this service should now be visible in the **Services** section:

Host ↑↓	Service ↑↓	Status ↑↓	Last Check ↑↓	Duration ↑↓	Attempt ↑↓	Status Information
crete.naginet	TRAP	PENDING	N/A	0d 0h 3m 52s+	1/3	Service is not scheduled to be checked...

6. Check that the `submit_check_result` script actually works, by invoking it with a test string on the monitoring server:

```
# /usr/local/nagios/libexec/eventhandlers/submit_check_result
crete.naginet TRAP 0 "Everything working"
```

After a short delay, if this has worked correctly, we should see the service change state in the web interface to reflect the test:

Host ↑↓	Service ↑↓	Status ↑↓	Last Check ↑↓	Duration ↑↓	Attempt ↑↓	Status Information
crete.naginet	TRAP	〔↑〕 OK	09-29-2012 20:30:28	0d 0h 0m 8s	1/3	Everything working

We now need to configure `snmptrapd` and `snmpd` to receive traps, and call the `submit_check_result` script for us:

1. Configure `snmpd` to pass received traps to `snmptt` by changing its configuration file `/etc/snmp/snmptrapd.conf`. The following configuration may work:

   ```
   traphandle default /usr/sbin/snmptt
   disableAuthorization yes
   donotlogtraps yes
   ```

2. Restart `snmpd` to apply this change:

   ```
   # /etc/init.d/snmpd restart
   ```

3. Configure `snmptt` to convert the IP addresses to hostnames, by changing the value for `dns-enable` to `1` in `/etc/snmp/snmptt.ini`:

   ```
   dns_enable = 1
   ```

4. Configure `snmptt` to use Net-SNMP at startup in `/etc/snmp/snmptt.ini`:

   ```
   net_snmp_perl_enable = 1
   ```

5. Configure `snmptt` to respond to an SNMP event by defining it in `/etc/snmp/snmptt.conf`. Here we've used the generic `linkDown` event defined by the OID `.1.3.t6.1.6.3.1.1.5.3`:

   ```
   EVENT linkDown .1.3.6.1.6.3.1.1.5.3 "Status Events" Normal
   FORMAT Link down on interface $1.  Admin state: $2.  Operational
   state: $3
   EXEC /usr/local/nagios/libexec/eventhandlers/submit_check_result
   $r TRAP 1 "linkDown for interface $1"
   SDESC
   A linkDown trap signifies that the SNMP entity, acting in
   an agent role, has detected that the ifOperStatus object for
   one of its communication links is about to enter the down
   state from some other state (but not from the notPresent
   state).  This other state is indicated by the included value
   of ifOperStatus.
   EDESC
   ```

   Depending on your distribution, there may already be a definition for a `linkDown` event, in which case you may only need to change the `EXEC` field.

6. From the monitored host, fire a test trap for a `linkDown` event. Substitute `olympus.naginet` for the name or IP address of your monitoring host. This will require the `snmptrap` utility to be installed on that host, and may require `root` privileges.

```
# snmptrap -v 1 -c public olympus.naginet .1.3.6.1.6.3.1.1.5.3
localhost 2 0 '' .1.3.6.1.2.1.2.2.1.1.1 i 1
```

Note that we use the `public` community string here; your own will likely differ.

7. Check the Nagios Core log file located at `/usr/local/nagios/var/nagios.log` to see if there's new output from the event handler:

```
[1348914096] EXTERNAL COMMAND: PROCESS_SERVICE_CHECK_RESULT;crete.
naginet;TRAP;1;linkDown for interface 1
```

```
[1348914100] PASSIVE SERVICE CHECK: crete.naginet;TRAP;1;linkDown
for interface 1
```

```
[1348914100] SERVICE ALERT: crete.naginet;TRAP;WARNING;HARD;3;link
Down for interface 1
```

```
[1348914100] SERVICE NOTIFICATION: nagiosadmin;crete.
naginet;TRAP;WARNING;notify-service-by-email;linkDown for
interface 1
```

If so, the same state should be reflected for the TRAP service in the web interface:

Host	Service	Status	Last Check	Duration	Attempt	Status Information
crete.naginet	TRAP	PASV WARNING	09-29-2012 22:21:36	0d 0h 33m 44s	3/3	linkDown for interface 1

With this done, we've confirmed that SNMP traps from the `crete.naginet` host can be received and processed by the `olympus.naginet` server. We can apply the same setup for other hosts that generate SNMP traps in our network by configuring them to send their traps to the Nagios Core monitoring server, and adding appropriate handlers for the expected traps.

If this didn't work, the first thing to check should be that your monitoring server is actually listening for checks on the relevant IP address, as `snmptrap` does not throw errors when it can not deliver traps. On Debian-derived systems, you should check that the `snmptrapd` process is actually running; it may require a change to `/etc/defaults/snmp` and a restart of `snmpd`.

How it works...

When an SNMP trap is generated and delivered to the monitoring server by whatever means, the `snmpd` daemon will pass it to the `snmptt` program for processing.

The `snmptt` handler checks if the event OID matches any of the traps for which it has defined events in `snmptt.conf`. In our example, it finds a handler defined for the OID `.1.3.6.1.6.3.1.1.5.3`, which corresponds to the `linkDown` event, with the number of the relevant interface as an additional argument in `$1`.

Using this information, it fires the `submit_check_result` handler that we installed in the first part of the recipe, setting the state of the `TRAP` service to `WARNING`, and including the information `linkDown` for interface `1`, as specified by the final argument to `submit_check _result` in the `EXEC` handler. The service can be set to notify the appropriate contacts or contact groups, just as it would for an actively monitored service.

If a trap arrives on the Nagios Core server for a host that Nagios Core doesn't know about, even if it has an event handler defined for `snmptt`, it will simply ignore it.

There's more...

In order to "clear" the state of the service and return it to `OK`, we can simply schedule an active check for it from the web interface, with **Force Check** selected:

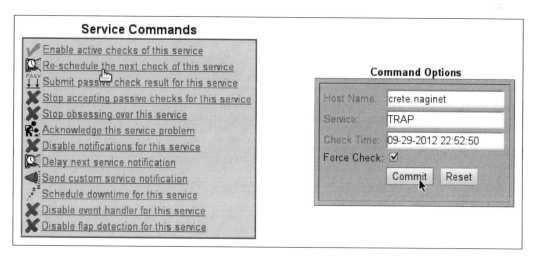

Because `check_command` is defined as `check-host-alive`, as long as the monitoring host is actually responding to `PING`, the service should assume an `OK` state:

Host ↑	Service ↑	Status ↑	Last Check ↑	Duration ↑	Attempt ↑	Status Information
crete.naginet	TRAP	OK	09-29-2012 22:56:31	0d 0h 0m 52s	1/3	PING OK - Packet loss = 0%, RTA = 1.12 ms

See also

▶ The *Submitting passive checks from a remote host with NSCA, Allowing and submitting passive checks,* and *Setting up an event handler scripts* recipes in this chapter

▶ The *Monitoring the output of an SNMP query* and *Creating an SNMP OID to monitor* recipes in *Chapter 5, Monitoring Methods*

Setting up an event handler script

In this recipe, we'll learn how to set up an event handler script for Nagios Core. Event handlers are commands that are run on every state change for a host or service (whether for all hosts or services, or just particular ones). They are defined in a similar way to notification commands and check commands for plugins.

In this example, we'll implement a simple event handler that writes the date, the host state, and the number of check attempts to a separate file for a single host. This is a trivial example to demonstrate the concept; a more practical and complex application for the use of event handlers is given in the *Setting up a redundant monitoring host* recipe, in *Chapter 10*.

Getting ready

You will need a server running Nagios Core 3.0 or higher. You should be familiar with defining new commands, as per the *Creating a new command* recipe in *Chapter 2* and the *Writing low-priority notifications to an MOTD* recipe in *Chapter 4, Configuring Notifications*.

How to do it...

We can set up a new event handler for the Nagios Core server as follows:

1. Change to the `objects` configuration directory for Nagios Core. In the quick start guide installation, this is `/usr/local/nagios/etc/objects`. Edit the file `commands.cfg`:

   ```
   # cd /usr/local/nagios/etc/objects
   # vi commands.cfg
   ```

2. Add the following command definition:

   ```
   define command {
        command_name     record_host_data
   ```

```
    command_line    /usr/bin/printf "%b" "$LONGDATETIME$:
$HOSTSTATE$ (attempt $HOSTATTEMPT$)\n" >>/usr/local/nagios/var/
states-$HOSTNAME$.log
}
```

3. Edit the file containing the definition for an existing host, in this example `delphi. naginet`. Add the `event_handler` directive with the value `record_host_data` to your host definition:

```
define host {
        use             linux-server
        host_name       delphi.naginet
        alias           delphi
        address         10.128.0.26
        event_handler   record_host_data
}
```

4. Validate the configuration and restart the Nagios Core server:

```
# /usr/local/nagios/bin/nagios -v /usr/local/nagios/etc/nagios.cfg
```

```
# /etc/init.d/nagios restart
```

With this done, the next time the host changes state (whether to a SOFT or HARD state) it should log the information in the `/usr/local/nagios/var/states-delphi.naginet. log` file:

```
Sat Sept 29 23:53:54 NZST 2012: DOWN (attempt 1)

Sat Sept 29 23:54:04 NZST 2012: DOWN (attempt 2)

Sat Sept 29 23:54:14 NZST 2012: DOWN (attempt 3)

Sat Sept 29 23:57:14 NZST 2012: UP (attempt 1)
```

How it works...

The `event_handler` command we defined is configured to use `printf` to write a line of text to a file named after the host. Its definition is built out of four macros:

  ▸ $LONGDATETIME$: This specifies the date and time, in a human-readable format

  ▸ $HOSTSTATE$: This specifies the state of the host (UP, DOWN, or UNREACHABLE)

  ▸ $HOSTATTEMPT$: This specifies the number of check attempts made so far for a host in a problem state

  ▸ $HOSTNAME$: This is the hostname itself (used to build the name of the file)

Note that this behavior is slightly different from notifications. Notification commands are only run when the number of `max_check_attempts` for a host or service has been exceeded, to alert somebody to the problem. Event handlers are run on SOFT changes as well as HARD changes, and hence can be used to keep more information about host performance that might be missed by the routine notifications.

Service event handlers can be defined in just the same way, by adding the `event_handler` directive to their definitions:

```
define service {
    use                  generic-service
    host_name            crete.naginet
    service_description  PING
    check_command        check_ping!100,10%!200,20%
    event_handler        record_service_data
}
```

In this case, we would probably want to use the macros for service states instead:

```
define command {
    command_name    record_service_data
    command_line    /usr/bin/printf "%b" "$LONGDATETIME$:
$SERVICESTATE$ (attempt $SERVICEATTEMPT$)\n" >>/usr/local/nagios/var/
states-$HOSTNAME$-$SERVICEDESC$.log
}
```

There's more...

As a shortcut, if there's an event handler we want to run on all hosts or all services, we can use the `global_host_event_handler` and `global_service_event_handler` directives in `nagios.cfg`:

```
global_host_event_handler=record_host_data
global_service_event_handler=record_service_data
```

This will apply the appropriate event handlers to all hosts and services, therefore running whenever a host or service changes state.

A specialized case of event handler for recording detailed performance data of plugins and checks is also possible using Nagios Core's Performance Data feature, as documented in the manual at `http://nagios.sourceforge.net/docs/3_0/perfdata.html`.

Performance data is written on every check rather than every state change, and is hence useful for assessing the performance of plugins and checks. Performance data is used by the **Nagiosgraph** utility, for example, discussed in the *Tracking host and service states with Nagiosgraph* recipe in this chapter.

See also

▶ The *Tracking host and service states with Nagiosgraph* recipe in this chapter

▶ The *Creating a new command* recipe in *Chapter 2, Working with Commands and Plugins*

▶ The *Writing low-priority notifications to an MOTD* recipe in *Chapter 4, Configuring Notifications*

Tracking host and service states with Nagiosgraph

In this recipe, we'll learn how to install and configure Nagiosgraph, a program that integrates with Nagios Core's performance data tools to produce graphs showing long-term information about how checks for hosts and services are performing.

Getting ready

You will need to be running a Nagios Core 3.0 or later server. Nagiosgraph will probably still work with older versions of Nagios Core, but the configuration may be slightly different. The `INSTALL` document included in the source for Nagiosgraph explains the differences in detail.

You should have a thorough understanding of defining hosts, services, and commands, and be able to install new software as the `root` user on the monitoring server. You should also be at least familiar with the layout of your Apache HTTPD server on the monitoring system; this recipe will assume it is installed in `/usr/local/apache`.

Because Nagiosgraph has many Perl dependencies, you will need to have Perl installed on your server, and you will likely also need to install a few Perl modules as dependencies. The package manager for your system may include them, or you may need to download them using the **Comprehensive Perl Archive Network** (**CPAN**): `http://www.cpan.org/modules/INSTALL.html`.

The server will need to already be monitoring at least one host with at least one service for the graphs to be any use. Nagiosgraph includes rule sets that translate known performance data strings into usable statistics. This means that graphing will work well for familiar plugins with a predictable output format such as `check_ping` or `check_http`, but might not graph data for less commonly used plugins without a little custom configuration.

This recipe is not a comprehensive survey of everything you can do with Nagiosgraph; if you like what this does, make sure to check out Nagiosgraph's documentation online at `http://nagiosgraph.sourceforge.net/`.

How to do it...

We can get some basic Nagiosgraph functionality for our monitoring server as follows:

1. Download the latest version of Nagiosgraph from its website at `http://` `nagiosgraph.sourceforge.net/`, directly onto your monitoring server, using a tool such as `wget`:

    ```
    $ cd

    $ wget http://downloads.sourceforge.net/project/nagiosgraph/
    nagiosgraph/1.4.4/nagiosgraph-1.4.4.tar.gz
    ```

2. Inflate the `.tar.gz` file and change to the directory within it:

    ```
    $ tar -xzf nagiosgraph-1.4.4.tar.gz

    $ cd nagiosgraph-1.4.4
    ```

3. As the `root` user, run the `install.pl` script with the `--check-prereq` option. This will give you a survey of any dependencies you may need to install via packages or CPAN. When you have installed all the prerequisites, the output should look similar to the following code snippet:

    ```
    # ./install.pl --check-prereq

    checking required PERL modules

       Carp...1.11

       CGI...3.43

       Data::Dumper...2.124

       File::Basename...2.77

       File::Find...1.14

       MIME::Base64...3.08

       POSIX...1.17

       RRDs...1.4003

       Time::HiRes...1.9719

    checking optional PERL modules

       GD...2.39

    checking nagios installation

       found nagios at /usr/local/nagios/bin/nagios

    checking web server installation

       found apache at /usr/sbin/apache2
    ```

These are all reasonably standard Perl libraries, so don't forget to check if packages are available for them before you resort to using CPAN. For example, I was able to install the RRDs and GD modules on my Debian system as follows:

```
# apt-get install librrds-perl libgd-gd2-perl
```

If you are having trouble getting `install.pl` to find your Nagios Core or Apache HTTPD instances, then take a look at the output of `install.pl --help` to run an installation specific to your kind of system. This is documented in more detail in the `INSTALL` file.

4. As the `root` user, run the `install.pl` script with the `--install` argument. You will be prompted many times for directory layout options. The default is shown in square brackets and should be correct for a typical Nagios Core installation, so to start with, simply press *Enter* on each option.

```
# ./install.pl --install
...
Destination directory (prefix)? [/usr/local/nagiosgraph]

Location of configuration files (etc-dir)? [/usr/local/
nagiosgraph/etc]

Location of executables? [/usr/local/nagiosgraph/bin]

Location of CGI scripts? [/usr/local/nagiosgraph/cgi]

Location of documentation (doc-dir)? [/usr/local/nagiosgraph/doc]

Location of examples? [/usr/local/nagiosgraph/examples]

Location of CSS and JavaScript files? [/usr/local/nagiosgraph/
share]

Location of utilities? [/usr/local/nagiosgraph/util]

Location of state files (var-dir)? [/usr/local/nagiosgraph/var]

Location of RRD files? [/usr/local/nagiosgraph/var/rrd]

Location of log files (log-dir)? [/usr/local/nagiosgraph/var]

Path of log file? [/usr/local/nagiosgraph/var/nagiosgraph.log]

Path of CGI log file? [/usr/local/nagiosgraph/var/nagiosgraph-cgi.
log]

URL of CGI scripts? [/nagiosgraph/cgi-bin]

URL of CSS file? [/nagiosgraph/nagiosgraph.css]

URL of JavaScript file? [/nagiosgraph/nagiosgraph.js]

Path of Nagios performance data file? [/tmp/perfdata.log]

URL of Nagios CGI scripts? [/nagios/cgi-bin]
```

```
username or userid of Nagios user? [nagios]

username or userid of web server user? [www-data]

Modify the Nagios configuration? [n]

Modify the Apache configuration? [n]

...
```

After the preceding selections are all made, the files should be installed with appropriate permissions set. The final part of the output gives instructions for adding configuration to Nagios Core and Apache HTTPD, which we'll do next.

5. Change to the Nagios Core configuration directory. In the quick start guide installation, this is /usr/local/nagios/etc.

```
# cd /usr/local/nagios/etc
```

6. Edit the core configuration file nagios.cfg, and add the following directives at the end of the file:

```
# process nagios performance data using nagiosgraph

process_performance_data=1

service_perfdata_file=/tmp/perfdata.log

service_perfdata_file_template=$LASTSERVICECHECK$||$HOSTNAME$||$SE
RVICEDESC$||$SERVICEOUTPUT$||$SERVICEPERFDATA$

service_perfdata_file_mode=a

service_perfdata_file_processing_interval=30

service_perfdata_file_processing_command=process-service-perfdata-
for-nagiosgraph
```

7. Change to the Nagios Core objects configuration directory. In the quick start guide installation, this is /usr/local/nagios/etc/objects.

```
# cd /usr/local/nagios/etc/objects
```

8. Edit the commands.cfg file, and add the following command definition:

```
# command to process nagios performance data for nagiosgraph

define command {

    command_name process-service-perfdata-for-nagiosgraph

    command_line /usr/local/nagiosgraph/bin/insert.pl

}
```

9. Edit the httpd.conf file for your Apache HTTPD server to include the following line at the end:

```
Include /usr/local/nagiosgraph/etc/nagiosgraph-apache.conf
```

In a local install of Apache HTTPD, this file is normally in `/usr/local/apache/conf/httpd.conf`, but its location varies by system. On Debian-derived systems it may be `/etc/apache2/apache2.conf`.

10. Validate the configuration of both the Apache HTTPD server and the Nagios Core server, and restart them both:

```
# /usr/local/apache/bin/apachectl configtest
# /usr/local/apache/bin/apachectl restart
# /usr/local/nagios/bin/nagios -v /usr/local/nagios/etc/nagios.cfg
# /etc/init.d/nagios restart
```

11. Visit `http://olympus.naginet/nagiosgraph/cgi-bin/showconfig.cgi` in your browser, substituting your own Nagios Core server's hostname, to test that everything's working. You should see a long page with configuration information for Nagiosgraph:

---

nagiosgraph configuration on olympus.naginet

30 Sep 2012 16:28:58 NZDT

PERL modules

        required

☐   Carp: 1.11 ☐
☐   CGI: 3.43 ☐
☐ Data::Dumper: 2.124 ☐
☐ File::Basename: 2.77 ☐
☐   File::Find: 1.14 ☐
☐ MIME::Base64: 3.08 ☐
☐   POSIX: 1.17 ☐
☐   RRDs: 1.4003 ☐
☐ Time::HiRes: 1.9719 ☐

        optional

☐   GD: 2.39 ☐

nagiosgraph

☐   ngshared.pm: ok ☐
☐   version: 1.4.4 ☐
☐ nagiosgraph.conf: ok ☐
☐ RRD directory: ok ☐
☐   log file: ok ☐
☐   CGI log file: ok ☐
☐   map file: ok ☐

Environment

```
DOCUMENT_ROOT=/var/www
GATEWAY_INTERFACE=CGI/1.1
HTTP_ACCEPT=text/html,application/xhtml+xml,application/xml;q=0.9,*/*;q=0.8
HTTP_ACCEPT_CHARSET=ISO-8859-1,utf-8;q=0.7,*;q=0.3
HTTP_ACCEPT_ENCODING=gzip,deflate,sdch
```

---

12. If everything is working up to this point, the only thing left to do is to define an action URL for the services that you want to graph, so that you can click to go directly to the graphs for that service from the Nagios Core web interface.

The tidiest and most straightforward way to do this is to define a service template:

```
define service {
        name        nagiosgraph
        action_url  /nagiosgraph/cgi-bin/show.cgi?host=$HOSTNAME$&serv
ice=$SERVICEDESC$
        register    0
}
```

Then, you can have the services you want graphed inherit from it, as well as from any other templates they use, by adding `nagiosgraph` to the value for the `use` directive:

```
define service {
        use                  generic-service,nagiosgraph
        host_name            corinth.naginet
        service_description  PING
        check_command        check_ping!100,10%!200,20%
}
```

You should do this for all the services for which you want graphing.

13. Validate the configuration and restart the Nagios Core server again:

```
# /usr/local/nagios/bin/nagios -v /usr/local/nagios/etc/nagios.cfg
# /etc/init.d/nagios restart
```

With this done, visiting the **Service** section of the web interface should include action icons after each graphed service:

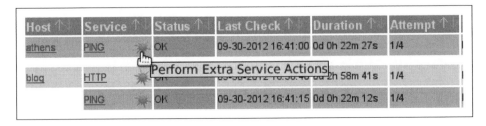

Clicking one of these should bring up a graph interface; for example, a service using `check_ping` might show something similar to the following screenshot:

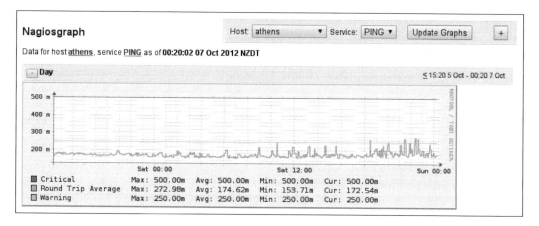

Note that it includes two line bars to show the thresholds for `CRITICAL` and `WARNING` state as well as the actual response time. Also note that the preceding graph is several days old; it will take a while to build up enough data to see a perceptible line, and you may not see any graphs until performance data has actually been received from Nagios by Nagiosgraph.

Don't forget that graphs won't work out of the box for every service. If Nagiosgraph doesn't know how to parse the performance data for a check, it will show a red error text instead of graphs. We'll mention an approach to fixing this in the *There's more...* section.

How it works...

The configuration changes in the preceding section prompt Nagios Core to log performance data for every check on every service, using the `service_perfdata_file_processing_ command` directive. This command, named `process-service-perfdata-for-nagiosgraph`, is defined to pass data to the `bin/insert.pl` script included in the new `/usr/local/nagiosgraph` directory.

This script in turn parses performance output, such as the following output from a typical service using `check_ping`:

```
PING OK - Packet loss = 0%, RTA = 174.19 ms
```

Nagiosgraph extracts numeric information from the performance data, according to the templates defined in `/usr/local/nagiosgraph/etc/map`, using Perl regular expressions. This data is recorded using Perl's bindings for the RRD library, and graphed using the GD2 library, with an appearance similar to graphs produced by MRTG.

The `action_url` directive uses macros for each service to define a URL for each service that shows its graphs. In our example, for a service PING on host `corinth.naginet`, `action_url` would expand to the following:

```
action_url    /nagiosgraph/cgi-bin/show.cgi?host=corinth.
naginet&service=PING
```

This isn't the only possible use of `action_url`, of course; it just happens to be a useful one in our case. You can make `action_url` go anywhere you'd like for a given host or service.

There's more...

If you don't intend to define any other kind of action for services, you may like to change the `action.gif` image to something more descriptive than the default red splotch. The Nagiosgraph sources include a possible alternative icon, but you can use any GIF image you wish.

```
# cp nagiosgraph-1.4.4/share/graph.gif /usr/local/nagios/share/images/
action.gif
```

You may well be running some kind of check that Nagiosgraph isn't able to graph, because it doesn't understand the format of the performance output, and can't extract numeric information from it. The default mapping rules cover output from quite a few standard plugins, but if you know a little about Perl, then you may be able to add more rules to `/usr/local/nagiosgraph/etc/map` to process other kinds of plugin output.

Besides the examples in the map file, which include instructions for writing new output checks, there are more examples of such definitions included in the `/usr/local/nagiosgraph/examples/map_examples` file.

If you're comparing Nagios graphing solutions, another popular solution to try could be **PNP4Nagios**, available at `http://docs.pnp4nagios.org/pnp-0.6/start`.

See also

- ▶ The *Getting extra visualizations with NagVis* recipe in this chapter
- ▶ The *Monitoring Nagios performance with Nagiostats* recipe in *Chapter 10, Security and Performance*

Reading status into a MySQL database with NDOUtils

In this recipe, we'll learn how to install the **NDOUtils** extension to Nagios Core, in order to have all of Nagios Core's configuration and data written into a MySQL database. This allows easy development of custom reports and interfaces for Nagios Core data with languages, such as Perl and PHP, and their standard interfaces to the popular MySQL server, rather than needing to interact with Nagios Core's own logs or its data format. Some plugins, such as NagVis, use this format to read information about Nagios Core configuration and objects.

Getting ready

You will need a Nagios Core server version 3.0 or later. NDOUtils will probably still install and work on older versions of Nagios Core, but the installation process is slightly different; see the `INSTALL` file included in the NDO source for information on this.

Nagios Core uses its event broker functionality to write information to the socket for the MySQL database to pick up. You will need to have compiled Nagios Core with the `--enable-event-broker` flag:

```
$ ./configure --enable-event-broker
$ make
# make install
```

If you are unsure whether you compiled with this flag, it is probably a good idea to recompile and reinstall Nagios Core from your original sources with this installed. Don't forget to back up your previous installation in case of problems.

In order to compile the `ndomod` part of NDOUtils, you will need to have the MySQL client libraries and headers installed on the Nagios Core server. You will also need to have a MySQL server ready to store the data. The MySQL server does not have to be running on the same host as Nagios Core, but the Nagios Core server should be able to connect to it.

Finally, you should take note of the opening paragraph of `README`, which at the time of writing points out that NDOUtils for Nagios Core 3.0 is still officially in beta; you should read the note and be aware of the risks in installing it. In my own experience, however, the code is very stable. There are also no guarantees at the time of writing that this procedure will work correctly with the unreleased Nagios 4.0.

How to do it...

We can install the NDOUtils package for Nagios Core as follows:

1. Download the latest NDOUtils `.tar.gz` from its Sourceforge site at `http://sourceforge.net/projects/nagios/files/ndoutils-1.x/`.

   ```
   $ wget http://downloads.sourceforge.net/project/nagios/ndoutils-
   1.x/ndoutils-1.5.2/ndoutils-1.5.2.tar.gz
   ```

2. Unpack the `.tar.gz` file and change directory into it.

   ```
   $ tar -xzf ndoutils-1.5.2.tar.gz
   $ cd ndoutils-1.5.2
   ```

3. Run `./configure` and build the software. Note that there is no install target; we will be performing the installation manually.

   ```
   $ ./configure
   $ make
   ```

4. Read the output of `./configure` carefully if the build fails, to determine if you are missing any dependencies on your system. The output of `./configure` should end with something similar to the following code snippet:

   ```
   *** Configuration summary for ndoutils 1.5.2 06-08-2012 ***:

   General Options:
   -----------------------

   NDO2DB user:     nagios
   NDO2DB group:    nagios
   Review the options above for accuracy.  If they look okay,
   type 'make' to compile the NDO utilities.
   ```

5. On the MySQL server, create a database to store the Nagios Core information, and a user to access it. In this example, the MySQL server is running on the same host as the Nagios Core server (`olympus.naginet`), so the access will be done from `localhost`.

   ```
   mysql> CREATE DATABASE nagios;
   Query OK, 1 row affected (0.10 sec)
   mysql> CREATE USER 'ndo'@'localhost' IDENTIFIED BY 'mPYxbAYqa';
   Query OK, 0 rows affected (0.62 sec)
   mysql> GRANT ALL ON nagios.* TO 'ndo'@'localhost';
   Query OK, 0 rows affected (0.02 sec)
   ```

We have used a random password after `IDENTIFIED BY`. You should generate your own secure password.

6. Run the `installdb` script in the source to create the various tables Nagios Core will use. Use the database details established in the previous step:

    $ cd db

    $ ./installdb -u ndo -p mPYxbAYqa -h localhost -d nagios

    ** Creating tables for version 1.5.2

    Using mysql.sql for installation...

    ** Updating table nagios_dbversion

    Done!

    Don't be concerned about the following error message; it is because you are installing the extension for the first time:

    ```
    DBD::mysql::db do failed: Table 'nagios.nagios_dbversion' doesn't
    exist at ./installdb line 51.
    ```

7. Copy the compiled `ndomod` module into the `/usr/local/nagios/bin` directory:

    # cd ..

    # cp src/ndomod-3x.o /usr/local/nagios/bin/ndomod.o

8. Copy the sample configuration for the module into `/usr/local/nagios/etc`:

    # cp config/ndomod.cfg-sample /usr/local/nagios/etc/ndomod.cfg

9. Make sure it is readable only by the `nagios` user:

    # chown nagios.nagios /usr/local/nagios/etc/ndomod.cfg

    # chmod 0600 /usr/local/nagios/etc/ndomod.cfg

10. Edit your `nagios.cfg` file:

    # vi /usr/local/nagios/etc/nagios.cfg

11. Add a `broker_module` definition to the file, and check that the `event_broker_options` directive is set to `-1`:

    ```
    broker_module=/usr/local/nagios/bin/ndomod.o config_file=/usr/
    local/nagios/etc/ndomod.cfg
    event_broker_options=-1
    ```

Note that the `broker_module` and `config_file` definitions should be on the same line, but `event_broker_options` should be on its own line.

With this done, the broker module ought to be successfully installed, and we can move on to installing the `ndo2db` daemon.

12. Copy the `ndo2db` binary into the `/usr/local/nagios/bin` directory:

    ```
    # cp src/ndo2db-3x /usr/local/nagios/bin/ndo2db
    ```

13. Copy the sample configuration for the daemon into `/usr/local/nagios/etc`:

    ```
    # cp config/ndo2db.cfg-sample /usr/local/nagios/etc/ndo2db.cfg
    ```

14. Make sure it is readable only by the `nagios` user:

    ```
    # chown nagios.nagios /usr/local/nagios/etc/ndo2db.cfg
    # chmod 0600 /usr/local/nagios/etc/ndo2db.cfg
    ```

15. Edit the configuration file as installed:

    ```
    # vi /usr/local/nagios/etc/ndo2db.cfg
    ```

16. Change the values in `ndo2db.cfg` to reflect the database details:

    ```
    db_host=localhost
    db_port=3306
    db_name=nagios
    db_user=ndo
    db_pass=mPYxbAYqa
    ```

17. Test the `ndo2db` daemon by starting it and verifying it is running with `ps -e` or `pgrep`:

    ```
    # /usr/local/nagios/bin/ndo2db -c /usr/local/nagios/etc/ndo2db.cfg
    # ps -e | grep '[n]do2db'
    32285 ? 00:00:00 ndo2db
    # pgrep ndo2db
    32285
    ```

    If it works, you should add this command into your system's `init` scripts, so that the daemon is started at boot time.

18. Validate the configuration and restart the Nagios Core server:

    ```
    # /usr/local/nagios/bin/nagios -v /usr/local/nagios/etc/nagios.cfg
    # /etc/init.d/nagios restart
    ```

With this done, inspecting the database tables in MySQL should show they have been filled with information from Nagios Core, for example the `nagios_services` table:

```
$ mysql --user=ndo --password --database=nagios
mysql> select count(1) from nagios_services;
```

```
+----------+
| count(1) |
+----------+
|       54 |
+----------+
1 row in set (0.00 sec)
```

How it works...

NDOUtils is in fact a collection of components, two of which we installed in the previous sections:

- ▶ `ndomod` is used as a broker module, for writing events and data from Nagios Core to a UNIX socket in `/usr/local/nagios/var/ndo.sock`. It runs as a module of the Nagios Core server.

- ▶ `ndo2db` is used as a database backend, for reading the events and data from the UNIX socket to which `ndomod` writes, and applying them as MySQL database operations. It runs independently as a daemon on the system, and performs the MySQL connection and transactions.

`broker_module` updates these tables as plugins are run, hosts and services change state, notifications are issued, and other Nagios Core behavior takes place. It covers most data of interest quite comprehensively. Note that it includes:

- ▶ Configuration directives
- ▶ Details for types of Nagios Core objects
- ▶ Properties and current states of hosts
- ▶ Acknowledgement and scheduled downtime information
- ▶ Notification history and complete logging

The main reason to install NDOUtils is to put Nagios Core's data into a standardized format, so that it can be read and processed by external applications, whether in simple table-style reports or completely new application interfaces to the Nagios Core data. This tends to be much easier than custom building a Nagios Core CGI of your own!

There's more...

Another recipe in this chapter, *Writing customized Nagios Core reports*, applies NDOUtils after its installation by demonstrating some example MySQL queries for retrieving useful data and summaries from its tables, including an example of writing a report in Perl, and a simple RSS feed in PHP.

To get the most out of NDOUtils, it's a good idea to take a look at its documentation, which includes a complete breakdown of the contents of the MySQL tables: `http://nagios.sourceforge.net/docs/ndoutils/NDOUtils.pdf`.

See also

> ▸ The *Writing customized Nagios Core reports* and *Getting extra visualizations with NagVis* recipes in this chapter

Writing customized Nagios Core reports

In this recipe, we'll explore some simple applications of the NDOUtils database by trying out some queries, and change one of them into both a simple report in Perl, and also into a PHP-based RSS feed.

Getting ready

This recipe assumes you have NDOUtils already installed, and that your Nagios Core 3.0 (or later) server is monitoring at least a few hosts and services, so that the queries we try actually return some data. You should also have some means of executing MySQL queries on the database server. The `mysql` command-line client will work just fine; a tool such as phpMyAdmin might make the data a little easier to explore.

How to do it...

We can explore some queries against the NDOUtils databases as follows:

1. Retrieve the content and date/time of the latest ten notifications:

   ```
   mysql> SELECT start_time, long_output FROM nagios_notifications
   ORDER BY start_time DESC LIMIT 10;
   ```

2. Retrieve the content and date/time of the latest ten host or service comments:

   ```
   mysql> SELECT entry_time, comment_data FROM nagios_commenthistory
   ORDER BY entry_time DESC LIMIT 10;
   ```

3. Count the number of hosts currently in the OK state:

   ```
   mysql> SELECT COUNT(1) FROM nagios_hoststatus WHERE current_state
   = 0;
   ```

4. Retrieve the names of all hosts currently in scheduled downtime:

```
mysql> SELECT display_name FROM nagios_hosts JOIN nagios_
hoststatus USING (host_object_id) WHERE scheduled_downtime_depth >
0;
```

Note that the syntax of this query assumes a MySQL version of at least 5.0.12.

5. Return a list of all host names and the number of services associated with them:

```
mysql> SELECT nagios_hosts.display_name, COUNT(service_id) FROM
nagios_hosts LEFT JOIN nagios_services ON nagios_hosts.host_
object_id = nagios_services.host_object_id GROUP BY nagios_hosts.
host_object_id;
```

We could implement a Perl script to print the latest ten notifications using the DBI module as follows:

```perl
#!/usr/bin/env perl

# Enforce Perl best practices
use strict;
use warnings;

# Import database modules
use DBI;
use DBD::mysql;

# Get connection to database
my $nagios = DBI->connect(
    'dbi:mysql:dbname=nagios;host=localhost',
    'ndo',
    'mPYxbAYqa'
) or die "Could not connect to database";

# Define an SQL query to run
my $query = q{
    SELECT
        notification_id, start_time, name1, long_output
```

```
            FROM
                nagios_notifications
            JOIN
                nagios_objects USING (object_id)
            ORDER BY
                start_time DESC
            LIMIT
                10
    };

    # Execute query and retrieve notifications
    my $notifications = $nagios->selectall_hashref(
        $query,
        'notification_id'
    ) or die 'Could not retrieve notifications';

    # Print each notification
    foreach my $id (keys %{$notifications}) {
        my $notification = $notifications->{$id};
        printf {*STDOUT} "%s - %s: %s\n",
            $notification->{start_time},
            $notification->{name1},
            $notification->{long_output};
    }

    # Exit successfully
    exit 0;
```

Saved into a file `latest-notifications.pl`, we could run it as follows:

```
$ chmod +x latest-notifications.pl
$ ./latest-notifications.pl
2012-10-06 10:11:27 - blog: PING OK - Packet loss = 0%, RTA = 160.31 ms
2012-10-06 10:48:17 - athens: PING OK - Packet loss = 0%, RTA = 155.82 ms
2012-10-06 14:08:17 - athens: PING WARNING - Packet loss = 16%, RTA =
171.79 ms
2012-10-06 14:13:17 - athens: PING OK - Packet loss = 0%, RTA = 164.39 ms
2012-10-06 10:56:17 - athens: PING CRITICAL - Packet loss = 28%, RTA =
164.65 ms
```

```
2012-10-06 10:38:17 - athens: PING CRITICAL - Packet loss = 28%, RTA =
166.10 ms

2012-10-06 10:06:27 - blog: PING WARNING - Packet loss = 16%, RTA =
163.72 ms

2012-10-06 13:39:27 - blog: PING WARNING - Packet loss = 16%, RTA =
163.78 ms

2012-10-06 13:44:27 - blog: PING OK - Packet loss = 0%, RTA = 167.10 ms

2012-10-06 13:29:27 - blog: PING CRITICAL - Packet loss = 28%, RTA =
159.55 ms
```

Similarly, we could implement a crude RSS feed for notifications using PHP5 with PDO MySQL as follows:

```php
<?php

// Get connection to database
$nagios = new PDO(
    'mysql:host=localhost;dbname=nagios',
    'ndo',
    'mPYxbAYqa'
);
// Define an SQL query to run
$query = '
    SELECT
        start_time, name1, long_output
    FROM
        nagios_notifications
    JOIN
        nagios_objects
    USING
        (object_id)
    ORDER BY
        start_time DESC
    LIMIT
        10
';

// Retrieve all the notifications as objects
$statement = $nagios->prepare($query);
```

```php
$statement->setFetchMode(PDO::FETCH_OBJ);
$statement->execute();

// Read the notifications into an array
for ($notifications = array(); $notification = $statement->fetch(); )
{
    $notifications[] = $notification;
}

// Send an RSS header rather than an HTML one
header("Content-Type: application/rss+xml; charset=utf-8");
echo '<?xml version="1.0" encoding="UTF-8"?>';

?>
<rss version="2.0">
    <channel>
        <title>
            Latest Nagios Core Notifications
        </title>
        <link>
            http://olympus.naginet/nagios/
        </link>
        <description>
            The ten most recent notifications from Nagios Core
        </description>
<? foreach ($notifications as $notification): ?>
        <item>
            <description>
                <?= htmlspecialchars($notification->name1); ?>: <?=
htmlspecialchars($notification->long_output) ?>
            </description>
            <pubDate>
                <?= htmlspecialchars(date('r',
strtotime($notification->start_time))) ?>
            </pubDate>
        </item>
<? endforeach; ?>
    </channel>
</rss>
```

Saved in a file named `latest-notifications.php`, we could subscribe to this in our favorite RSS reader, such as **Liferea** (`http://liferea.sourceforge.net/`):

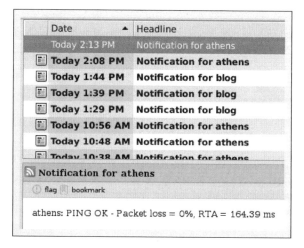

Date	▲	Headline
Today 2:13 PM		Notification for athens
Today 2:08 PM		**Notification for athens**
Today 1:44 PM		**Notification for blog**
Today 1:39 PM		**Notification for blog**
Today 1:29 PM		**Notification for blog**
Today 10:56 AM		Notification for athens
Today 10:48 AM		Notification for athens
Today 10:38 AM		Notification for athens

Notification for athens

ⓘ flag bookmark

athens: PING OK - Packet loss = 0%, RTA = 164.39 ms

How it works...

The examples given in the preceding section are just to get you started with very simple reports; there is a wealth of data available in the NDOUtils database to explore. Here are some other possibilities:

▶ A breakdown of all the hosts in your system and their states, ordered by name, presented in an HTML table

▶ A list of all the hosts that have been down more than once in a month

▶ The percentage of uptime for all hosts

See also

▶ The *Reading status into a MySQL database with NDOUtils* and *Getting extra visualizations with NagVis* recipes in this chapter

Getting extra visualizations with NagVis

In this recipe, we'll explore how to go beyond the default network map discussed in *Chapter 8*, to get a lot of visualization power with the extension NagVis. NagVis can use the NDOUtils backend to build custom maps in various styles.

NagVis is most likely of interest to you if you're interested in visualizing Nagios data more extensively, particularly if you're having problems with the scalability of the included Nagios Core status map. The default status map works well for smaller networks, but can struggle with rendering larger ones in a timely fashion.

A complete survey of NagVis' functions would not be possible in one recipe, but this one will walk you through downloading, installing, and configuring the extension to give you a simple **automap**, in order to get you started.

Getting ready

You should have a running Nagios Core server with version 3.0 or later, and have the NDOUtils backend successfully installed and populating a MySQL database to which you have administrative access. This is discussed in the *Reading status into a MySQL database with NDOUtils* recipe in this chapter.

In order for the automap to be much use, you will need a network with at least a few parent-child relationships—see the *Creating a network host hierarchy* recipe in *Chapter 8* for details on how this is done.

NagVis includes an installation script that deals quite well with different systems' installations of Nagios Core. However, it still requires certain dependencies, specifically:

▶ Apache with `mod_php` on the same server as Nagios Core

▶ PHP 5.3 or newer, with the following modules: `gd`, `gettext`, `mbstring`, `mysql`, `pdo`, `session`, `sqlite`, and `xml`

▶ The Graphviz graph visualization software, with the following modules: `circo`, `dot`, `fdp`, `neato`, `twopi`

▶ SQLite 3

You may need to consult your system's documentation to install all these dependencies; check your system's package manager, if there is one. For Ubuntu and other Debian-derived systems, the following packages generally suffice:

```
# apt-get install apache2 libapache2-mod-php5 libgd2-xpm libgd2-xpm-dev
php5 php5-gd php5-mysql php5-sqlite graphviz sqlite3
```

On systems such as CentOS and Fedora, the following packages may work:

```
# yum install php php-gd php-gettext php-mbstring php-mysql php-pdo php-
sqlite php-xml graphviz graphviz-gd graphviz-php
```

It is difficult to anticipate the exact packages needed for all systems; searching your package manager for keywords (for example `php sqlite`) may help.

How to do it...

We can install NagVis with an NDO backend as follows:

1. Download the latest sources for NagVis from `http://www.nagvis.org/downloads`:

   ```
   $ wget http://downloads.sourceforge.net/project/nagvis/NagVis%20
   1.7/nagvis-1.7.1.tar.gz
   ```

2. Inflate `.tar.gz` and change directory to within it:

   ```
   $ tar -xzf nagvis-1.7.1.tar.gz
   $ cd nagvis-1.7.1
   ```

3. Run the `install.sh` script as `root`:

   ```
   # ./install.sh
   ```

4. The script will attempt to find your Nagios Core installation, and will ask you to specify a location for the new NagVis files. In our case, the defaults are correct and acceptable, so we can simply press *Enter*.

   ```
   -- Checking paths --

   Please enter the path to the nagios base directory [/usr/local/
   nagios]:

     nagios path /usr/local/nagios   found

   Please enter the path to NagVis base [/usr/local/nagvis]:
   ```

5. The script will attempt to find all of the prerequisites needed and will alert you if any are not found. If this is the case, you should abort the installation with *Ctrl + C* and install them before trying again.

   ```
   -- Checking prerequisites --

   PHP 5.3                                found

     PHP Module: gd 5.3                   found

     PHP Module: mbstring compiled_in     found

     PHP Module: gettext compiled_in      found

     PHP Module: session compiled_in      found

     PHP Module: xml compiled_in          found

     PHP Module: pdo compiled_in          found

     Apache mod_php                       found

   Graphviz 2.26                          found

     Graphviz Module dot 2.26.3           found
   ```

```
       Graphviz Module neato 2.26.3              found

       Graphviz Module twopi 2.26.3             found

       Graphviz Module circo 2.26.3             found

       Graphviz Module fdp 2.26.3               found

   SQLite 3.7                                    found
```

6. The script will prompt you for an appropriate backend to configure as NagVis' data source. In this example, the only one we want is the ndo2db backend. Press *n* for all the others.

```
-- Checking Backends. (Available: mklivestatus,ndo2db,ido2db,merli
nmy) --

Do you want to use backend mklivestatus? [y]: n

Do you want to use backend ndo2db? [n]: y

Do you want to use backend ido2db? [n]: n

Do you want to use backend merlinmy? [n]: n

   /usr/local/nagios/bin/ndo2db (ndo2db)   found
```

7. The script will attempt to detect your Apache HTTPD settings. It does a good job with most systems, but you should check the results are correct before you press *Enter*. It should also be safe to allow it to create an Apache configuration file for you.

```
-- Trying to detect Apache settings --

Please enter the web path to NagVis [/nagvis]:

Please enter the name of the web-server user [www-data]:

Please enter the name of the web-server group [www-data]:

create Apache config file [y]:
```

8. The script will give you a summary of its intentions for installing the software, and will ask you to confirm. Do so by pressing *Enter*:

```
-- Summary --

NagVis home will be:              /usr/local/nagvis

Owner of NagVis files will be: www-data

Group of NagVis files will be: www-data

Path to Apache config dir is:  /etc/apache2/conf.d

Apache config will be created: yes

Installation mode:               install

Do you really want to continue? [y]:
```

9. Restart the Apache HTTPD server:

```
# apache2ctl configtest
# apache2ctl restart
```

If all of the above goes correctly, once the installation is finished, you should be able to visit the NagVis configuration page on `http://olympus.naginet/nagvis/`, substituting the hostname for your own Nagios Core server:

You can log in with the default username `admin` and the password `admin` to take a look at some of the demo maps.

There is a little more to go yet before we can get our automap working:

1. On the server, edit the `/usr/local/nagvis/etc/nagvis.ini.php` file:

   ```
   # vi /usr/local/nagvis/etc/nagvis.ini.php
   ```

2. Find and change the following directives under the `backend_ndomy_1` section, adding the values you used for your ndo2db installation:

   ```
   ; hostname for NDO-db
   dbhost="localhost"
   ; portname for NDO-db
   dbport=3306
   ; database name for NDO-db
   dbname="nagios"
   ; username for NDO-db
   ```

```
dbuser="ndo"
; password for NDO-db
dbpass="mPYxbAYqa"
; prefix for tables in NDO-db
dbprefix="nagios_"
; instance name for tables in NDO-db
dbinstancename="default"
```

Make sure that all the preceding values are uncommented (they should not be preceded by a semicolon).

3. Log in to the NagVis web interface, and click on **Manage Maps** under the **Options** menu:

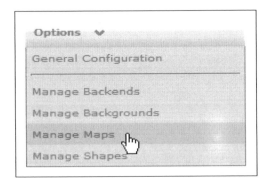

4. Under **Create Map**:

    1. For **Map name**, enter the value Automap.

    2. For **Map iconset**, choose **std_small**.

    3. Leave **Background** blank.

    4. Click on **Create**.

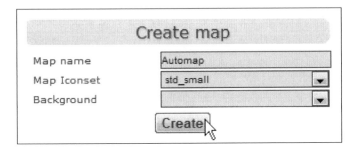

The page should refresh to a blank screen, because we have not yet elected a data source for the map.

5. Click on **Map Options** under the **Edit Map** menu.

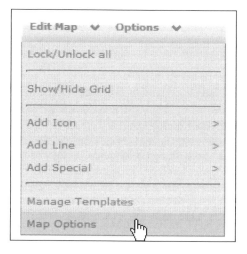

6. In the resulting dialog:

    1. Check the **sources** checkbox, and change the value to `automap`.

    2. Check the **backend_id** checkbox, and choose the value **ndomy_1**.

    3. Scroll down to the bottom and click on **Save**.

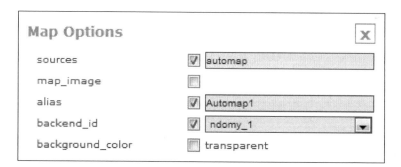

With this done, the page should refresh and show you a map of your network, automatically generated from your configuration, in a similar style to the Nagios Core web interface status map. You should also be able to hover over individual nodes to see their details.

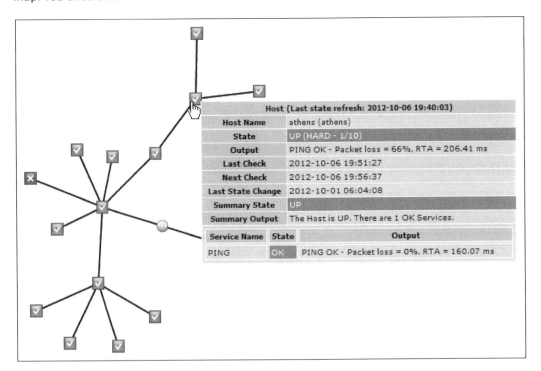

How it works...

NagVis' automap is generated from the data in the database that we established in the NDOUtils recipe. It generates the map in much the same way that the default status map does, but is more scalable for larger networks. The parent and child relationships defined in the configuration are included, to make a tree-style map.

There's more...

The use of NagVis could fill an entire book in itself, and the automap is only one of many possible maps, including defining one's own backgrounds, icons, labels, and hover behavior. For more detail on how to make customized maps as well as other styles of automaps, consult the NagVis documentation at `http://www.nagvis.org/doc`.

See also

- ▸ The *Reading status into a MySQL database with NDOUtils* and *Writing customized Nagios Core reports* recipes in this chapter
- ▸ The *Creating a network host hierarchy* and *Using the network map* recipes in Chapter 8, *Understanding the Network Layout*

Index

Thank you for buying
Nagios Core Administration Cookbook

About Packt Publishing

Packt, pronounced 'packed', published its first book "*Mastering phpMyAdmin for Effective MySQL Management*" in April 2004 and subsequently continued to specialize in publishing highly focused books on specific technologies and solutions.

Our books and publications share the experiences of your fellow IT professionals in adapting and customizing today's systems, applications, and frameworks. Our solution based books give you the knowledge and power to customize the software and technologies you're using to get the job done. Packt books are more specific and less general than the IT books you have seen in the past. Our unique business model allows us to bring you more focused information, giving you more of what you need to know, and less of what you don't.

Packt is a modern, yet unique publishing company, which focuses on producing quality, cutting-edge books for communities of developers, administrators, and newbies alike. For more information, please visit our website: www.packtpub.com.

About Packt Open Source

In 2010, Packt launched two new brands, Packt Open Source and Packt Enterprise, in order to continue its focus on specialization. This book is part of the Packt Open Source brand, home to books published on software built around Open Source licences, and offering information to anybody from advanced developers to budding web designers. The Open Source brand also runs Packt's Open Source Royalty Scheme, by which Packt gives a royalty to each Open Source project about whose software a book is sold.

Writing for Packt

We welcome all inquiries from people who are interested in authoring. Book proposals should be sent to author@packtpub.com. If your book idea is still at an early stage and you would like to discuss it first before writing a formal book proposal, contact us; one of our commissioning editors will get in touch with you.

We're not just looking for published authors; if you have strong technical skills but no writing experience, our experienced editors can help you develop a writing career, or simply get some additional reward for your expertise.

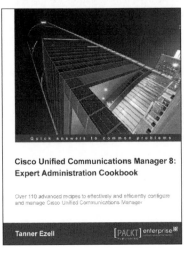

HP Network Node Manager 9:
Getting Started

Manage your network effectively with NNMi

Marius Vilemaitis

[PACKT] enterprise 88

HP Network Node Manager 9: Getting Started

ISBN: 978-1-849680-84-4   Paperback: 584 pages

Manage your network effectively with NNMi

1. Install, customize, and expand NNMi functionality by developing custom features

2. Integrate NNMi with other management tools, such as HP SW Operations Manager, Network Automation, Cisco Works, Business Availability center, UCMDB, and many others

3. Navigate between incidents and maps to reduce troubleshooting time

4. Screenshots and step-by-step instructions to customize NNMi in the way you want

BackTrack 5 Cookbook

Over 90 recipes to execute many of the best known and little known penetration-testing aspects of BackTrack 5

Willie Pritchett   David De Smet   [PACKT] open source ✤

BackTrack 5 Cookbook

ISBN: 978-1-849517-38-6   Paperback: 236 pages

Over 90 recipes to execute many of the best known and little known penetration-testing aspects of BackTrack 5

1. Learn to perform penetration tests with BackTrack 5

2. Nearly 100 recipes designed to teach penetration testing principles and build knowledge of BackTrack 5 Tools

3. Provides detailed step-by-step instructions on the usage of many of BackTrack's popular and not-so-popular tools

Please check **www.PacktPub.com** for information on our titles

Printed in Great Britain
by Amazon.co.uk, Ltd.,
Marston Gate.